Adams combines a lifetime of experience in some of the world's most troubled spots with academic rigor and a passion for peace to share this remarkable narrative. From Air Force jet mechanic in Vietnam to UN peacebuilder in Kosovo, and now as a concerned citizen in a divided and troubled United States, he provides informed perspective with astute analysis, and he puts the current complex challenges in context and offers pathways to resolution. I enjoyed his first book, and this one is even better. I highly recommend it to anyone who seeks solutions to the conflicts in a complex and challenging world.

> Charles F. "Chic" Dambach, Former President
> and CEO, Alliance for Peacebuilding, author of *Exhaust
> the Limits: The Life and Times of a Global Peacebuilder*.

In a timely treatise for those who care about the future of America if not our world, James Adams does a masterful job of helping us understand how the same dynamics of national self-destruction over there present an existential threat to our own experiment in self-governance over here. Also, this richly researched and thought-provoking work offers a navigational guide on how the methodologies of experienced, scholarly practitioners like Jim, based on lessons learned from conflicts all over the world, can help put us back on the road to positive peace right here at home. Read this before it's too late!

> Christopher Holshek, Colonel, U.S. Army Civil Affairs (Ret.),
> Vice President, Narrative Strategies LLC, author of Travels with Harley -
> *Journeys in Search of Personal and National Identity*,
> and founder of the National Service Ride project.

James Adams concludes his first book, *Analytic Reflections from Conflict Zones: A Cautionary Tale for a Polarizing America and World*, with this admonition: "…this is a cautionary tale for an increasingly polarized America—a hard-won model of democracy, now at risk." His second book endeavors to address this burgeoning risk by providing a tour de force of the concepts and theoretical constructs that have been developed to describe and explain the intricacies of international intervention into internal conflicts that threaten regional and international security.

His central argument is that a combination of Johan Galtung's negative and positive peace measures for addressing the root causes of conflicts (i.e., coercive suppression of hostilities combined with institutionalization of mechanisms for resolving conflict) if applied with a judicious combination of both realism and idealism is the path to self-sustaining peace, both globally and here at home.

Michael Dziedzic
Adjunct Professor, George Mason University: Co-Editor of
The Quest for Viable Peace: International Intervention and
Strategies for Conflict Transformation

Peace and Conflict

Citizens Edition

James R. Adams

HAMILTON BOOKS
Bloomsbury Publishing Inc, 1359 Broadway, 12th Floor, NY 10018, USA
Bloomsbury Publishing Plc, 50 Bedford Square, London, WC1B 3DP, UK
Bloomsbury Publishing Ireland, 29 Earlsfort Terrace, Dublin 2, D02 AY28, Ireland

BLOOMSBURY and the Diana logo are trademarks of
Bloomsbury Publishing Plc

First published in the United States of America 2026

Copyright © Bloomsbury Publishing, 2026

Cover art by James R. Adams

All rights reserved. No part of this publication may be: i) reproduced or transmitted in any form, electronic or mechanical, including photocopying, recording or by means of any information storage or retrieval system without prior permission in writing from the publishers; or ii) used or reproduced in any way for the training, development or operation of artificial intelligence (AI) technologies, including generative AI technologies. The rights holders expressly reserve this publication from the text and data mining exception as per Article 4(3) of the Digital Single Market Directive (EU) 2019/790.

Bloomsbury Publishing Inc does not have any control over, or responsibility for, any third-party websites referred to or in this book. All internet addresses given in this book were correct at the time of going to press. The author and publisher regret any inconvenience caused if addresses have changed or sites have ceased to exist, but can accept no responsibility for any such changes.

ISBN: HB: 978-0-7618-9209-0
       PB: 978-0-7618-7477-5
       ePDF: 978-0-7618-8038-7
       eBook: 978-0-7618-7914-5

Typeset by Integra Software Services Pvt. Ltd.

For product safety related questions contact productsafety@bloomsbury.com.

To find out more about our authors and books visit www.bloomsbury.com
and sign up for our newsletters.

I dedicate this book to the courageous souls in conflicted lands who press on to bring peace and dignity to their people.

Contents

List of Illustrations	ix
List of Tables	x
Abbreviations	xi
Preface	xiv
Foreword	xvii
Acknowledgments	xix
Introduction	1

Part 1 The Human Perspective

1	A Broader Perspective/a Shared Awareness	7
2	A Few Words about Conflict	11
3	Qualifications and Certain Observations	13
4	The Straight Path and Ditches	21

Part 2 Thoughts, Moments, Places

5	Fate	31
6	Vietnam	35
7	Mayor's Citizen's Assistance Center	37
8	Sudan	39
9	Somalia	49
10	Rwanda	81
11	Kosovo	91
12	Afghanistan	117

Part 3 The Conceptual Perspective

13	Who Would Manage an Intervention in the United States?	131
14	Stabilization and Peacebuilding Operations Basics	139
15	Operationalized Negative and Positive Peace	145
16	Peacebuilding and Intent	151

17 The Case of Bosnia and Herzegovina	157
18 Interventions into the Recent Bosnian War	169
19 Assessing a Negative and Positive Peace Status	187
20 Implications, Conclusions, and Recommendations	227
21 What Now?	235
Appendix: A Day at Boot Camp Peace-in-Our-Time	239
References	247
Index	255
About the Author	260

Illustrations

9.1	Automatic Prejudice Default Levels	52
11.1	Sample Intervention Structure: Kosovo	102
14.1	The War Is Over, But the Peace Has Yet to Be Won	140
14.2	Core Components of Peace Operations	141
14.3	Conceptual Model of Peace Operations: Civil Order—Social Justice	143
15.1	Conflict-Management Range, Positive-Peace Process Added	149
16.1	Sustained Problem-Solving Dialogue	153
19.1	War to Sustainable Positive Peace Continuum Model Grand Total Means: All Structural Elements + All Relationship Elements	192
19.2	Adapted Conflict Nested Paradigm Determination	217
19.3	Humanitarian and Peace Operations Activity Levels	219
19.4	Intervention Assessment and Approach Selection	221

Tables

14.1	Conceptual Model of Peace Operations (CMPO)	141
15.1	Operationalized Negative and Positive Peace	146

Abbreviations

APC	Armored Personnel Carrier
BiH	Bosnia and Herzegovina
CAR	Conflict Analysis and Resolution
CHW	Community Health Worker
CMF	Comprehensive Multilevel Framework
CMOC	Civil-Military Operations Center
CSO	US Department of State Bureau of Conflict and Stabilization Operations
DOD	US Department of Defense
DRT	District Reconstruction Team
EU	European Union
FBiH	Federation of Bosnia and Herzegovina
FOB	Forward Operating Base
FRY	Federal Republic of Yugoslavia
HQ	Headquarters
IC	International Community
ICFY	International Conference for the Former Yugoslavia
ICRC	International Committee of the Red Cross
IDP	Internally Displaced Persons
IFOR	NATO Implementation Force
INGO	International Nongovernmental Organizations

IO	International Organizations
IOM	International Organization for Migration
IPTF	International Police Task Force
KFOR	NATO Kosovo Force
KLA	Kosovo Liberation Army
LCO	Local Communities Officer
LNGO	Local NGO
MCO	Municipal Communities Office
MPICE	Measuring Progress in Conflict Environments
MVI	Medical Volunteers International
NATO	North Atlantic Treaty Organization
NGO	Nongovernmental Organizations
OECD	Organization for Economic Development
OHR	European Union Office of the High Representative for BiH
OSCE	Organization for Security and Cooperation in Europe
Oxfam	Oxford Committee for Famine Relief
PISG	Provisional Institutions of Self-Governance
PRT	Provincial Reconstruction Team
PTSD	Post-Traumatic Stress Disorder
R2P	Responsibility to Protect
RPF	Rwanda Patriotic Front
RPG	Rocket-Propelled Grenade
RS	Republika Srpska
S/CRS	US Department of State Office of the Coordinator for Reconstruction and Stabilization

SNA	Somalia National Army
UN	United Nations
UNAMIR	United Nations Assistance Mission for Rwanda
UNHCR	United Nations High Commissioner for Refugees
UNICEF	United Nations Children's Fund (formerly United Nations International Children's Fund)
UNMIK	United Nations Interim Administration Kosovo
UNOSOM	United Nations Operation in Somalia
UNPA	United Nations Protected Area ("Safe Area")
UNPROFOR	United Nations Protection Force
UNSCR	United Nations Security Council Resolution
US	United States
USAID	United States Agency for International Development
USSR	Union of Soviet Socialist Republics
WFP	United Nations World Food Program

Preface

This book is for concerned citizens.

I was working for the United Nations in Kosovo as a civil affairs officer assigned to community-level minority issues and protection when a local citizen asked me why I worked in such places, meaning conflict zones. I replied, "It's a job ... and because I don't want my country to have to need someone like me back home." Meaning, among other things, that I worked to address problems overseas so that they would remain overseas; so that my country—the United States—would not need someone specializing in post-conflict reconstruction and civil society building.

My first book, *Analytic Reflections from Conflict Zones: A Cautionary Tale for A Polarizing America and World* (2021), was my retirement "note-to-file" in response to the conflict patterns that I had witnessed in conflict zones overseas over many years in peacekeeping operations; I delayed publication to add some commentary on more recent troubling conflict patterns that I was seeing back home in the United States. That book is mostly intended for academics, students, and stabilization and peacebuilding professionals, although I attempt to explain things on a human level.

It is clear to me now that a shared basic understanding of peace and conflict fundamentals is needed by all concerned citizens. My mostly hypothetical response to the question posed to me above by the Kosovo citizen in the early 2000s is no longer so hypothetical.

Serious conflicted political and cultural reality in the United States, and elsewhere, is too close for comfort. Despite what are often good intentions, democracy and civil and human rights, principles, and practices—the basic ingredients of a free society and country—are under threat.

Therefore, in this second book, I have distilled out some academic-dedicated material that is in my first book (although it might not seem like that at first glance) and have recast what I have to say with all concerned citizens in mind.

I will take this Citizens Edition and message on the road, engaging as many people, organizations, conferences, and communities as possible—not because I like public speaking particularly, but because I believe that what I have to say is necessary in these challenging times.

While reading this book, think about how the specific explanations or scenarios that I describe apply to conflicted political or cultural circumstances that you are seeing or experiencing. Similar human dynamics apply whether they take place on your street corner, in your community or nation, or globally, the difference is mostly a matter of scale and intensity.

Also know that many other people elsewhere have seen these circumstances before, and many are working on solutions.

The point of this book is to learn from others' experience and to think about peace and conflict differently, and that all experiences count since human fundamentals (emotions, perceptions, narratives, basic human needs) are involved in every circumstance and at all levels. I believe that US citizens, and others, need to be better aware of peace and conflict dynamics and of the consequences of taking certain paths. People need to know what to expect.

I believe that a shared awareness of key conflict and peacebuilding fundamentals, and of extremism and polarization consequences, is needed among governmental and nongovernmental representatives (civilian and military) as well as the general public.

It occurred to me to title this book *Agitations*—supposing that some are considering charging down a path to societal or national self-destruction. If setting your own house on fire (community or nation) to make a cultural or political point is your first impulse and preferred method of communication, then I ask that you pause that impulse and to listen to what I have to say; listen to the voices of many who have gone down that path before you and have experienced regret and untold pain.

My observations and peace and conflict conceptual knowledge come from many years of boots-on-the-ground experience in conflict zones, listening to citizens and intervenors in conflict zones, and studying the work of those who have been thinking about such things for a long time.

My specialization is analyzing stabilization and peacekeeping operation environments—that is the language I know. I translate lessons available from such circumstances as best I can for consideration by those now challenged by serious polarization and fragmentation stresses.

I make the distinction, in the different parts of this book, between a "human perspective" and a "conceptual perspective" in order to speak freely about experiences and observations from a human level standpoint initially, followed by conceptual-theoretical explanations supposing that such explanations are helpful to our overall understanding of what is going on in our complicated world. I sprinkle in various ideas of my own about what might be done, or thoughts about what others are doing to improve our circumstances.

I do not have all the answers, but I can offer some insight and suggestions, and perhaps some comfort. One suggestion is to consider a broader perspective generally with regard to peace and conflict and humanity. I try to humanize the discussion.

By the way, I am sure that there is something in this book to annoy and to please everyone. It is a decidedly different approach to the subject of peace and conflict. My hope is that you will take-to-heart the parts of this book that speak to you. I offer what insights I can.

Foreword

This Citizens' Edition of "Peace and Conflict" is not for academics, who can spend pages debating the kind of "positive peace" we might aim for, or the differences between conflict resolution and conflict transformation.

Jim Adams' "career" has been rather different and in many ways his journey through life has been unique. Starting young with his participation in the ill-starred and divisive US intervention in Vietnam, he then switched to field work in civil affairs, development and peacebuilding with USAID, the UN and other international nongovernment organizations, and undertook practical relief work in some of the worst and most violent situations around the globe.

He has met and interacted with refugees and IDPs, warlords, local government officials, military peacekeepers, traumatized civilians, overworked doctors and other relief workers striving to make impossible situations a little less lethal.

In places such as Somalia, Kosovo and Afghanistan, he has witnessed at first hand some of the successes—and the frequent failures—of various forms on international humanitarian intervention whereby the international community—that elusive entity—has tried to mitigate some of the worst effects of violent and intractable human conflicts.

Writing his first book, *Analytical Reflections from Conflict Zones*, Jim Adams had the chance of reflecting on all the various lessons that need to be learned—and passed on—from the numerous local-level situations of mistrust, hostility and violence that he had witnessed in environments where the aspirations of divided communities and the ambitions of their leaders have clashed and led to widespread destruction and death.

Now, as Adams once feared, his own country is polarized, rife with hostility and lack of trust, on the brink of mass violence and thus in danger of suffering many of the ills that afflicted former Yugoslavia, Afghanistan, Somalia and other war zones in which he has worked.

His latest book simply asks what lessons from Kosovo, Bosnia, East Timor or Sudan might be helpful in Chicago, Sandy Hook, Los Angeles, Boulder—or your hometown.

There are answers to that question and many can be gleaned from, this "Citizen's Edition" but the book and the author warn that some remedies are difficult, some are long term and others demand sustained effort.

Are we up these challenges, as we come to the 250th anniversary of the Republic?

Christopher Mitchell
George Mason University, Virginia

Acknowledgments

I would like to express my gratitude for the support of the Carter School for Peace and Conflict Resolution at George Mason University, which enabled me to better understand the conflict and peacebuilding dynamics that I was witnessing in the field. I single out for particular appreciation my esteemed academic advisor and dissertation committee chair, Dr. Dennis Sandole, whom I relied on for many years in the endeavor. Also, I want to say thank you to my other committee members, Dr. Kevin Avruch and Professor Dave Davis, both of whom advised patiently while indulging my often unorthodox conceptual approaches.

I want to express my appreciation to the diplomats, the international and local organization representatives, and the Bosnian citizens, who kindly gave me the benefit of their time, wisdom, and thoughts about difficult memories during interviews in Bosnia and Herzegovina.

Finally, I want to thank my sister Lynette, brother-in-law Dusty, niece Yvonne, nephew John, and friend Donna for their untiring support above and beyond the call of duty.

Introduction

With bullets bouncing off the house and rocket-propelled grenades going off around town, I asked myself: "How the hell is anybody supposed to meditate around here with all this racket going on?"

Shortly thereafter, in exasperation I uttered, "How the hell is anybody supposed to read around here with all this racket going on?"

After an unsolicited moment of reflection, it occurred to me that maybe such questions were a little selfish—that maybe there is another way to do peacekeeping. Such were my contemplations while sitting in the United Nations Humanitarian Division compound in Mogadishu, Somalia, on Christmas Day of 1994.

After further annoying moments of reflection, I was determined to take a course of action to become better informed about conflict and peacebuilding, and so I sought out those who had been thinking about such things. The idea had occurred to me before, but it was now time to act. Thereafter, in between work in conflict zones, I earned a master's degree and a PhD in Conflict Analysis and Resolution (CAR) at George Mason University, specializing in the analysis of stabilization and peacebuilding operation environments. I carried out my doctoral field research in Bosnia and Herzegovina (BiH).

Generally, humanitarian relief, stabilization, and post-conflict reconstruction operations are intended to help bring about the normalization of life in the aftermath of wars. My first book, *Analytic Reflections from Conflict Zones* (2021), was to be a simple reflection on my experience over the years in that line of work, and an opportunity to share my framework for better understanding and tracking peace and conflict dynamics, and planning for peacebuilding—a retirement note-to-file so to speak.

I figured that that would do it. I would write a memoir of sorts for peace and conflict scholars, students, and professionals, and then declare victory and go home.

I learned soon enough, however, that my home, America, has a problem. Humanity has a problem. This complicates things. More needs to be said. More needs to be done. The porch and rocking chair would have to wait. Troubling political and societal trends in America compelled me to add commentary on the American domestic situation to my review of humanity's problems, at least to the extent that I had the ability to comment.

This book, *Peace and Conflict: Citizens Edition*, is a continuation of that effort. It is still about my time working in some of the world's most intractable conflict zones while making efforts to better understand peace and conflict. It is also a cautionary tale about the consequences of unchecked impulses toward prejudice, intolerance, hatred, authoritarianism and fascism, extremism, and vengeance.

Particularly, now, this is a cautionary tale for an increasingly polarized America—a hard-won model of democracy, now at risk. America, despite its historic place of democratic moral leadership and innovation, cannot claim exception to self-destructive political dynamics.

I have argued in my conceptual work that a broader perspective in the discourse on peace and conflict is needed globally. In *Analytic Reflections from Conflict Zones*, I added the United States as a country of concern. This time I focus on communicating the necessary to the public at large—to all concerned citizens.

Essentially, I see a need to make a better understanding of peace and conflict more accessible through personal human-level expression—an effort to help prevent our deteriorating national discourse from sliding into the worst manifestations of destructive conflict.

An added complication now is that internet-connected societies are subject to ever-greater misinformation and disinformation influences that drive much of the political and societal fragmentation and extremism dynamics today (leadership included).

In these circumstances, we have much to learn from others elsewhere who have endured destructive levels of aggressive nationalism, polarization, and evolving extremism, where things got entirely out of hand and an international intervention was called for to quell the horrible violence captured on the news. This is the perspective that I offer as well as some hopeful encouragement and suggestions for improving our circumstances.

An America so internally conflicted that intervention is required to save it from itself is something that probably few have contemplated, beyond perhaps a small collection of the US Department of Defense (DOD) and law enforcement analysts preoccupied with remote-scenario war gaming.

What would an intervention look like in the United States? When would such a thing be called for? Who would carry it out? Is such a thing even thinkable? I will address these questions in due course.

Probably, such questions have been given little thought since the American Civil War—until lately.

> I have seen the consequences of caustic discourse, deep societal division, and the dehumanization of others that, when taken to their logical extreme, slice through families, societies, and nations, leaving destruction and decades of tragedy. Nationalistic and ethnic-racial passions are stirred to hatred and violence, and identities and circumstances are weaponized for political ends.
>
> Such a path, if taken unrestrained, leads down the avenging-angel road to its logical extremes—civil strife, civil war, hundreds of thousands killed and maimed, and millions made internally displaced or refugees, plus the inevitable perpetuation of cycles of violence. Rule by mob is not a circumstance you want to find yourself in.
>
> (Adams 2021, xiv)

The two paragraphs just above are pulled from *Analytic Reflections from Conflict Zones*; the paragraphs were originally intended for discussion about serious conflict and international interventions in foreign lands. I did not expect to be quoting myself in connection with conflict and intervention in America in my rocking chair retirement years.

Analytic Reflections from Conflict Zones links the consequences of political polarization, extremism, and trends toward fascism (strong leader + propaganda + mobs + institutional degradations) with similar patterns that I have witnessed in conflict and "post"-conflict zones overseas.

When I was recently asked to share my thoughts on polarization and extremism in America, my first thought was that it is not my area of expertise. My core specialization is explaining peace and stabilization operation dynamics, presumably in foreign lands.

In any case, I delayed the publication of my first book to backtrack and add some commentary on conflict patterns that I see in the United States lately that concern me—a possible future history of failed state status, or a possible failed democracy.

What I see happening now in America is the early-stage genesis of such a history in the making. The implications for the United States—and for the rest of the world—are profound. As I say, the United States, despite its historic place of democratic leadership and innovation, cannot claim an exception to this destructive dynamic—therefore my first book, and now this Citizens Edition.

Also, the purpose of this Citizens Edition is to reach a wider audience of concerned citizens with a less academic message and an affordable book.

To begin, I think it is time for some conflict-consequences insight and reality-checking in the United States, as well as mention of efforts for hope of a more peaceful outcome. The lessons to be learned are not new. It is time to step back and consider a broader perspective.

Part One

The Human Perspective

1

A Broader Perspective/a Shared Awareness

It has become clear to me that the journey of individuals, societies, and nations cannot be separated from humanity's journey overall. It is one and the same journey, really. A great stream of collective bits and pieces of experience, emotions, and observations, past and present, that eventually, unavoidably, merge and speak of ancient repetitions by individuals and nations, of acts of kindness and wisdom, and of acts of arrogance and foolish destruction.

In this greater stream, it is the dynamics of hatred, polarization, and emerging extremism in present-day America and elsewhere that concern me most—particularly the impulse for self-righteous indignation, a sense of superiority, and its primal holdover, vindictiveness, from which all manner of vile forces emerge, seeking release and justification.

Extremism and polarization can facilitate convenient blame and assuage the stings of perceived slights and wrongs. But such a path is laid with traps for the arrogant and overly prideful—even for the innocent. At the end of the avenging angel road lays the lonely ruin of individuals and the graveyard of empires. Nazi Germany took it to the bitter end. The global refugee movements and earnest efforts at genocide of the Second World War are evidence of this.

Grievance-based lashing out without actual evidence or a basic understanding of conflict or peacebuilding dynamics, or a serious consideration of consequences, will, most likely, lead to destruction and regret. The above dynamic seems to apply whether the conflict is internal or across international borders. The Russian invasion of Ukraine is likely to become a future case in point.

Concerning conflict in America: The world cannot afford to lose the hope and the role model of democracy, of a free people, that the United States represents historically in the world, even with its numerous flaws. People living under the iron heel of authoritarian regimes around the world need the kind of hope and encouragement toward a free society that the United States has promoted in the past, despite some notable lapses in judgment to support certain dictatorships and an ill-chosen war or two.

Still, the torch of freedom needs American leadership. The torch of freedom needs the continued American practice of democracy and its active support for basic civil and human rights as envisioned by our founding fathers in the US Constitution and Bill of Rights, despite notable omissions and the flaws of their own characters and time.

Nevertheless, the struggle of American democracy (ideally) of respect for the basic human dignity of all needs to be demonstrated. This effort that we have inherited from our forefathers and foremothers down to this day, despite our own human flaws and clashes, must continue. It needs to be seen—for humanity's sake, and for America's sake.

As I say, I believe that a shared awareness of key conflict and peacebuilding fundamentals, and of extremism and polarization consequences, is needed among governmental and nongovernmental representatives (civilian and military) as well as by the general public. A brief common language with an illustrated framework can more readily facilitate such awareness—literally, a common picture.

I expect that a shared awareness (beyond conventional mediation and expedient political settlements) will result in fewer misunderstandings and less frustration during normalization or reconciliation efforts, and during reconstruction, if needed. Or at least, a shared informed awareness will encourage more functional working relationships by virtue of there being fewer uninformed people groping around in the dark, scaring each other.

Better awareness by citizens about conflict and peacebuilding fundamentals also offers some immunity to divisive, bombastic rhetoric, and agendas. In terms of perspective, after years of living and working in conflict zones and after much academic/scholarly contemplation, an unembellished revelation came to mind—*war is the road rage of humanity*. I mean this to be taken literally. After a time, it occurred to me that even road rage (the tiny wars) and courteous driving are examples of the passions of war and peace, albeit on a nonlethal (usually) personalized scale.

As such, it has also become clear to me that the elements and dynamics of conflict are similar whether at the individual, societal, or global level, given that human fundamentals are involved at all levels—emotions, perceptions, narratives, basic human needs.

Reactionary deep-origin rage is about parts of humanity enduring injury and, in turn, striding the avenging-angel road—a road to hell if taken to its logical extreme—one paved with stones of arrogance, self-righteous indignation, and injury. It is also about magnificent moments of the human spirit and can become strong evidence for hope.

Conflict, regardless of location, has the commonality of human fundamentals; what applies in foreign lands applies in America as well. To extend the idea of conflict commonalities, the war currently impacting Ukraine has deep origins in historical traumas, lingering assumptions of imperial procurement prerogatives, and traditional realpolitik/geopolitical calculations.

Such dynamics played out in the break-up of the former Yugoslavia, Bosnia and Herzegovina (BiH) in particular. American leaders and citizens would do well to heed the lessons available from the wars of the former Yugoslav republics—painful lessons still being taught.

In connection with the current conflict in Ukraine, it has serious potential to escalate across Europe, and the dominant combatant, Russia, has major power status with nuclear weapons to brandish at those inclined to intervene. In any case, territorial procurement and deep-origin rage conflicts have much to say about humanity's state of mind, in the past and now, both domestically and globally.

The shooting has started, so it is too late to work out a preventative strategy in Ukraine. It might even be too late to achieve a negative peace status (international intervention and suppression of violence) since the intervention force would likely be seen as a combatant by Russian President Vladimir Putin. Unless the invading combatant relents or Ukraine submits, the conflict will play itself out sooner or later.

An additional complicating factor is that Ukraine is now a test-bed for measuring the strength of autocratic governance impulses (Russia) versus the political will to resist of open democracy-oriented societies (Ukraine and Western nations), generally speaking. Authoritarianism lashing out, whether at the individual, community, or on a national level, is an innate human impulse. Lashing out is simpler, faster, and easier than reasoned, peaceful relationship-focused alternatives.

The Second World War was also a collision of resentments and ambitions driven by conflict entrepreneurs. *This is a dangerous moment for humanity with some people apparently inclined to authoritarian iron-fisted solutions for resolving conflict, and some inclined to collaborative relationship-improvement solutions to conflict.*

From another perspective, it appears that the current Russia/Ukraine conflict is more of an authoritarian-governance impulse versus a representative-governance impulse projected to a global scale—that is to say, internalized grievances and convictions within individuals and societies worldwide according to, primarily, an authoritarian impulse versus a relationship-improvement impulse (negative peace versus positive peace-oriented tendencies).

Therein lies a possible explanation as to why some people in democracies support Putin's invasion of Ukraine, and some people in authoritarian-dominated societies are opposed to the invasion of Ukraine. A dichotomy, it seems, is at work in the United States also—*a dichotomy that reflects the very essence of the American experiment in democracy—sorting out differences and choices mutually, fairly, and non-violently versus authoritarian rule.*

2

A Few Words about Conflict

Conflict is pervasive. Like oxygen to the brain, it is necessary for clarifying things. Like fire, it can be used in constructive or destructive ways. Conflict is a fact of life. It is omnipresent nature—human, animal, and environmental. We need to aim for constructive conflict.

What is needed now are efforts by which to more readily assess and discuss circumstances from a more informed standpoint, a more civil standpoint, and to find a viable balance within "constructive conflict" (Kriesburg and Dayton 2016)—not total apathy, and not total war, which at either extreme indicates abandoned hope. Another perspective on this approach has been described as constructive dissent.

The general idea of *constructive conflict* is a respectful joint collaboration of conflict parties on mutually worked-out, mutually fair and beneficial solutions, which involve efforts to understand others' perspectives, and to experience working on and solving mutual problems together.

Usually, such collaborations are assisted by informed conflict resolution process facilitators/mediators who are not focused on immediate political settlements but instead on mutual understanding and relationship change.

An underlying objective is to change chronic destructive relationship dynamics to positive constructive relationship understanding and behavior.

It seems that it often takes generations to heal from destructive approaches to conflict. Perhaps, also, a psychosocial educational and healing effort (counseling for community and national leaders) could be advanced concerning territorial procurement assumptions and generational harms done. There have been, and are, some efforts underway in this regard, but they are relatively small scale and underfunded.

Peacebuilding efforts can only go so far without some genuine understanding of the underlying psychosocial dynamics. Such an understanding on the part of intervenors, and ultimately by conflict parties themselves, is essential to getting at chronic destructive underlying forces, and dealing with barriers to the humanization of others. This kind of knowledge and effort is essential to understanding constructive conflict and human relationship-based positive peace.

Humanity is in need of balance. Our impulses are in need of balance. Ultimately, I am talking about humanity's search for balance. Conflict in Ukraine, Kosovo, Bosnia and Herzegovina (BiH), the United States, and elsewhere, although painful, is an opportunity to further such a process.

A broader perspective is needed on war, when things have already gotten out of hand, and on peace, which is often misunderstood and mislabeled. There are various levels of conflict and different kinds of peace. Distinctions between negative peace and positive peace need to be made so that authoritarian leadership cannot so easily pass off negative peace as real peace or positive peace.

My intent is to help fractured societies better see the elements and dynamics of their conflict circumstances and peacebuilding possibilities, and to engage in a more civil, constructive discourse.

Having a better understanding of peace and conflict dynamics and their thresholds can better enable people to move toward functional working relationships.

I do not have all the answers to our human dilemmas. I am not aware of easy solutions to society's ills. What I can contribute are some experience-derived observations, illustrated frameworks and models, and recommendations that I believe can be helpful in efforts toward a more informed civil discourse. Some thoughts, I have already mentioned above. Others are to follow.

I should also mention that after a certain point while working in conflict zones, I began to see that I am a participant in the conflicts that I have witnessed, and that I can be part of the solution, if I choose, regardless of scale. My books are also about that revelation and the ongoing process of understanding. The effort is a work in progress.

But probably, I should back up here and say a little more about myself and my qualifications to have such thoughts.

3

Qualifications and Certain Observations

Beyond my time in the US Air Force in Vietnam as an aircraft mechanic, I have served overseas in conflict zones in a civilian capacity as a humanitarian-aid worker, operations officer, and civil affairs officer for nongovernmental organizations (NGOs), the International Organization for Migration (IOM), and the United Nations (UN) in East and Central Africa (Sudan, Somalia, Rwanda, Uganda), and in Kosovo. Generically speaking, I was a field officer.

Much of the time, I liaised with or advised embassy staff and civil-military operation units on the return and resettlement of refugees and internally displaced people, minority-population issues and protection, and civil society building/rebuilding at the municipal level. I was embedded with the US Army in Afghanistan as a crisis, stabilization, and governance officer for the US Agency for International Development.

During the years that I was focused on emergency relief and civil affairs reconstruction work overseas, I spent little time tracking current affairs back in the United States. I voted by absentee ballot for general elections, listened to BBC news radio, and watched TV news broadcasts when satellite services and electricity were available. If we could get football and Oprah via satellite, that was a plus. I read old copies of the *International Herald Tribune* and the *Economist*.

Although I was in the United States from time to time, I was focused internationally and on my studies. So, when I did eventually return from full-time work overseas around 2012, I was struck by the dramatic increase of hostile and often belligerent voices shouting and lashing out in town halls, and on American TV, radio, streets, and social media.

A vein of coarse language, belligerent partisanship, strident nationalism, and barely concealed ethno-racism that had long been around but subdued had burst open into the mainstream discourse, seemingly nearing a point of normalization. It is not just words but often a harsh, threatening tone that has found a new level of acceptability and channels of release.

Around 2015, I found that I had successfully aged beyond those years appealing to employers in my usual trade, and that I did not have the teaching experience to compete for an academic position paying more than minimum wage. I needed some cash and a change of pace to clear my head. Driving a semi-truck on the open road, perched high in the cab of an eighteen-wheeler, and seeing America up close for a while seemed the thing to do.

So, I went to truck-driving school, got a commercial driver's license, and hit the road in a semi-truck. Now, I did learn soon enough that operating a semi "over-the-road" is a tough way to make a living with the absurd number of hours involved, demanding requirements, every sort of foul weather and traffic condition, extreme deadlines, and, often as not, low pay in the post-union era.

However, traveling the highways and byways and truck stops of the country did, as it turns out, afford me a unique opportunity to listen in on conversations and get a feel for the national discourse, if not the heartbeat, of working America. Politics, the economy, immigration, and elections were favored topics for lamentations when trucking, law enforcement, and football were not enough.

When not otherwise distracted by responsible driving and navigation, I listened to the radio and the steady stream of commentary above rumbling motor and changing gears as counties and states passed underneath my wheels, of which at least one was at any given time plotting a slow loss of air for overnight-flat inconvenience or an immediate gunshot burst of tire-blowout drama.

Although the scenery constantly changed and local radio stations offered varying shades of dialect and political or religious persuasion as I drove on, the tone of opinions shared on the airwaves seemed to get increasingly passionate, abrasive, and intolerant.

There was a diversity of opinion offered. Some of the sentiments that I heard have the true ring of authenticity matching that which eventually led to the kind of societal disintegration and destruction that I have seen elsewhere. It is difficult to identify exactly the moment that it fully hit me that some of the rhetoric that I was hearing—that I am still hearing—here in the United States is actually dangerous.

But I am increasingly reminded of the divisive rhetoric used by some leaders in countries which eventually fell into open violence, war, ethnic cleansing, and sometimes earnest efforts at genocide—and the eventual need for someone like me. Bosnia and Kosovo again come to mind.

Now, before marching off into the book, I want to introduce a few crucial points.

Despite political polarization being new, fresh, and alarming to many Americans, it is nothing new in the world. It is a well-known stress. It is a repetitive historical and global phenomenon as constant as the rise and fall of empires and nations.

All is not lost, though. At the same time, I have also seen the resilience of people and of nations who have come back from the gravest circumstances to find a kind of normalcy again. It takes dedication, the help of friends, and patience. It requires a change in the caustic tone of discourse between those of differing opinions. Wise leadership is helpful.

Also, there is widespread confusion about national, ethnic, and racial identity, which greatly exacerbates civil unrest and accommodates easy political manipulation. Fundamentally, race is the color of skin and physical traits; ethnicity is cultural tradition; and nationality is country of origin or naturalization. Race, ethnicity, and nationality are often aligned in the popular imagination, but it is less and less the case in reality.

There are many kinds of culture: ethnic culture, race culture, national culture, work culture, military culture, arts, music, criminal, political, academic, sports, religious, city, rural, Western, Eastern, realists, idealists, love cultures, hate cultures, etc. And there is a great deal of mixing and matching of cultures. There is clashing of cultures. It can all get quite mixed up as clashes of paradigms are prone to happen. I make some distinctions.

Examples of relevant sentiments expressed in earlier conflicted eras and places are most notably in association with the fascist movements in the years leading up to and during the Second World War that led to massive loss of life, destruction, and displacement. Similarly, divisive ethnopolitical sentiments expressed during the breakup of the Yugoslav republics in the 1990s echo the hate and blame rhetoric used by Italian dictator Benito Mussolini (1883–1945).

Mussolini, an admired authoritarian and fascist, pioneered modern fascism in Italy in the years prior to the Second World War—practices that were later adopted by one of his most ardent admirers, Adolf Hitler (1889–1945). Sometimes, when I saw and heard President Donald J. Trump, I saw and heard Mussolini and former president Slobodan Milosevic (1941–2006) of Serbia.

In other words, it is a style of leadership that promotes blame, character assassination, exclusion, division, aggressive nationalism, and coarser instincts, particularly toward immigrants, minority groups, intellectuals, activists, and a free press. Such a practice does not lead to a good end.

Democracy is based on trust that truth is being held forth. There are differences in perceptions of truth, of course, but knowingly purveying falsehoods for personal or political gain is reckless and dangerous at any level.

As I say, it has become clear to me that the elements and dynamics of conflict are similar whether at the individual, societal, or global level, given that human fundamentals are involved at all levels—emotions, perceptions, narratives, needs. Likewise, the elements and dynamics of peace are similar at different levels.

The distinction is mostly a matter of scale and the use of force (negative peace), or positive peace, which is essentially constructive conflict and dialogue and relationship improvement—the idea being to get at the underlying causes and conditions of a conflict, enabling citizens to coexist peacefully and meet their respective needs and potential.

As I say, *what is needed now is a broader perspective* by which to assess and discuss circumstances from a more informed standpoint, a more civil standpoint, and to *find a viable balance within constructive conflict.*

This book is also about serving "in the field" (overseas, abroad, away from home). "Field officer" is a generic term for someone who carries out foreign-affairs tasks on behalf of an organization or government outside of one's home country. Diplomats and specialized embassy or civilian staff work "in the field"; military officers and troops work in theaters of operation.

This can be one and the same place and task depending on security circumstances. I include some explanation about foreign affairs work overseas to better illustrate stabilization and peacebuilding efforts, my own work, and its relevance to what is happening in the United States now, or potentially could happen in the future.

Fieldwork covers tasks in various sectors: governance, security, rule of law, the economy, and social welfare, requiring a wide range of skills, for example: political and civil affairs, security, finance, business, medicine, engineering, education, agriculture, logistics, and more.

Sometimes, embassy or government agency staff carry out the tasks; sometimes they oversee and contract out the work to international or local aid organizations such as Save the Children or Oxfam (originally founded in Britain in 1942 as the Oxford Committee for Famine Relief) or commercial contractors. Some organizations prefer to remain independent of government or military affiliation or funding.

The work can take place anywhere along a continuum from emergency and disaster relief to post-conflict reconstruction and long-term development. The demobilization of former combatants and the return and resettlement of refugees and internally displaced persons are included.

In complete failed-state circumstances, in which there is no national or local government to interact with, or there is a collection of warring or competing self-declared authorities and militias, intervention interactions can be venturesome and dubious. Finding legitimate counterpart representation becomes an interesting question.

Field staff serve in wide-ranging conflict circumstances: war, ethnic cleansing, natural disasters, and refugee crises. Add to this, imperial-colonial enterprises, territorial acquisitions and partitioning, an assortment of nation-building or nation reassignment projects, and human-security issues (a newer term for an ancient problem). Further, add provision for basic human needs: food, water, shelter, protection, dignity, jobs, healthcare, education, and so on.

Now one can begin to understand a different kind of journey, a different kind of perspective—that of the field officer or field staff. Over time, a broader perspective is gained on the realities of conflict and the human condition.

With regard to deep societal fracturing and political polarization, military troops and civilian field staff have seen these stresses before. Things get out of hand somewhere, sometimes with a strong push from an emerging leader with authoritarian impulses and associated disinformation campaigns. Sometimes, fracturing comes from multinational corporation mischief, sometimes from misguided geopolitical ambitions by rival nations, and, easily enough, the result is tragic—ethnic cleansing or worse.

The people of Bosnia and Kosovo know of this. The people of Somalia know of this. The people of Pakistan, India, Russia, China, Europe, Afghanistan, Rwanda, Latin America, Africa, and the Middle East know of this. Those who have real knowledge of the American Civil War and its aftermath have an understanding of its consequences. Nearly all indigenous populations know of this.

I think it is time for some conflict-consequences insight and reality checking in the United States. The lessons to be learned are not new.

In the end, the journey of a humanitarian-aid worker, or soldier, or refugee, or migrant is humanity's journey—the constant flow of adjusting populations, forced or voluntary, internal or external. Perhaps population movement is humanity's most enduring trait.

There is an historical perspective involved here, and a human perspective, a meeting of realism and idealism—what I refer to as *human realism*. It is a useful meeting place, I think, for engaging in common-ground discussions about changing things for the better in stressful times.

I have played a small part in this ongoing story of the ages, that is to say, international post-conflict intervention. But it is a revealing part. The story began long ago and courses through the history and lives of nations, families, and individuals. This story is about the search for freedom, adventure, home, and security. Naturally, it contains descriptions of virtues and vices.

To repeat my earlier observation: *War is the road rage of humanity.* It is about parts of humanity enduring injury and, in turn, striding the avenging-angel road—a road to hell if taken to its logical extreme—one paved with arrogance and pain. *It is also about magnificent moments of the human spirit and strong evidence for hope.*

Humanity's journey is about desperate acts of cruelty and kindness, ambition, power, commerce, crime, and corruption; it is about hopes and dreams, nightmares, honest theft, greed, callousness, and the jostling of earnest convictions.

In my opinion, peace guaranteed by the hammer alone (negative peace), or by mutually assured destruction, or by futile isolation, is no longer a viable bet, domestically or internationally.

This rush of elements is ever present and relentless amid the gaming of empires and the forces of nature. Sometimes, it is not a happy result for human beings. But sometimes it is. It has always been this way. Often, it has been for the benefit of one at the expense of another.

There are broader implications to consider. Now that we, humanity, have attained technical global interconnectedness, we are experiencing periodic civilizational crises together, globally, in real time. Weapons of mass destruction are everyone's problem now, and there is no putting that genie back in the bottle without international collaboration—and that requires leaders talking to each other.

There is no taming civilizational crises, or international terrorism, or riotous nature by going it alone. This can only be done through a basic display of respect at a human level and collective effort.

This book aims to contribute toward that effort—toward a judicious balance of negative and positive-peace initiatives (I will explain), which is only possible through the development of common understandings. I believe that the insights and frameworks that I have acquired from others, and those of my own that I have developed and field tested, contribute to clarity.

Sometimes, the journey is humanity's search for redemption and happiness. Sometimes it is a reach for revenge. But it is always a search for balance.

For these reasons, I write this book for a wider readership—one that is less technical, more personal, conversational, and conveyed in human-level terms.

This book reflects a field officer's journey and perspective, and it is a cautionary tale for an America at a crossroads in its own journey. But, in the end, it is about humanity's journey and search for balance—in freedoms, in dignity, in civility, in fairness.

I am writing about understanding conflict and war and peace differently, and about changing our national discourse for the better.

I am writing about seeing ourselves differently, as humans.

Ultimately, I am writing about survival, evidence for hope, and what possible futures we are choosing for our children.

I hope that sharing my thoughts and journey will be helpful to you in yours. In fact, I invite you—one concerned citizen to another—to join me in sorting things out as to what is going on—to contribute toward a more helpful way of looking at conflict, and to a more constructive way of communicating with each other in our personal, national, and global discourse.

After my human-perspective contemplations offered humbly and mercilessly in Parts I and II, I offer some conceptual frameworks and models in Part III for those who might find them useful. My intent is to help conflicted societies better see the elements and dynamics of their conflict circumstances and their peacebuilding options—thereby being better able to move on from destructive discourse and political polarization toward functional working relationships, and the eventual normalization of conditions.

Finally, along with an analysis of discord, this book conveys words of hope and encouragement from citizens in conflict zones: words that somehow, eventually, manifest in the human calculus on the kinder side of life, often as not by one individual at a time—one concerned citizen at a time.

How do I explain my arrival at this point of view? How do I explain constructive conflict and finding common perspective in an era of polarization and broken discourse? It has not been a straightforward path—and so I explain it this way.

4

The Straight Path and Ditches

In the course of this book, I will careen between the straight path of scholarly explanation and the miserable but comforting ditches of failure and redemption intended to capture those who stray—those who fall short in unemotional responses to insult or threat.

I will do this while commenting on the dubious nature of humanity, international interventions, and myself by way of example.

I find the sampling of myself—the individual I am most familiar with—useful for relating the one to the many in a larger tide of human experience, of which conflict and intervention, and the expressions of realism and idealism, have, apparently, always been constants. This self-sampling enables me to stay grounded and, at the same time, to declare myself an author of some self-importance, should I have need of any.

First, I should clarify that, like most human beings, I am one thing, and then I am another—like the peaceful motorist who, in a split second, is rendered a raging cursing idiot by a vehicular affront to his or her sensitivities. Or, perhaps, like every other basic human unit, I am stamped with certain portions of virtue and of vice.

What is important to remember is that I am both and that I need to focus on what I want my world to be. Whether in peace or in war, or tranquilly motoring along and then abruptly agitated into an instinctive display of self-righteous indignation on the highway, each of me has anecdotes to make the case for respective opposing convictions. I argue with myself, state my cases, and draw a picture of worlds that are and of the worlds to be.

To rest, I must focus and choose one. If I do not, I will condemn myself to eternal drifting between impulses to war, tepid acceptance of boot-enforced negative peace, or doing nothing and settle for witless chaos with an occasional taunting glimpse of genuine peace in passing—a positive peace, as it is said.

This is not a textbook, and yet it is. It includes historical elements, citations, models, graphics, conflict and peacebuilding theory, analysis, recommendations, and a reference list. At the same time, my intent is to convey the personal on-the-ground reality of conflict and of intervention. The challenge of this book is to get a coherent blend of conceptual description and human-level expression—in other words, a mix of realities, which, after all, is the human condition.

This is not an autobiography, and yet it is to the extent that I describe my own immersion into conflict environments and my evolving perspective on humanitarian, military, and political intervention. I convey scholarly and practical insights, stories, wisdom, and warnings of my own, and those of others in conflict zones who want to be heard. I reflect on other circumstances before and since that have relevance to a broader understanding of conflict and peacebuilding, applied to either international interventions or domestic troubles here at home.

All events, names, people, places, general timing, and attributed statements are real (some paraphrased, some exact in quotes). If protection discretion is called for, or I do not have permission to share names (e.g., my field research interviewees), then I omit personal identification details. Or it might be that I simply do not recall a name or exact date from years gone by, in which case I just provide information as needed to make a point.

Also, I figure that if I am to legitimately comment on conflict, intervention, peacebuilding, and the human condition from a personal-experience perspective, including mention of other's failed projects, then I better declare myself human now and owner of mistakes of my own, lest someone point them out before I do, and undue excitement is generated in the age of Twitter/X.

So, I do hereby confess retroactively and preemptively to all manner of fault, ill-word, judgmental glare, and misjudgment, so that from here on I can offer, with sufficient righteousness, tips on how humanity might proceed more constructively.

I'll expand on Johan Galtung's (1969) concepts of negative peace and positive peace, along with an explanation of how I operationalized the concepts for use in assessing the status of peace and stabilization environments. But, for the moment, I offer the following points about negative and positive peace.

Essentially (in my adapted version), *negative peace* is the result of the coerced suppression of hostilities and violence by political settlement and/or armed action or presence that establishes and maintains a "stable" political/security situation.

In other words, it is the use of force, or threat of force, to stop a war or keep a lid on violence and major civil disorder until other arrangements can be made. *Positive peace* is the successful establishment of ongoing nonviolent mechanisms, institutions, and relationships among conflict parties to address contentious issues and get at the underlying root causes and conditions of a conflict, while enabling the pursuit of individual and group potential and dignity (institutionally and relationship-wise).

Sustainable positive peace would indicate that intervention by outsiders, including assisted stabilization, is no longer needed. Negative peace, if not transitioned into a positive-peace status at some point, will inevitably erupt into violent civil disorder or war, perpetuating chronic cycles of violence and negative peace, and needless tragedy.

It seems that conflicts, large or small, compel a personal response/reaction, and therefore a choice and, ultimately, accountability.

After a time, it occurred to me that the grander aspects of war and peace also apply to the tiny wars of road rage—a perspective that I find useful when risking contemplation of personal accountability for conflict of any sort.

Note: by way of full disclosure, I accept the part about personal responsibility, but under protest of course.

In regard to my earlier declaration that I am one thing and then I am another, I am also saying that I sometimes find myself pulled by opposing convictions within myself that are taken to be held by a realist or an idealist about the viability or justification of intervention. This includes opposing convictions about the use of force, lethal or nonlethal, or not, and opposing convictions about humanitarian and reconstruction aid that saves innocent lives and too often simultaneously empowers opportunists, warlords, war criminals, and despots.

It includes opposing convictions about intervening, or not, in another nation's sovereignty in order to deal with humanitarian emergencies, civil abuses, atrocities, and war crimes. The same can be said, I think, with regard to family, community, or nation-level conflicts and interventions.

Fundamentally, convictions are tested by questions around being the world's police officer, social worker, or judge (with or without a United Nations (UN) mandate). Or about being your brother's keeper. Or about whose truth is more real. And about the true nature of the motivations underneath. Such questions are always immediate. Interventions, field staff, and conflict-zone populations are continuously subject to the social and political dynamics of intervenor governments and constituencies back home. There is a linkage of impact both for better and for worse.

As I said in the Preface, "I believe that a shared awareness of key conflict and peacebuilding fundamentals is needed among governmental and nongovernmental representatives (civilian and military) as well as the general public." So, additional objectives of this book are to provide a brief common language to aid civil discourse and an illustrated framework to more readily facilitate such awareness—a common picture.

Initially, unbeknown to me, a US government interagency taskforce was developing a conflict-assessment approach similar to mine about the same time, which it called "Measuring Progress in Conflict Environments (MPICE)" (approximately 2006–8), published as a paper under US Institute of Peace (2008) auspices as *Interagency Metrics Framework for Assessing Conflict Transformation and Stabilization*. But, as I have been told, the initiative died, along with their use of the term conflict transformation, because interagency planning died in regard to international interventions, and due to interagency rivalry issues at that time. I adapted some elements of the MPICE framework and further developed my own, which I will briefly outline in Part III.

A few more initial thoughts on perspective: with regard to war as humanity's road rage, it is a rage that simultaneously releases and entraps. It is offended innocence. Deeper origins are often concealed, conviction the stronger. Individual. Community. Nation. World. Scale does not seem to matter.

Rage—it is human emotion and our quickened sense of justice and injustice. A humanity at war with itself. An emotion well-practiced. Deeply held. Easily set loose.

Whether of the individual scope or worldly, peace is a nice idea, but not realistic. That seems to be the general assumption. Yet, peace is something I can do, we can do, if we choose. It is a matter of focus. I keep telling myself this because I do not much like the alternatives.

This book describes my recommendation to humanize realism, to give more backbone to idealism, and to make conflict transformation transparent—in essence, find the equilibrium in our midst, draw the picture and tell the story of constructive conflict—a concept explored in depth by Louis Kriesburg and Bruce W. Dayton (2016). It is acknowledgment of our virtues and vices, and a realistic yet humane approach to reckoning with each other, with our respective demons, and without the wasteful destruction of lives and property and so much emotional wear and tear. It is to refocus.

Conflict is past, present, and future. In this context, whether in the field or back home (wherever that may be), whether knowingly or unknowingly, conflict, and our response to it, is likely perceived and described in realist and idealist terms.

Conflict is a common thread that tracks through all manner of human interaction, from the schoolyard fight to global war—pitched as an eye for an eye and a tooth for a tooth; hawks and doves; sticks and carrots; freedom or subjugation; survival, or just simple earned karma.

Conflict is a common thread that runs from thoughtful explanation through firm shouts of tough love, to caustic angry bellowing, to cold lethal delivery. Conflict includes all manner of manipulation, innocent or not.

Realism (negative peace), although often a protector and a sometimes necessary short-term measure, is often of little use in creating anything beyond itself—think military intervention and most law-enforcement approaches. Idealism, although often empathetic, creative, and visionary, is, often enough, naive and ineffective. Realism and idealism passions expressed more robustly are both, from time to time, violently hurled with declarations that there was no other choice.

Either approach, if pushed to extremes or completely to the exclusion of one from the other, leaves wreckage in its wake. So, I argue for humanizing realism, bracing idealism, and making conflict transformation transparent—in other words, thinking in terms of *human realism*. Explaining the why and how of this process and graphically illustrating it comprise the technical objective of this book.

War and peace. Chaos and equilibrium. Rage—the embodiment of fierce and delicate emotions that drift back and forth, back and forth, back and forth. Seeking vengeance. Seeking equilibrium. Sometimes seeking redemption.

I see human realism as acknowledgment of humanity's dual capacity for constructive and destructive interaction. It is full awareness, not just realism, and not just idealism. It suggests insight, deliberate pause, and a tendency toward more balanced encounters. Human realism can allow choice, deliberate mutual awareness, and mutual acceptance; and sometimes, mutual redemption.

I define *human realism* as the proven capacity of humanity to deliberately engage in inconsiderate, competitive, selfish, win/lose acts at others' expense for the personal gain of wealth, resources, territory, power, prestige, or survival.

The term also encompasses the proven capacity of humanity to deliberately engage in considerate, more collaborative, constructive processes to understand, to change, to overlook or forgive, and to engage in a more meaningful discourse for managing and resolving differences.

In the interest of full disclosure, if tasked to specify every suspect encounter, incident, indignity, or close call, and the resulting foul urge for revenge based on duly earned self-righteous indignation on behalf of my innocent self, I suppose I could provide a list. If such irritations and resulting foul urges were to be analyzed for theoretical relevancy, I suppose I could narrow down some for consideration in terms of conflict generation, escalation, management, settlement, and resolution or transformation as the case may be.

In some cases, I would say that resolution has simply been granted by the passage of time (otherwise known as aging) and the fact that the parties concerned, me included, have gone on to other things and have largely forgotten, or have chosen to ignore, earlier differences or resentments.

Such ignoring, of course, does not account for those remnants of unpleasant experience that might still be lurking around somewhere in my person, not informing me of their presence or intentions, and occasionally bothering me to the point that I feel compelled to tell some innocent bystander to go to hell.

Occasionally, I suspect that such displays are festering remnants of unresolved matters (individual or continental) between the ancients that are passed down to grandfathers and eventually on to modern cousins of some description. In any case, it might explain some stern stares in ancestral family photographs, a variety of invasions, and Uncle so-and-so's drunken mean streak.

You might have noticed by now my occasional grasping at bits of snarky humor to, perhaps, deflect closer scrutiny of an ancient remnant of my own, or to fatten up my arguments. However, experience has shown me that, at times, humor can work as an antidote to hardening hearts and closing minds. It can divert attention from brinksmanship long enough for those concerned to look up and see something different.

I in no way mean to lessen the seriousness of the pain of conflict of any kind. The most serious kinds of conflict are deeply destructive to the psyche, bone deep, and require a sensitive touch. Sometimes, humor eases a return to openness, but it is a fine-edged tool to be handled with care. My motivation, ultimately, is to support efforts at transforming destructive conflict into constructive conflict before tragic inevitability sets in.

In effect, it is to acknowledge virtue and vice in all of us—with or without humor—to acknowledge the absurdities of life, and to draw a picture of a reality beyond over-simplified realism or over-simplified idealism. *It is an effort to identify missing pieces before it is too late.*

What follows is a chronology of thoughts, moments, and places that I have encountered in my journey to better understand peace and conflict, myself and others, and the human condition. It is a chronology that began before I knew I was on a journey.

Part Two

Thoughts, Moments, Places

5

Fate

Inevitable. Beyond management. Without fault, or reason for praise. A soldier's gradual acceptance of "It is what it is" as the most basic of coping strategies. Such is fate.

I started out in Oklahoma, born into a large family. We moved around often. It seems my mother felt that it was prudent to stay a step ahead of ex-husbands. I enjoyed ample amounts of freedom of movement, which might explain my independent streak, resourcefulness, and being a terrible student in my youth. We did a stint in an orphanage. I lived with different sisters on occasion; ran away from home when I was sixteen years old; lived with one of my sisters and brothers-in-law for my last two years of high school in Ocean Springs, Mississippi.

In my junior year, I decided to take up music. I was first-chair trombone. Rumor had it that this was because I was the only trombone player in the band. Our band director assigned me two friends. He might have been concerned that he would lose his only trombone if I were left to my own devices.

Over the course of my youth, I was introduced to Jesus at least three times. One occasion involved being baptized among the faithful by Brother Ellis in a nice little pond on the Oklahoma prairie. Of course, I do not want to make assumptions, but I figured that that put me and Jesus on a first-name basis.

My family had just moved into the neighborhood when I was about twelve years old, and I, according to my custom, preferred to leave the neighborhood bullies to their own affairs by minding my own business. However, being the new kids on the block, my big brother and I were inevitably invited to the seemingly timeless ritual of territorial defense and early manhood testing provided by resident bullies everywhere.

Now, my older brother, being an experienced bully himself, took naturally to the regimen of guerrilla or full-frontal-assault warfare with the installed collection of neighborhood bullies in various combinations of one, two, or three-on-one, as the occasion provided. My policy, as I carried it out, was to tell the assorted bullies, in particular two boys from Texas who lived next door, to "leave me the hell alone, stupid."

The bully collective expressed, as a whole, philosophical positions (to which my brother concurred) that I was a wimp (also known as Stringbean), evidently based on their appraisal of my neutral nonalignment policy and less-than-ominous stature. The collective members, individually or in packs, consequently harassed me in the time-honored tradition of bully-neutral party relationships. I seemed to have been quite skilled at providing suitable provocative commentary in service to the neighborhood, since some of the boys and at least one girl in my elementary school also got in a lick or two on occasion. This routine went on for a while.

Then, one morning, it all changed. Something snapped in me, as is wont to happen, when a lovely eleven-year-old neighbor girl (whom the less-than-ominous me secretly admired) and I were sitting on the front porch together observing an exemplary altercation in my front yard in which two bullies (the Texans of next door) and my big brother were engaged in full two-on-one battle (I should clarify that the purpose of Oklahoma is to keep an eye on Texas).

Witnessing the altercation, the lovely and concerned eleven-year-old girl said to the unengaged and generally unimpressed nonaligned neutral, "Aren't you going to do something?" To make a long story short, following a brief—so this is what fate is like—gaze into her sincere eyes, I charged into the fray in progress and forthwith proceeded to execute a rapid and quite professional-like Muhammed Ali number on the younger Texan (my peer in the lineup), quickly dispatching him into submission, decisively changing the balance-of-power equation, and bringing the altercation to a momentous halt.

Later that same day we were all (collective bullies and former nonaligned neutral) to be found playing eight-ball pool together for the first time in the Texans' garage next door. And, also for the first time, having a normal conversation.

I do not know exactly what psychological and physiological dynamics transpired that day, but I know that a conflict transformation of sorts occurred. After that day, for the remaining year or so that we lived in the neighborhood, I do not recall another hostile encounter between me, my brother, and the neighborhood bullies, including the Texans. Our relationship had changed.

I suspect that we were lucky and that the conflict elements in play during that scenario were of a low enough intensity, and in the context of a generally less violent era, that things did not lead to more serious consequences that would have precluded the transformation. And that circumstances allowed space for a wimp-turned-lethal-fighting-machine shock value to have a positive effect.

At the same time, there may be some kernel of basic human truth in the episode that might translate from an adolescent rivalry scenario to a serious adult conflict of much greater consequence, supposing that adult/gang/national/global rivalries might be carried out in ways and with emotions and motivations that are not entirely dissimilar to adolescent rivalry.

6

Vietnam

Like many other strong, fresh, male youths of draftable qualities sitting among rows of similar kind on a US government chartered Flying Tigers' DC-8 and enjoying the attentions of stewardesses while winging our way through the night over moon-shimmering and pearled Pacific waters to Vietnam, I was entirely innocent of any carnal knowledge of war or politics. Finished high school, low draft number, joined the US Air Force, boot camp, aircraft maintenance tech. school, nine months' on-the-job training, volunteered for Vietnam, the Air Force obliged with a Flying Tigers' seat.

In 1971, preliminaries of war came with briefings on military logistics, communicable diseases, base security, tricks of the enemy, assignment of a defensive position, and access to an M16 in case of base perimeter breech, and the way-of-things generally at Cam Ranh Bay Air Base, Vietnam. Supplementary lessons in reality were occasionally provided by the Viet Cong with Russian 105 rockets launched onto the base from atop the mountain across from Cam Ranh Bay.

I was not a combat soldier/airman. Nevertheless, ear-shattering incoming rocket blasts, sirens, and overhead flares drifting down on little parachutes in the middle of the night erased any illusory doubt that someone was trying to kill us, and it was no joke.

After a while, guys who had been in-country longer, me included, stopped bothering to jump off our bunks and run for the blast walls. A waste of effort. It was already too late. We mostly made do with just rolling over and cussing and cursing, knowing that come tomorrow our F-4s would toss bombs onto the offending mountaintop across the bay and we could get uninterrupted sleep again for a while.

> Direct knowledge of realism is useful.
> More specific knowledge of war and politics came later.
> Real understanding came much later.

7

Mayor's Citizen's Assistance Center

Citizens have expectations. One of those expectations is to be able to march into City Hall and pound on a desk (for democratic emphasis), while expressing a community or personal grievance, conviction, request, or inquiry of one sort or another. At least that was the custom in the mayor's office in San Francisco, California, while I was assistant director of the Mayor's Citizen Assistance Center there in the mid-1980s. It was a job, as it turns out, that entailed processing many of the same expectations and tasks familiar to local governments everywhere, including those in war zones.

The difference being that, in war/conflict zones, which entail an international intervention, such things are handled by United Nations (UN) civil affairs and political affairs officers, international police, and UN military contingent officers, or by coalition military commanders and their civil affairs staff, depending on security circumstances and mission mandate.

The primary distinction between the expectations and associated services dispensed in San Francisco and those in war/post-conflict zones is the obvious presence of destruction, deep civil strife and violence, warlords, militias, refugees and displaced persons, unrestrained organized crime and corruption, and extreme shortages of food, shelter, water, fuel, electricity, healthcare, jobs, banks, social services, schools, and coffins.

In fact, citizens might be compelled to notice the absence of government, law enforcement, and the rule-of-law entirely. And there are typically many thousands or millions suffering from post-traumatic stress disorder (PTSD) due to prolonged exposure to serious long-term traumatic events and pressures. Presumably, anarchists and a select variety of extremists would feel quite at home.

8

Sudan

One never knows what might transpire on a Sunday after church when going into an Irish pub for a discussion about tribalism. An acquaintance from a little Presbyterian neighborhood church of the sort that espoused freedom of thought (had a woman minister) and I walked around the corner to a pub to talk a little about his time as a volunteer in Somalia in response to famine and civil war that had a grip on the Horn of Africa in the mid-1980s.

My friend had just mentioned to me that a Somali, whom he had known in Somalia, had recently paid him a visit in town and suggested that they go to "his tribe's bar" (my friend's) to catch up on things. The idea that someone would naturally think of an American pub as a tribal gathering place (in the literal sense) was an intriguing idea, so off we went to discuss tribalism.

After about twenty minutes of descriptions and discussion, Maria Eitz, the director and founder of Medical Volunteers International (MVI), walked into Yancy's Saloon for her customary after-mass keoke coffee. Unbeknownst to me, she lived in the neighborhood and MVI was based in San Francisco. My acquaintance introduced us and described our conversation. Maria did some reminiscing, and after a little while divulged that she was looking for someone to replace a departed field manager at a famine-initiated child-survival project in Sudan. There was a pause, my friend looked at me, looked at her, looked at me, looked at her again, and said while pointing to me: "There's your man."

Now, it so happens that my tenure as a mayoral appointee was ending at the mayor's office anyway since Mayor Dianne Feinstein's final term in office was at hand, and the broom of expedient political transition was fast approaching. To make a long story short, a few weeks later I found myself in the desert near the Eritrean border in the Red Sea Province of Sudan. It was my introduction to African-style low-intensity conflict, floods, sandstorms, diseases, corruption, foreign-aid dilemmas, political intrigue, and, otherwise, some very nice people.

The task was managing a United Nations Children's Fund (formerly United Nations International Children's Fund) (UNICEF)-sponsored child-survival project that was set up a few years earlier to provide emergency relief and, later, to support district medical authorities in setting up mobile community health services and training local community health workers. I handled administration, logistics, and government relations; the medical staff handled medical tasks and training.

Uncle Saleh's Restaurant/We Remember the British

In 1987, having left Port Sudan early and bounced or jolted through the desert on Tokar Road, which could still offer some British colonial asphalt on occasion, I arrived in Tokar—ancient village, more recent colonial town and fort, and current Sudanese government district headquarters. Tokar—where stories of battles with British colonial forces are proudly and boldly told and are available for the asking.

Such stories, from the local Hadendowa tribe's point of view, are still matters of living memory, given that the British-Egyptian Sudan campaigns, or Sudanese Mahdist Holy War (1881-98), depending on one's point of view, are still passed down to descendants as relatively fresh news.

Many Hadendowa still carry on the nomadic life but ride their camels into town from time to time for provisions and a cup of tea at Uncle Saleh's Restaurant (Uncle Saleh was my interpreter's uncle).

The scene was somewhat reminiscent of a small desert town in the American Old West near the Mexican border—stark sunlight and broad dusty dirt streets lined with old mudbrick buildings that edged up to the vast thornbush-decorated desert. British colonial engineers designed exceptionally wide streets in the new part of town to allow sandstorms to blow through with less obstruction, thus not burying so many walls.

Ancient black, brown, and reddish volcanic rock mountains sit on the horizon staring back, pondering the fleeting human activity.

But, instead of horses tied up at Uncle Saleh's Restaurant and cowboys relaxing on the benches out front, there were camels and Hadendowa tribesmen sipping tea in traditional white robes and turbans. They had swords and daggers strapped to their sides. Northern Sudan is mostly comprised of a dark-skinned Arabized people. You could, however, say that it was a mixed group at the restaurant, since there were also patrons in modern street clothes, and a roughly equal number of Toyota 4x4 pickup trucks and camels tied up out front.

As we dismounted our dusty road-weary Toyota, my interpreter exchanged godly greetings with a couple of the white-robed figures while introducing me and mentioning my interest in local history.

One of the white-robed and turbaned ones, sitting with one leg up on a bench and being confident of his local folklore and unspoken gestures, offered a few keen insights on local history ending with a raised arm and heavenwardly pointed finger, which then arched down in a slicing motion across his throat, continuing the arch until his hand rested with familiar ease on the sword at his side, which was waiting patiently in its weathered leather sheath. He accompanied this historically meaningful gesture, and reference to bygone battles with British colonial forces, with a warm, affectionate smile and a nod of welcome to Tokar and the ancient land of the Hadendowa.

Having exchanged greetings with the locals we entered Uncle Saleh's Restaurant, although there was a slight delay at the entrance as three or four goats ran out, apparently for their lives. Uncle Saleh's was renowned for an excellent breakfast, lunch, and supper of goat meat, lamb, eggs, spicy beans (*ful*), feta cheese, and assorted vegetables and greens. One could tell that the menu items were fresh, as evidenced by the goat hides and leg bones drying in the sun just outside the door, as well as by the assortment of astute, keen-eyed cats lurking about, and everyone knows that cats are finicky eaters.

In the otherwise dimly lit restaurant, a large collection of the sun's rays were reaching down through gaps in the tree-limb and thatch roof, further animating Uncle Saleh who was expertly maneuvering ingredients to, around in, and from large wok-like pans over charcoal-fired mudbrick grills. At least one cat was peeping through a roof gap, keeping lookout over the whole affair, I suppose.

The essential local history, delivered in so few words by the white-robed and turbaned one, eloquently spoke to the historic battles and persevering memories in the Tokar area. His viewpoint also spoke to the broader colonialization exercise known as the Scramble for Africa—primarily a nineteenth-century phenomenon but extended into the twentieth century with some facilitation by the First World War and the Second World War.

The more polite description given to the enterprise was providing Civilization, Commerce, and Christianity to the assumed grateful inhabitants of the "dark" continent. The UK, France, Belgium, Germany, Portugal, Italy, and Turkey (the Ottoman Empire) all competed in efforts to enhance, or hang on to, their territories and resources in Africa—apparently an ancient practice and rite of passage for self-respecting empires everywhere. Everyone is doing it, as the saying goes.

A young America had its turn at expansion, having procured most of its land from native Americans. Also, a very sizable piece of the new-world continent was procured from Mexico by war—lands which had earlier been procured from native populations in Mexico by Spanish conquistadors.

It can get confusing to keep track of procurements. In fact, it can get quite tedious to keep track of procurement-conflicts since most of history is defined by conflicts driven by procurements, or from another perspective, economic, resource, population, and migration pressures. Then there are the more dubious motivations of power, control, greed, glories, and adventure that must be factored in, and are assumed benefits of procurement.

The battles and skirmishes conducted across Sudan in the 1880s, with major engagements near Tokar and Suakin at EL Teb and Tamai, involved British army soldiers and sailors (Nile River/Red Sea), along with loyal British colonial forces from Egypt, India, Australia, Canada, and other colonies, arrayed against a multitude of Sudanese tribesmen.

It seems that empire building and maintenance were and are, likely as not, driven by robust racism—innocent or otherwise. That is to say, sincere convictions that one's preferred race or ethnicity is utterly superior to unpreferred races or ethnicities, and that God assumes that this is so. To quote a British army commander in the Suakin-Tokar area in 1885, while welcoming Australian colonial forces to the fight: "We honor the feeling which led you to war against the desert and its savage inhabitants … the race to which you belong" (qtd. Gambier-Parry 2006, 234).

The story gets more complicated though. It always does. Egypt was nominally ruled at the time by the Ottoman Empire via the Sultan-appointed Khedive of Egypt, who nearly bankrupted autonomous Egypt through corruption and mismanagement. This prompted the UK to take measures to more exactly control Egypt, which had Ottoman–Egyptian Condominium authority over Sudan. The motivation was to protect British economic and strategic interests in the Middle East (otherwise known as geopolitics), which included the Suez Canal and the Red Sea, and other vital transit routes to far-flung British colonies around the world. Also of interest was the favored Egyptian cotton and other commodities grown in Egypt and Sudan.

Adding to the complication was the inclination of many Sudanese to be free of all colonial forces in Sudan (including the Egyptian garrison at Fort Tokar). All of this, not surprisingly, led to a popular Sudanese uprising initiated by Muhammad Ahmed, an early Islamist and a self-appointed Guided One (Mahdi) of Islamic prophecy, who declared the uprising a jihad against foreign occupiers.

Muhammad Ahmed added further complication by declaring that it was his God-ordained destiny to convert the rest of humanity to Islam by persuasion or by the sword.

The Mahdist forces initially won major battles against British-Egyptian forces (1881–96), including the taking of Khartoum and the killing of British Major-General Charles Gordon (the former imperial governor of Sudan), forcing a British retreat. This turn of events shocked the British Empire and led to the creation of an Islamic Mahdist state in the Sudan.

Muhammad Ahmed died in 1896. Nevertheless, Mahdist-inspired Sudanese tribes carried on fighting under Osman Digna until, eventually, the British army and colonial forces regained total control of the Sudan in a second campaign, resulting in the Anglo-Egyptian Condominium of 1899, which lasted until 1956 when Sudan was granted full independence.

There was a brief moment of imperial-military self-doubt after the British defeat in their first Sudan campaign, as reflected in Major Gambier-Parry's (2006) memoir on the battles near Suakin and Tokar:

> The most extraordinary rumours reached us from England about the government being pressed to withdraw from the Sudan altogether, and give up the destruction of the tribes, against whom we had no real quarrel. We hardly credited this, though, and we could not believe that the enormous outlay and loss of life would have been allowed unless the government had some decided aim in view.
>
> (Gambier-Parry 2006, 234)

I suppose that comfort should be taken by all concerned that the stated aim of destruction of the tribes was not meant to be taken personally.

Major Gambier-Parry's reflection echoes other moments of national self-doubt by other nations at other times and places: Vietnam, Afghanistan (Soviet and American), and Iraq. Although some of the subsequent wars were not empire-expansion specific, the character of racist-sentiment-driven wars does resonate to a degree with present-day intercultural "forever" wars.

Although genuine rapport and respect do develop between some occupying troops and local troops and citizens, I have heard ample racist remarks from soldiers in war zones, and respective constituencies back home, directed toward war-zone populations (friend and foe). The racist impulse is still alive and well.

I offer a few other observations. After the first loss to war of close comrades-in-arms or family members, war becomes very personal to those who directly suffer the losses. This applies to any conflict scenario, international or domestic. The emotional impact often creates an exceptionally strong impulse to rage, and an exceptionally strong barrier to humanizing opponents or to reach non-violent solutions. The pain goes deep, resonating in one's bones. This is the nature of violence.

The sweep of world history—or "clash of civilizations," to use Samuel Huntington's (2011) phrase—is essentially the endless repetition of the same conflict. It is the road rage of humanity continually clashing with itself—without empathy, without really understanding the conflict situation, without awareness of alternatives, and without sufficient control over counterproductive impulses.

Some add—without respect for the basic humanity or dignity of others (Hicks 2011).

He Said Yes

Communication

On one occasion, several representatives from a distant village came to our organization's MVI house in Tokar seeking agricultural tools for their village. International organizations (IO) often distribute materials and implements to affected populations due to war, famine, natural disasters, epidemics, and refugee movements. Often as not, it is a combination of calamities that compels action, otherwise known as a complex emergency, which often requires a broad coordinated response from organizations and governments—broadly speaking, foreign aid.

In 1987, the area of Tokar, and East Africa in general, was still recovering from the impact of major drought and famine conditions (over 1 million dead), which prompted MVI to establish a child-survival project in 1984.

On this occasion I called my interpreter, Uncle Saleh's nephew, for assistance (unfortunately, I do not recall his name). He duly listened to the village delegation's explanation of their mission, their circumstances, and their request, and translated. I thanked them for their visit and laudable efforts to help their village.

I then explained that MVI was purely a medical services organization and had no gardening or farming implements, or expertise in the subject. I specified, however, that Oxfam, a British nongovernmental organization (NGO), had an office in town specializing in support for agricultural projects like gardening and farming, and that they should go see Oxfam.

My interpreter translated. Curiously, they kept repeating their circumstances and request for tools, and in each attempt became more agitated. This went on for a while to the point that I was not involved in the discussion at all, and the delegation members were becoming quite animated, waving their arms and shouting. I brought the proceeding to a halt and asked my interpreter what was going on, and what they had said. My interpreter then calmly declared: "He says yes."

Clearly, there was more going on than I was made aware of. It turned out that my kind interpreter wanted to spare me from indelicate expressions associated with a variety of painful, history-bound episodes that, apparently, the principal delegate felt compelled to share. He needed to vent pent-up frustrations about many things that had nothing to do with gardening tools.

The point of this story is that communication, on any scale, be it family, community, nation, or global, with friends, strangers, or enemies (especially enemies), is always susceptible to misunderstandings and the influence of painful history-bound circumstances, and subsequent complications. This applies to conflict of any kind—international stabilization operations and peacebuilding, as well as domestic civil unrest; in particular, those involving cross-cultural encounters. American civil unrest included.

Also, I am certain that civilian local residents who have endured years of serious trauma are as likely to be tormented by PTSD as soldiers returning from war or police officers who are constantly exposed to violence.

To perhaps state the obvious, as much as it is possible, it is important to establish trust. It is important to be honest and as clear as possible, and to get clarification on statements and intentions when needed.

Of course, all of the above is easier said than done. I have to remind myself of this point often enough.

Spies

I suppose I could take it as flattering to be thought of as a spy. But no—I am not, nor have I ever been, a spy. Toward the end of my time in Tokar, our NGO was investigated by the Sudanese national police for possible spying. I never found out what I was supposed to be spying on, but I suspect that I was caught up in general police-state paranoia wherein all foreigners are suspected spies, with the added complication that, three weeks earlier, economic sanctions had been placed on the government of Sudan by the United States and the United Kingdom for corruption involving foreign aid to the country.

My organization was one of only a few American NGOs in the country at the time, and therefore an easy target for retribution for, and a distraction from, the sanctions if some evil doing could be attached to an American or British NGO.

Over the course of several weeks, one of our nurses was arrested after taking photographs of her Sudanese friends in the local market. The charge was taking photographs of poverty, which is illegal in Sudan. Given that Tokar is mostly a traditional stick-and-mudbrick-building village, old stick mudbrick buildings are impossible to miss when taking photos of friends in town. State police made an unannounced search of our house, and interrogated staff and other people in town.

Now, I have to admit that it might have looked a little odd to police that, when they entered our compound (with AK-47s in hand), I was in the yard dumping papers into a big barrel with a big fire in it and stirring the stuff around with an iron rod.

For clarification, the famine-drought emergency had passed, and we were in the process of transitioning the mobile community health clinic capacity over to district health officials, including all equipment, trained local staff, and vehicles, so I was consolidating all needed reports and files and burning all unneeded papers and trash.

I should also mention that Tokar District, which borders Eritrea (then part of Ethiopia), was a sensitive security area, to the extent that Eritrean rebels fighting Ethiopian troops in northern Ethiopia transited back and forth through Tokar District (mostly open desert) to their safe havens north of the border in Sudan, and Sudanese rebels fighting Sudanese troops moved through the area to their safe havens south of the border in Ethiopia—a rebel foreign exchange program, of sorts.

In any case, the national police were determined to find something on us, and local police were determined to protect us, knowing that we were not spies and that the investigation was unwarranted. About a month later, we handed the project over to local health authorities and left the country. Three weeks after that (April 1989), General Omar al-Bashir overthrew the government of Sudan in a military coup d'état. In April 2019, he himself was overthrown in a military coup, and was imprisoned on corruption charges.

I mention this episode to offer a suggestion that it is a good idea to be careful about freely talking "about" sensitive security matters with folks around town when working in countries with insecurities and police-state tendencies.

Except for the spying investigation drama, my experience in Sudan was quite positive. The people of Sudan were unfailingly kind, gracious, and friendly. Local authorities looked after me when, on two occasions, I was in the hospital (malaria, etc.), and were quite supportive and appreciative overall of our efforts.

9

Somalia

It was April 1993, and my first job in Somalia, as project manager, was to oversee the completion of an emergency-reconstruction project already underway in Baidoa. It was sponsored by the US Agency for International Development (USAID) and private donors in the United States. It consisted of rebuilding a community health worker (CHW) training facility in town and the rehabilitation of a former agricultural extension station outside of town, which was to become a multipurpose community facility and orphanage.

The CHW training facility was completed without incident. The multipurpose facility was a different matter. Legal ownership of property—governmental or private, recent or many decades in dispute—is a major complicating factor in post-conflict peacebuilding and reconstruction. In former socialists' countries and former colonies, for example, the former Yugoslav republics (Kosovo and Bosnia), many former state or worker-owned businesses, factories, and properties are in ownership dispute and greatly complicate normalization and peacebuilding efforts.

The day after the multipurpose facility was completed in Baidoa, it was looted and taken over by a local sub-clan claiming that the land was taken from them by the Somali government without compensation in the 1950s (under Italian colonial control at the time). Somalia's independence came in 1960. After lengthy discussions among local authorities (the District Council had just been re-established by the UN mission in Somalia), clan elders, chiefs, and UN officials, the sub-clan occupiers were informed that United Nations Operation in Somalia (UNOSOM) troops (a French Foreign Legion unit in Baidoa at the time) would remove them from the facility if they did not leave.

I do not know what political arrangements were made between local authorities and clan members, but the occupying group vacated the property. In the interim, work continued on the CHW training facility in town.

At the opening day ceremony for the multipurpose facility about three weeks later, with a newly trained advisory board, local dignitaries, donor representatives, and local residents in attendance, speeches were made, and pledges offered. Not far into the program the new district commissioner got mad and stormed out of the proceedings, having been under the impression that he was to get the keys to the donated pickup truck for the facility but did not.

A rising cacophony of flung opinions and arm waving ensued. Fortunately, a local band and performers were waiting in the wings, so I prompted them to jump right in and expedite their harmony and reconciliation-themed play. It is always good to have a band standing by.

We Are Fighters, Not Singers

In traditional Somali society, there are consistent and rapid responses to a conflict depending on what clan, and clan level, a particular threat emanates from. Although not specific to Somali clan dynamics, Vamik Volkan (1999), a psychologist, comments on group cohesion and social identity dynamics in relation to conflict, which I think is relevant here:

> When one large group interacts with another, "we-ness," whether it is described with reference to religious, ethnic, national, or racial affiliation, acts as an invisible force in the unfolding drama ... Similarly, individuals are not usually preoccupied with their large-group identity until it is threatened. When a group is in continuing conflict or even at war with a neighboring group, members become acutely aware of their large-group identity to the point where it may far outweigh any concern for individual needs, even survival. It is the psychology of we-ness that may provide valuable insights into why and how large-group identities can act as an invisible force ... Large groups, like individuals, regress under shared stress; they fall back on primitive ways of behaving.
>
> (Volkan 1999, 25–7)

Volkan most likely had Europe and Asia's twentieth-century wars in mind. His expressions of "we-ness" under stress in conflict, however, are well captured in the Somali, saying: "I against my brother, my brother and I against the family, my family against your family, and my tribe against your tribe." I saw this saying play out in real time on several occasions, depending on where the threat was coming from.

All Somali clans claim to have descended from Abraham and have subsequently subdivided into five major clans and dozens of sub-clans (families/tribes). According to tradition, every child must memorize their exact lineage divisions down from Abraham. Depending on the level of a clan or sub-clan engagement in insult or threat from someone in another group, the response/retaliation is inevitably at the same level.

In one instance, two neighboring business owners in Baidoa from the same major clan but from differing sub-clans got into an argument over the repair of a common wall. The interaction digressed to a fight, and within minutes members of the opposing sub-clans were running to the scene from all over town (women and children included), waving sticks, guns, knives, and rocks while converging on the shop to support their respective sub-clan. Within about twenty minutes, seven people were dead and emergency evacuation procedures had been initiated for internation aid workers in town, me included. The incident did not involve members of rival clans outside of or above the particular sub-clan level involved.

Although not with the precision that Somali clans or sub-clans divide and oppose on short notice, similar group dynamics were demonstrated consistently in Bosnia, Kosovo, and Rwanda between ethnic groups. And, more recently, apparently between many on the right and left in American cities, with ample representation by excited extremists on both sides.

Apparently, automatic prejudice defaulting can be seen in conflict divides of all sorts: war, politics, religion, sports, race and ethnicity, urban and rural divides, gender, occupations, and regional dialects, etc. There seems to be no limitation on likely differences that can be called into the service of prejudice, hatred, and instant righteous hostility—the apparent constants being an adversarial-comparison imperative, a timely excuse or trigger event, and agitation by poor leadership.

My mention of poor leadership specifically brings to mind a well-known practice by some leaders or influential persons (conflict entrepreneurs), to incite groups against each other for political or personal gain. Leaders prone to authoritarianism and fascism are particularly fond of this practice.

Many of my interviewees in Bosnia, across ethnicities, told me that their relationship with their Serb, Croat, or Bosniak (Muslim) neighbors, colleagues, or classmates was fine, even close, until historical resentments and fears, and newly invented ones, were regularly stoked by hardline nationalist leaders pushing their own agendas. It is clear that the consequences of war, violence, chronic prejudice, and discrimination embed animosity and injuries deeply into the psyche, generating ongoing cycles of violence, unless somehow interrupted.

I capture these phenomena in the psycho-social-oriented model in Figure 9.1.

Scholastic disclosure: I saw an illustration years ago with some of the indicators in my figure below, but the emphasis was on the dynamics of humiliation. I have forgotten the source and have not been able to find it again. However, whether focused on humiliation or prejudice (closely related dynamics), the context and results appear to be essentially the same in the violentization process, including in a peace and stabilization operation environment.

The Default Levels indicated in the left section of Figure 9.1 are broad categorizations meant to be generally representative categories of identity that might contain further deconstructed identities. For example, the community level might include urban versus rural people, or military versus civilian groups, or any given in-group versus an out-group positioned in a minority role.

Opportunities to exercise automatic default prejudice seem virtually limitless given the highly refined capacity of humans to thinly slice human distinctions for any given occasion.

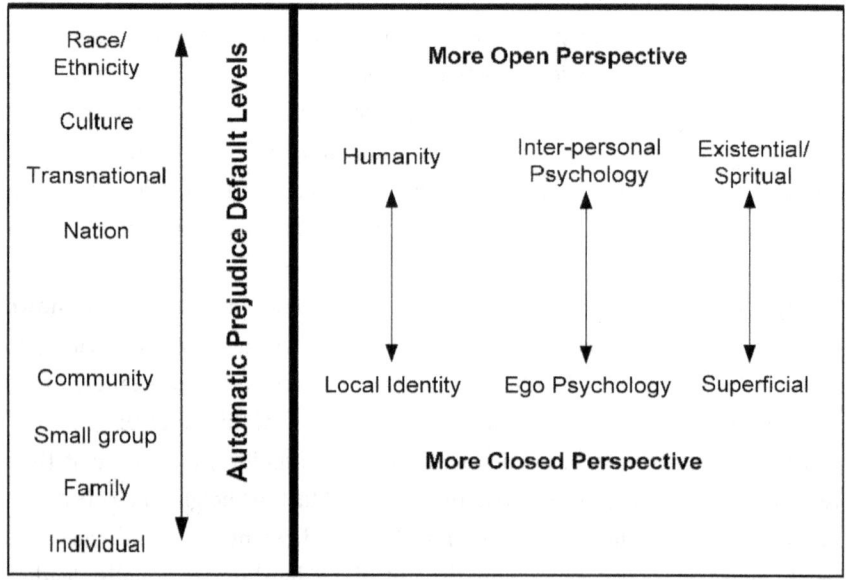

Figure 9.1 Automatic Prejudice Default Levels.
Source: Chart designed by James R. Adams, 2012.

The section on the right of Figure 9.1 reflects a broader more open worldview (upper part) in contrast with a narrower more closed worldview (lower part). No model can adequately capture all elements or nuances of any concept. I only qualify with regard to this model that having a feel for various perspectives seems helpful and more constructive overall. In any case, I suggest that a broader perspective in general is more conducive to peaceful relations.

I believe that the principles of division indicated in the prejudice default model are alive and well in all human societies—large or small.

Violence

Moving beyond prejudice to actual violence, I find Lonnie H. Athens' (2003; 2017) theory of violentization helpful in explaining much of what I have seen in conflict circumstances, particularly his application of violentization theory to communities (see Athens and Ulmer 2003).

The key points that Athens and Ulmer put forth are the assumptions of "domination" and "subordination," and the need for "institutionalizing" such perspectives as defense mechanisms following prolonged exposure to a violentization process on any level.

The insidious nature of the violentization process, as Athens and Ulmer (2003) argue, is that being subjected to violence and subjecting others to violence in an ongoing pattern of domination and forced subordination become desirable and second nature to those caught up in the cycle. This dynamic of violentization, I believe, explains much of the difficulty in stopping or reversing a protracted conflict cycle.

In a discussion among several elders and myself in Baidoa, the topic turned to the United Nations' military presence, which included military units from twenty-eight different countries. One of the elders rhetorically asked, why is the Indian Army in Somalia? (One of the largest UN contingents in the country), then, not waiting for an answer, declared, "We are fighters, not singers." The other elders nodded their heads in agreement and contributed various comments to the effect that Indian Army troops did not stand a chance against Somalis.

This sense of traditional warrior violence strength—although notionally subject to traditional warrior code-of-conduct constraints, such as no harm is to come to women and children—appears to be an endemic process of domestic violentization that was overwhelmed by full-blown civil war and ample modern weapons.

I argue that taking violentization dynamics into account is an essential conflict and peacebuilding assessment task. Violence is an integral ingredient of war and, often, civil strife, and it is usually not susceptible to remedy by ignoring it, or by forcing it below the radar into an enforced (frozen) negative peace where it hibernates in the hearts and minds of the afflicted, until stimulated into predictable resurrection by political opportunists and conflict entrepreneurs—as was demonstrated effectively in Bosnia and across Yugoslavia, not to mention the earnest efforts of fascist leaders in Europe prior to the Second World War.

I first heard the apt phrase "frozen peace" from Kurt Basseneur, a Balkans policy expert and one of my interviewees in Bosnia. Violence, at its worst, is human passion or rationale gone awry, or, perhaps worse, conscience gone dead. To be clear, though, the use of violence is complicated. Controlled violence is the very essence of law enforcement (the use of necessary means to protect life and property), although community policing and de-escalation communication (insight policing) are increasingly used. I believe that, in essence, the same principle applies to the stabilization phase of an international stabilization intervention.

Negative peace and positive peace are sometimes opposite sides of the same peacebuilding coin—in the first instance to get control of violent destructive conflict, and in the second to move dynamics beyond negative peace to the establishment of positive peace/constructive-conflict processes.

To say the least, people are often not at their best in the stabilization phase of an intervention after long periods of violence, stress, and trauma. All manner of violence can be encountered on a daily basis before and during the early stages of an intervention.

Numerous theories have been generated by scholars and practitioners who have studied the dynamics of violence, paradigms, values, and other belief systems that might be considered natural and thereby innate human behavior.

I believe that all concepts pertaining to violence are relevant and collectively account for much that can be associated with war, violent disorder, and enforced/frozen negative-peace environments (for concept details, see Adams (2021) *Analytic Reflections from Conflict Zones*).

Galtung (1969) makes an interesting observation that "structural [institutional] violence seems to be more 'natural' than structural peace," and "personal violence is perhaps more 'natural' than personal peace" (179). In this regard, Galtung's observations echo Athens' sentiments concerning the reasons for violence among individuals and communities.

Athens' (1992) theory of "violentization" explains processes by which an individual progresses, for a variety of reasons, through stages of increasing capacity and inclination for violent acts in interaction with others. Later, Athens (1997) expands his violentization theory to explain dynamics of violence at the community level, with implications for societal levels.

His later refinement of violentization theory (Athens and Ulmer 2003; Athens 2017) expands his commentary to encompass societal-level structures, which should be of interest to those trying to understand the current civil unrest in America, particularly organized hate group violence as well as increased individual random acts of violence.

A number of factors need to be taken into account. Stabilization and peace operations are very complex, multinational, multicultural, multilevel, political, and security-sensitive enterprises with continuous interaction between individuals, communities, and societal-level entities, often in violent, hazardous conditions.

Athens and Ulmer's (2003) edited volume includes an article by psychiatrist Matthew Dumont, who "explores the broader social and cultural implications of Athens's ideas for human nature, mental illness, and authority" (43–52). Also, Richard Rhodes explains, using Athens' violentization theory, the progression of ordinary German citizens into specialized Nazi SS mass killers (Athens and Ulmer 2003, 93–106). Athens also notes that Joshua Sanborn, a historian, discusses violentization and "parallels between the socialization toward violent behavior of criminals and soldiers" (Athens and Ulmer 2003, 107–24).

With stabilization and peacebuilding in mind (international or local), I separate discussion of Athens' theory into two parts: (1) Athens' theory of violentization of the person (as I refer to it) and (2) Athens' application of violentization theory to community, which I think is useful in analyzing societal-level dynamics.

Athens and Ulmer's (2003) violentization theory of the person consists of four stages: (1) brutalization, (2) defiance, (3) violent dominance engagement, and (4) virulency (8–18).

During "violent subjugation," authentic or would-be subjugators, such as fathers, stepmothers, older siblings, neighbors, or schoolmates, use or threaten to use physical force to make a perceived subordinate accept their domination.

The second elemental experience that comprises brutalization is "personal horrification." During this experience, perceived subordinates do not undergo violent subjugation themselves, but they witness someone close to them, such as a mother, brother, close friend, neighbor, or schoolmate, undergo it.

"Violent coaching" is the final elemental experience that comprises brutalization. During this experience, a superordinate places himself in the role of coach and assigns a perceived subordinate to the role of novice. The coach instructs novices that they should not try to avoid, appease, ignore, or run from their would-be subjugators, but instead physically attack them (Athens and Ulmer 2003, 8).

The second stage of the violentization, defiance, entails a moment of "epiphany," whereby a victim that has endured the various elements of brutalization, including violent coaching, makes a "mitigated violent resolution" that it is better to "kill or gravely harm" someone else than to let them do the same to him or her. At this point, the victim has completed a personal psychological reorganization and moves on to the "violent dominance engagement" stage.

This stage involves a potentially prolonged series of events involving the establishment of dominance over another or others, or the failure to do so:

> Unlike brutalization, but like defiance, a violent dominance engagement is also a unitary yet nuanced experience. Dominance engagements arise when disputes break out over dominance, but, despite appearances to the contrary, such disputes do not occur instantaneously. Instead, they arise over a process that has a minimum of three basic steps: (1) dominance-claiming gestures; (2) a would-be subordinate must resist being cast in the subordinate role; and (3) one of the two would-be superordinates must decide to overcome the others' actual or anticipated resistance to performing the subordinate role.
>
> (Athens and Ulmer 2003, 12–14)

Athens and Ulmer (2003) elaborate on a fourth step:

> Virulency is the fourth and final stage of violentization of the person process. After making this new violent resolution, he is transformed from a person who would only resort to violence to resist his or an intimate's debasement or violent subjugation to a person who relishes any opportunity to violently subjugate others. Undergoing the malevolency experience marks not only the completion of the virulency stage, but the entire violentization process. At the end of this stage, a "violent" individual matures into an "ultra-violent" one and, in the process, discovers a complete "cure" for his earlier personal disorganization. Ultra-violent criminals live and die by a motto that turns the golden rule on its head: "Do onto others as they have done onto you, but do it to them first."
>
> (Athens and Ulmer 2003, 17–18)

Athens (1997) concludes by positioning his violentization concept in relation to the broader, ongoing debate on the nurture-versus-nature argument. He considers the human relationship with one's environment to be developmental: "Because of the conscious, interdependent, and developmental nature of this relationship, children, like adults, always play a proactive rather than merely a passive role in their own violent transformations and in the transformations of the larger communities in which they live" (22–7, 115–20).

Athens believes that human beings are complex thinking entities that respond to biological, environmental, psychological, and other influences through experience, knowingly participating in their own violentization process and are responsible for their actions.

In his application of the violentization theory to community (society), Athens argues that the "violentization process" is relevant to understanding violence dynamics in communities, and that it has serious implications for societal wellbeing. He breaks his points down into the "Basic Building Blocks of Communities" (dominance, institutions, and socialization), and "Communal Change Processes" (Athens and Ulmer 2003, 19–38).

Athens introduces his *"minor community"* categories entailing *"civil minor community," "turbulent minor community,"* and *"malignant minor community."* He elaborates on how minor-civil, turbulent-minor, and malignant-minor communities fluctuate and transition, "evolving" or "devolving" into any one of the other minor community categories—that is to say, a more-or-less violent-minor community, or one in basic chaos.

Finally, Athens (2003) concludes by warning of the dangers of increasing violentization at community and societal levels, given our "shrinking" world, and that it is in everyone's interest to support the research and development of programs to help transform malignant-minor communities into civil ones, and prevent civil communities from evolving into turbulent or malignant ones (37).

Put another way, it is in everyone's interest, except perhaps criminal organizations, to shift circumstances from destructive conflict processes to constructive conflict processes. *In this regard, Athens has described a core task of conflict prevention, stabilization, and peacebuilding, regardless of scale. Present-day America should take note.*

The chronic violent conflict in Somalia reflects fundamental ills and destructive traps in which international and indigenous injustices have degraded normal civil restraints and are matched with the near limitless availability of AK-47s to fulfill wishful thinking in dark moments.

Perhaps people elsewhere will recognize the avenging-angel syndrome in themselves, which, if left unchecked, will also lead them to the logical extreme of taking the avenging-angel road to hell.

Welcome to UNOSOM

In May 1994, I am again in Somalia, this time as a humanitarian affairs officer with the United Nations' Operation in Somalia (UNOSOM II).

As a matter of convenience, I sometimes use the term "peacekeeping" to describe a UN mission since it is a term much better known among the general public. But the original definition of peacekeeping (separation and observation of combatants), for example, after the 1948 Arab–Israeli war, has long since lost its literal meaning.

Following decades of frustrating efforts at trying to apply the term "peacekeeping" to UN interventions in which there was precious little peace to keep, the UN devised more elastic terms to describe the more complex circumstances of post-Cold War/intra-state conflicts and subsequent interventions, such as "peace and stabilization" operations. Yet, peacekeeping as a term still survives in the popular imagination.

My first six weeks were spent in Mogadishu assisting the Humanitarian Division Return and Resettlement Unit with the return of internally displaced persons (IDPs) to their villages of origin, which had been overrun or evacuated during the civil war. I co-coordinated IDP return-and resettlement convoys out of Mogadishu in conjunction with Indian Army Colonel Chibber, through the Civil–Military Operations Center (CMOC).

He liaised with the military side, and I liaised with the civilian side. My boss liaised with UNOSOM civilian and military leaders, and key clan chiefs, elders, and respective warlords, as needed. Such operations involved moving about 3,000 to 4,000 IDPs on each occasion in local civilian transport trucks. The IDP convoys were escorted by UN military contingents (armored personnel carriers, tanks, fuel and water tankers, troop transports, and jeeps [all small, off-road vehicles tend to be called jeeps in Africa])—up to one hundred vehicles per convoy.

During this time, I was given a general orientation on UNOSOM and introduced to various local and international officials and individuals.

We Accept

Since the government in Somalia had completely collapsed during the civil war, vital national infrastructure components such as the Mogadishu International Airport and Seaport had become the private income-generation and extortion projects of the strongest clan militias, with periodic changes in management forced by rival clan militias. One of the international intervention's first tasks was to remove militias from vital infrastructure sites and re-establish normal operations.

For me, several statements and events stand out as symbolic of the overall character of the UN intervention during the time I was there. On one occasion, I accompanied the installed UNOSOM port commander, an American, on one of his daily trips to the Port of Mogadishu. The port is a large one, and it was busy. From the hillside upon which we stood overlooking the ocean, the port below was a vision of urgent human industry, with a multitude of ships at dock and waiting offshore with countless tons of emergency-relief food and supplies for offloading.

Also being unloaded and organized were thousands of vehicles and equipment of all kinds: trucks, tanks, helicopters, SUVs, water and fuel tankers, armored personnel carriers (APCs), and road and building-construction equipment.

There were thousands of large shipping containers whirling and shuttling about, containing avalanches of mobile and portable mission-support equipment and supplies, such as portable offices, living quarters, tents, refrigeration units, kitchen and laundry units, medical units and supplies, communications equipment, generators (many generators), convenience-shop containers, fuel, water, food, spare parts, small and large guns, mortars, and rocket-propelled grenade launchers, etc. Mountains of ammunition rounded out the delivery. Basically, every convenience essential for sustaining and protecting an international intervention of 28,000 military and civilian UNOSOM personnel in a desert country with extreme shortages of everything was piling onto shore.

Many of the vehicles were UN white (transferred from previous missions elsewhere) with large "UN" letters painted on the sides. Some still had the original camouflage paint of their respective coalition national armies.

The UN port commander, while describing the workings of the UNOSOM supply-and-distribution system, reflected on one occasion in which he gave a similar briefing tour to a warlord (I forget the name), who, after surveying the impressive scene of the supplies and equipment arrayed below him, and a suitable pause and nod, said: "We accept." That simple, direct statement captures the irony and dilemma of UNOSOM in the history of international humanitarian interventions.

It became very clear over time that the abundance displayed in the early days of UNOSOM II at the port was sincerely accepted as gifts to the people of Somalia (with the kind facilitation of warlords) and was expected by Somalis to remain in Somalia. This arrangement was sanctified by gesture of friendship and pledge of cooperation, and acknowledgment of duly paid foreign aid and military aid compensation, as was customary practice for past colonial right-to-rule, and more recent Cold War right-of-territorial presence liberties.

As Somali and international political and cultural paradigms clashed and misunderstandings and resentments multiplied over the coming months, relationships between all concerned increasingly soured and became increasingly dangerous. The withdrawal of the aforementioned abundance became increasingly problematic.

Roadblocks and Checkpoints

Further symbolic phenomena of Somalia, and internal conflicts most everywhere, are ever-proliferating roadblocks and checkpoints, which are usually one and the same thing except that checkpoints might have a sliver of legitimacy attached to them in that attention is paid to one's personal identity.

In Somalia, there was pretty much a roadblock/checkpoint for every self-respecting or want-to-be militia expressing a territorial opinion, interest in the clan identity of passing travelers, or interest in a share of the transiting goods, otherwise known as local taxation or extortion, depending on whether one is paying or receiving.

Commitments, alliances, and territorial maneuverings associated roadblocks/checkpoints were ever changing in location, duration, and intensity of enforcement. I recall two roadblock/checkpoint encounters in particular.

The first involved a short convoy of three large empty transport trucks and an armed UN escort of three or four vehicles. I was in the lead vehicle with two armed guards and my Somali interpreter. My Italian colleague was in another pickup truck behind me. Our task was to drive from the IDP-staging area in Mogadishu to the food warehouses at the port, load up the trucks with three months of food supplies and resettlement kits for 3,000 IDPs, then return to the staging area in preparation for an IDP return-and-resettlement operation two days later.

All was well as we were moving along a major street when, just as the first half of our convoy had passed through a checkpoint, armed militiamen, shouting and waving their guns, stopped the three transport trucks behind us. My interpreter and I got out of our pickup truck and walked back to the roadblock. With all the shouting and commotion, it was difficult to determine who was in charge. We were simply told that the trucks could not pass the checkpoint.

I insisted on talking to whoever was in charge. After about ten minutes, a man came up identifying himself as being in charge and a representative of the clan in control of that area. He also stated that the trucks could not pass. It seemed to mostly be a problem that the truck drivers/operators were of a rival clan not welcome in that part of Mogadishu.

I informed the militia officer-in-charge about our task and asked for his kind permission to proceed so that we could get the supplies needed for an IDP convoy of over one hundred vehicles and thousands of IDPs and troops. I told him that I hoped that we could get the supplies and move on schedule without having to involve the UN Force Commander and an armed UN intervention at the checkpoint. He saw the necessity and allowed us through.

We proceeded to the port and requested food supplies and resettlement kits. The clerk at the warehouse denied our request, saying that a new procurement form had been added and that we had to go to the shipping and receiving office to get one. I did so.

I was informed by the clerk at the office that the man who approves the additional form had gone home for the day and that it could not be issued until the next day.

I went back to the warehouse clerk and declared with all due conviction, "I am declaring an emergency! The trucks must be loaded now!" whereupon the startled clerk directed warehouse workers to load our trucks immediately. After being loaded, we made our way back through the same checkpoint we had been stopped at earlier, gave a respectful salute in passing, and, while proceeding to the IDP-staging area, only had to veer around one truck intent on backing into our path along the way. Bureaucracy and militias—a lethal combination.

The second roadblock that comes to mind was encountered about 4:30 a.m. two days later. It involved the convoy of about 3,000 IDPs (mostly families) mentioned above, escorted by a Pakistani Army unit. The plan involved leaving the staging area at 4:00 a.m., driving through Mogadishu, a sizable city, and eventually turning off for villages located about a hundred miles to the north. For security purposes, the route was undeclared.

I was in the lead vehicle, a Pakistani Army APC. Indian Army Colonel Chibber, of the UNOSOM CMOC, was in the command vehicle at the rear of the convoy as per standard convoy-operating procedure. Mogadishu was quiet as we rolled along very dark streets, there being no moon and Mogadishu having no electricity at the time. We saw few other vehicles on the streets.

Eventually, the convoy was fully stretched out, being about one hundred vehicles comprised of armed pickup trucks, jeeps, APCs, and transport trucks carrying UNOSOM troops and supplies. Transport trucks carrying IDP families and supplies were interspersed in-between military escort vehicles. We were proceeding along at a moderate speed when, after maybe thirty minutes, we came upon a roadblock in the street ahead, but no militiamen were in sight.

It is not good to stop a convoy on dark streets in a lawless town filled with competing militias. I shouted to our driver to keep going, to veer onto the sidewalk and go around the roadblock, and "don't stop, don't slow down for any reason." The roadblock/checkpoint guards were probably asleep or just away for the moment. Apparently, they woke up or came back after a while since shots were fired into the air at the roadblock after about half of the convoy had passed through.

Eventually, the entire convoy emerged out of town on the north side. After a short break, we headed on to the IDP villages of origin without further incident, except for a little dust up, literally, at the end of the trip.

That afternoon, within a mile or so of our final destination, the Somali truck drivers started breaking out of the convoy and racing for the rendezvous point, turning the last mile into a wild storm of billowing dust and roaring bucking rattling trucks.

The determined charge across the desert terrain was accompanied by the calamitous banging of resettlement-kit pots and pans and a riotous cacophony of righteous shouts from a multitude of bounding and rebounding men, women, and children clinging to the backs of the trucks. The drivers were wholly dedicated to taking creative advantage of every conceivable shortcut over bump and brush and dip in the desert to land at the finish line first and victorious.

It seems that it is a matter of great pride and honor to be the first vehicle to arrive on such occasions. Undoubtedly, one driver was so honored, but it took about an hour to rearrange all of the vehicles from the mash-up chaos of civilian and military vehicles and people and supplies and equipment to attempt an orderly disbursement of said people, supplies, and equipment. A successful homecoming. Most families had been gone for years.

Accidental Likert Scale Demonstration

Some of my time and attention as a humanitarian affairs officer in Mogadishu was spent interviewing people seeking small-scale project grants being made available by UNOSOM's Humanitarian Division. Subsistence in the aftermath of the famine and civil war was still precarious for many people, so a balance had to be struck between finishing-up elements of emergency relief and the introduction of community and small business development initiatives that would support the normalization of living circumstances for the average Somali family, hence small-scale development projects.

For example, a small bakery, a cement block shop, a sewing shop, a produce shop, a household essentials shop, a water well, a small metal shop, an auto repair shop, or a fishing boat and nets, etc. We pushed projects for women and women's groups as much as we could, being aware that the women, generally, were more likely to ensure that families and the broader community would benefit.

However, the interview I am thinking of in this instance involved five men, younger men who came to our office as a delegation from a village not far from Mogadishu. They were seeking project money. I forget the specific purpose, but what sticks in my memory is the particular rhythm of communication and the physical placement of the applicants/clients involved in the discussion on the bench across from me.

Social science methodology includes a tool called the Likert scale, which typically involves using a survey scale of one to five from which a person selects one of the numbers that best corresponds to a description of one's view or experience of something.

For example, "to what degree are you subjected to racism?" Possible answers could be (1) none, (2) very little, (3) moderately, (4) often and (5) constantly. The answers (numbers) are added up for each individual, and then all added together for total averages and statistical (data) calculations, which, in turn, hopefully, shed light on some question being studied. Nonacademic readers do not particularly need to know this, but the discussion scenario that I witnessed is relevant to mention here for a number of reasons concerning human communication, especially in a conflict zone.

The five men were sitting across from me on the same bench. What is notable is that they each employed different approaches in their pitches for project funds. A man at one end of the bench, let's call him Client One, took the most belligerent-hard line in the meeting—paraphrasing, here: "You have invaded my country and you are responsible for the deaths and misery!"

The man right next to him, Client Two, took a strong but slightly less belligerent tone, and so on from most belligerent at one end of the bench to most conciliatory at the other. Essentially, Client One was hardball negotiating, Client Five was just pleading for mercy, and the others, in-between, were in the ordered range of most belligerent to most conciliatory.

Client Three in the middle agreed with hardliner Client One when he spoke, and with pleading Client Five when he spoke. However, Client Three was also synthesizing some of the valid concerns of Client One with the blessings offered by Client Five.

The well-known practice of negotiation by hardball intimidation to get your "opponent" off balance, as admirably demonstrated by Client One, was recognized as such by his colleagues. Also recognized was the timid and uncertain plea for mercy as expressed by Client Five.

Client Three, by synthesizing the polar approaches and viewpoints expressed across the spectrum from most hardline to most conciliatory, did in fact sway the other petitioners to his moderated perspective, being respectful and businesslike with well-reasoned points. He did so in a fashion that satisfied the concerns of all present, including my own. It was an extraordinary exercise to witness.

The reason why this encounter still stands out for me is that it reflects the dynamics of hardball-softball approaches that people often take in their dealings with each other, or that communities or nations take with each other, and which are, often as not, misinterpreted.

The human dynamics that I witnessed in that encounter continue to elicit contemplation on my part and are reflected to a degree in my War to Sustainable Positive Peace Framework model, which uses a Likert-type one-to-seven (1–7) scale to measure the perceived status of structural and relationship elements in conflict and intervention environments.

Such a scale could be imagined by measuring the degree of progress, or not, gained by the five different approaches described above. Clearly, the moderated, well-reasoned approach was more effective overall in obtaining the needed buy-in and cooperation of all concerned.

Intervention approaches of any sort can be decisive in how well or badly things work out. International interventions are usually associated with serious crises, often created by a combination of complex factors, hence the term "complex emergency," which typically includes a collection of political crises + war + drought + famine + pandemic + economic collapse + natural disaster + refugee and IDP movements, etc.

This being the case, complex responses are usually needed, plus, a means by which to better determine the status of a situation, and to plan and track conflict and intervention dynamics. The accidental demonstration of the Likert-type scale that I witnessed in Mogadishu is a useful demonstration of how to best approach others when seeking aid or cooperation regardless of scale.

Your Face Is Your Passport

Below is an excerpt from a letter I wrote in May 1995 with regard to further observations that I had about UN peacekeeping operations in Somalia in 1994.

*****

After my initial six weeks in Mogadishu in 1994, an urgent need for a humanitarian officer developed in Beled Weyne, so UNOSOM sent me there. Things were going well enough. The local chiefs, elders, and authorities accepted my offer of support for small-scale humanitarian-aid/reconstruction projects (water, small businesses, medical clinics, etc.). They told me that I did not need to worry about roadblocks or security in their territory by informing me that "your face is your passport."

All was going well, except that about three weeks later we were pulled out in an emergency evacuation when about 500 Haber Gedir clan militiamen from General Aideed's Somalia National Army (SNA) from the region next over invaded and overran the Beled Weyne region. We were attacked, or rather the Somalis around us were attacked on Sunday afternoon, July 24, 1994.

About 7:30 a.m. on Sunday, our female cooks and cleaners started running around screaming, frantically pulling jewelry off their necks, ears, and arms, hiding it, and scurrying under the tents in the compound. Word was that Haber

Gedir forces were five miles away and closing in fast. It was a false alarm, of course, as explained to us by the UN Zimbabwean military unit commander camped across the road from our tiny UN civilian camp. Everything was fine.

Periodically a "technical" (a heavy machine gun-mounted pickup truck) of the local dominate clan, Hawadle, loaded with men and boys with AK-47s in hand, could be seen charging across the road in front of our UN camp heading north into the desert to deal with the Haber Gedir militia, which was now said to be fifty miles away and "wouldn't come around here anyway."

At 1:30 p.m., the report was that the Hawadle had pushed them back seventy miles and everything was fine. At about 2:00 p.m., the Beled Weyne district commissioner and regional governor (Hawadle clan) were demanding ammunition from the UN Zimbabwean commander, and masses of people could be seen a mile and a half to the west streaming out of town headed in our direction. And everything was fine.

Our local UN zone director (my boss) demanded that at least fifteen Zimbabwean soldiers come across the road and man the walls of our camp—a camp with a handful of tents on the desert floor. "Oh, not necessary, don't worry, everything is OK," we were told by the UN Zimbabwean camp commander. "The Haber Gedir won't come around here, and even if they do, we can handle it."

Bravely spoken, I think, for one in a camp sitting on the desert floor surrounded only by concertina wire.

At about 3:15 p.m., a Hawadle technical shot out of the desert flying across the road by our camp heading south for dear life. From our vantage point up on the lookout post for our camp, I asked one of our UN Somali guards if it was Haber Gedir. He said, "No, not Haber Gedir." About ten minutes later, men, women, and children from the small village across the road adjacent to the Zimbabwean military camp started running across that same spot on the road, scattering to the south.

A few minutes after that, decidedly lethal-looking battle trucks came roaring and rumbling out of the desert from the north in billowing clouds of dust carrying hundreds of armed militiamen. They momentarily stopped on the road a hundred yards or so from our camp. I asked our UN Somali guard again, "Haber Gedir?" He looked at me with a "today is the day" look in his eyes: "Yes, Haber Gedir."

The invading-force militiamen looked around for a minute or so, then turned our way and opened fire, rushing toward us then flowing around us like a river around a boulder, and on to Beled Weyne a mile and a half to the west. It seemed a good time to run downstairs and radio UN headquarters in Mogadishu that everything was not fine. However, for the moment it appeared that the invading militia was not interested in the UN military camp across the road, or our tiny UN civilian camp.

At dusk, the victorious SNA militia returned from town casually rolling along the road between our camps as if coming back from a friendly football match and picnic, smiling and cheerfully waving in a long, slow, relaxed parade of assorted anti-aircraft gun-mounted battle trucks. Each was outfitted with a large two- or four-cannon anti-aircraft gun, a 0.50 caliber machine gun on each corner, and dozens of AK-47 and rocket-propelled grenade (RPG) launcher-packing militiamen. Also, in the victory parade were numerous technicals (pick-up trucks) weighed down with militiamen happily waving AK-47s and RPGs.

Interspersed in the proceedings were dedicated crews driving, towing, or pushing just-liberated Hawadle trucks, tractors, earthmoving equipment, new and old cars, one newly procured artillery piece on wheels, and one lagging lone wobbly liberated bicycle bringing up the rear of the parade under the guidance of its new and inexperienced owner. It was pay day. Literally. The ancient spoils-of-war principle seemed effective enough in lieu of cash or checks as militia payroll.

Apparently, it was strategically convenient for them to set up camp for the night around our tiny civilian UN camp which contained a handful of modest canvas tents and we four UN officers. Our camp did have a seven-foot-high wall around it, which was nice. I think I have an idea of what a small animal surrounded by hungry lions feels like, as do seven UN local Somali guards.

Under our instructions, our Somali guards, of the clan not friendly with the Haber Gedir that day, hid under our kitchen tent. If the militiamen saw them in our compound, the chances of their turning unwanted attentions on us and coming in to get our Somali guards were high.

That night, between periodic small-arms fire in the dark and one blast around 3:00 a.m. from the just-liberated 105 howitzer artillery piece, it seemed prudent to ponder if I had done anything worthwhile in my life.

The next morning, the SNA militia commander informed the UN Zimbabwean contingent commander across the road that they (SNA) were here to stay, that they were setting up a new regional government, were our new partners, and to just relax and carry on business as usual. Except, of course, that we would be doing business with the Haber Gedir/SNA from now on, and not the Hawadle.

The Zimbabwean commander convinced the SNA commander that we four UN civilians had to return to Mogadishu for consultations, and that if his militia was going to be considered as a friendly militia—that is, one the UN could do business with—then he had to allow us to go. He agreed.

The non-Hawadle minority representatives from the west side of Beled Weyne across the river (which the Haber Gedir did not cross for a week or so) had consultations with the SNA of their own in mind. One of the first things we saw Monday morning was the passage of a delegation of elders from those minority groups somberly but purposefully walking from town to the SNA camp across the road from us to present their neutrality to the new masters in the area, and to pay obligatory survival homage.

Before we were evacuated, we made an arrangement with the Zimbabwean commander to get our UN Somali guards out of our camp and across the road into his camp. An Australian commando team of ten arrived at the nearby airstrip about 4:00 p.m. that afternoon on a US Air Force C-130 cargo plane. The Zimbabwean troops provided transport to the airstrip where we four UN civilians boarded and departed about an hour later.

The next morning, Tuesday, while the SNA commander was away from his camp, his militiamen could not restrain themselves any longer. They drove a battle truck through our front gate, breaking it down, taking over the camp, and looting our UN vehicles and equipment.

Our seven UN Somali guards were still hiding underneath the kitchen tent floor. Something had gone wrong. The Zimbabwean commander had not been able to get them across the road into his camp as planned. They remained hidden under the kitchen tent for three days and nights.

On Wednesday morning, the Zimbabwean commander persuaded the SNA commander, who had returned, that to be considered friends of the UN his militia needed to bring back the looted items and vacate our UN civilian camp. They brought everything back with the exception of one Toyota 4x4, which was nearing the Ethiopian border by then.

The decision was made in Mogadishu to close our post permanently, so a team of technicians was sent to Beled Weyne on Wednesday to start taking the equipment out. The UN zone director for Beled Weyne and I went back with them to find our national Somali staff, see if they were OK, and give them their final pay.

The SNA militiamen were no longer smiling as the UN technicians started breaking down our tents and pulling out computers, water pumps, communication equipment, vehicles, etc. I think the SNA and its militia really did not expect us to pull out and were decidedly agitated and at a loss about what to think about it. I am sure a sense of rejection added to the surly mood to come.

None of our local staff was around, except our UN Somali guards. So, I left a message for a Somali doctor in town (whom I trusted, and who was treated as a neutral by all clans) to find our senior Somali staff officer and bring him to the Zimbabwean camp on Thursday at noon (the arrival time of the final equipment removal team and evacuation flight). The SNA "political officer" agreed to allow them both safe passage to the Zimbabwean camp to meet me.

The next day, Thursday, I returned to Beled Weyne, again compliments of the US Air Force C-130 and the ten Australian commandos, for the final evacuation flight. Unfortunately, we arrived three hours later than expected and the Somali doctor had to leave before I got there. Fortunately, however, the day before, the Zimbabwean commander had hidden our now six UN Somali guards (one had gone over the wall in the night) in a UN truck underneath equipment from our camp and driven them across the road to his camp and hid them there. I talked with our Somali guards for a while. They did not like their odds for survival.

By Thursday afternoon, the mood of the militiamen swarming around the camp, really a barely controllable mob, had turned distinctly sour. Some of them were fighting with each other and their commanders because UNOSOM was being allowed to haul off their spoils of war—stuff that they figured they owned now. After all, they conquered the place, didn't they?

The look in their eyes was sobering. Hundreds of surly, bleary-eyed, half-stoned militiamen/boys milling around. The atmosphere was very tense, peculiar—like just before a dark, brooding sky spits out a tornado. Only it had a distinct human quality—heavy, evil, harsh, resonating in my bones. It is the only time that I have felt such jarring, instinctive fear. My survival mechanism had kicked in and told me I had one.

The likelihood of our six Somali guards being captured and shot was high if the Zimbabwean camp was overrun. During the afternoon of the invasion a few days earlier, we had seen Haber Gedir militiamen standing around the rim of a nearby ravine watching something just out of our line of sight. The periodic single-shot reports coming from the ravine were clear enough indication of executions.

I talked with our Somali guards, the Australian commando team leader, and the Zimbabwean commander; we agreed to take our Somali guards with us to Mogadishu if we could get them on the plane. After having them change into civilian clothes, we managed to conceal them in the bottom of a Zimbabwean open-top APC, white with UN markings, and slowly make our way out of the Zimbabwean camp and along the road to the airstrip, passing hundreds of decidedly agitated, red-eyed, half-stoned SNA militiamen chewing khat, a mildly narcotic leaf.

After maybe twenty minutes, we arrived at the dirt airstrip. I had our six UN Somali guards pretend to be local laborers and, one by one, get up and carry a piece of equipment from the APC into the cargo hold of the C-130 and stay onboard to receive the rest of the equipment being carried in. After the equipment and everyone were onboard, the Australian commandos and I boarded, the engines started, and the cargo ramp closed. We taxied and took off without incident, turning south for Mogadishu.

We landed at Mogadishu Airport a couple of hours later and caught the last helicopter shuttle to the UN compound. It was not a straightforward process, given that the six UN Somali guards we brought with us were of a clan not welcome in Mogadishu, so we maintained a low profile. Upon disembarkation from the airport shuttle helicopter at the UN compound, our six Somali guards and I quietly walked to our transit staff quarters.

Outside of the UN compound walls, a couple of local militias were negotiating something with rocket-propelled grenades and small-arms fire—providing "Somali music," as the guards described it—while we walked. The oldest of the guards expressed our sentiments at that moment well enough: "Bullshit, bullshit, bullshit!" I informed my boss that we had six guests.

Two days later the SNA militia overran the Zimbabwean UN camp in Beled Weyne, executing one soldier to make their point, then taking tons of ammunition, fuel, four armored-personnel carriers, trucks, communications equipment, generators, and weapons—everything they had. The 120 Zimbabweans were outnumbered about five to one.

The day before, Friday, UNOSOM had decided to send a rapid-reaction force for reinforcement of the Zimbabwean camp. Up until then, UNOSOM had been having consultations with the SNA in Mogadishu, who assured them that everything was fine, nothing to worry about. However, the Pakistani rapid-reaction force was still loading their cargo and supplies, including live goats, onto the aircraft on Friday evening when it got too late to depart that day, so the rescue mission was cancelled for the day.

The SNA militia overran the Zimbabwean camp the next morning. One week later, the SNA militia stripped the Zimbabwean troops down to their underwear and sent them walking south down the road where they were eventually intercepted by a mobilized UN military unit.

You Are against Kismayo

For my next assignment, I was sent to General Mohammed Said Hersi Morgan's (former Minister of Defense) territory, Kismayo, in the Lower Juba Region. I was introduced to General Morgan and his entourage of exceptionally young colonels and an assortment of very young ministers of finance, culture, and tourism, etc. Pleasantries and pledges of cooperation for the good of the Somali people were exchanged.

In a subsequent meeting some weeks later with the very young colonels and ministers, one of my tasks was to inform the general's younger brother, for the fifth time, that I could not approve a second bakery for his local community organization. "There is a limited amount of funds," I said. "I must be fair and give as many others as possible a chance for funding a first project before issuing a grant for a second project to anyone."

"You are against me," he said.

I asked: "Isn't it fair to give others an equal chance and spread the projects around?"

"I will bring General Morgan," he said. "You will have to talk to General Morgan."

"Do you want me to be unfair to the others?" I asked.

Putting his hands up to his head, almost covering his ears, he shouted: "You are against Kismayo, you are against Kismayo."

Security by Militia Has Its Issues

While posted in Kismayo, UNOSOM asked me to provide coordination on my end for an IDP return-and-resettlement movement coming from Mogadishu IDP camps to the northern part of the Lower Juba Region, a movement of approximately 300 miles and four days over rough roads.

It involved about 3,000 IDPs along with resettlement kits (kitchen utensils, mattresses, blankets, garden tools, seeds, etc.) being transported by approximately forty local civilian trucks to a rendezvous point about one hundred miles to the northwest of my location. A three-month supply of food for each family would be transported by UN Indian Army trucks from a guarded warehouse in Kismayo.

A new idea was being tried—security for the IDP convoy would be provided by contracted militias instead of a UN military contingent. The food and resettlement kits would be distributed at a rendezvous point a few miles outside of the primary return destination. I would oversee the distribution of supplies to each family head at the distribution point.

The operation was completed, but not without some complications. The first complication occurred at the UN warehouse in Kismayo where local clan truck drivers blockaded the warehouse gate with their vehicles. Associated clan militiamen declared that no Indian Army truck would move; that their clan's trucks would transport the food to the distribution point.

The demand was delivered with the traditional death threats. It is assumed that any major interference with a UN operation is sanctioned by the primary clan chief/warlord in the region, which was General Morgan in the case of Kismayo at that time.

The real problem was that the IDP convoy was already en route from Mogadishu to the IDP rendezvous point, and the food and supplies had to be at the distribution point early the next afternoon. An additional problem was that the truck driver's "union," also clan-based, demanded that laborers from their clan load the food, not the ten minority Bantu laborers already employed at the warehouse. We only had a few hours to sort out the problem and get the trucks loaded for an early departure the next morning.

As described earlier, most militias, in a former colony/lawless state, look differently at humanitarian aid than do foreign-aid organizations and workers. The militia objective is often to convert aid to useable commercial tender—the easy way or the hard way. The easy way in a lawless state is by theft or force. Traditional militia negotiation tactics are to create facts on the ground, issue death threats, and, generally, fine-tune the art of brinksmanship.

UNOSOM was not inclined to use force to break the blockade of the warehouse. I had to do the necessary, the expedient, the distasteful.

I negotiated an agreement with the truck drivers to use Indian Army drivers and trucks for transport this time, but to contract their clan's drivers and trucks next time. The local clan laborers would load the trucks this time; the Bantu would load next time. The Bantu in Kismayo are among the most discriminated-against minorities in Somalia, hence the few jobs for Bantu laborers at the warehouse.

I paid the Bantu loaders anyway while they watched the "superior clan" laborers load the trucks. Spirited insults and historical opinions were exchanged between the local dominant clan and Bantu laborers while the loading was carried out.

We departed the next morning for the rendezvous point with the loaded Indian Army trucks and military escort. All was fine, the weather sunny. We arrived at the designated rendezvous point, a large field, on schedule. One complication—there was no IDP convoy and no IDPs, only two militia lieutenants standing at the crossroads.

They informed me that, for the convenience of the UN, we were to hand over all of the food and supplies to them, and they would distribute everything themselves to the IDP families now waiting with the convoy trucks in a nearby town. The considerate militia lieutenants had gathered all of the food/resettlement kit claim-tokens issued to each IDP head of family and presented them to me as a sign of sincerity and efficiency.

I thanked them for their consideration and informed them that the food and supplies could only be distributed to IDP families directly at the designated rendezvous point, and that I would radio UNOSOM Headquarters (HQ) in Mogadishu about the situation and await further instructions. Heated declarations of offense were expressed by the lieutenants concluding our meeting.

The distribution was rescheduled for the next afternoon at the designated rendezvous point. The UNOSOM Force Commander, Humanitarian Division Chief, and an assortment of UN military and civilian officials helicoptered in for the occasion, along with a variety of high-level clan and militia dignitaries. There was no further objection to the arrangement.

Back in Mogadishu at the Return and Resettlement Unit

In November 1994, UNOSOM was pulling out of Kismayo, and the head of the IDP Return and Resettlement Unit was leaving Mogadishu, so I was sent back to Mogadishu to take over that operation. Sometime in December, I was assigned to work with the International Organization for Migration (IOM), an intergovernmental organization tasked by the UN to take over IDP return-and-resettlement operations in Somalia.

The temporary IOM representative and I kept the existing UNOSOM Resettlement Unit local staff and opened up an IOM office in Mogadishu. This occurred two weeks before all international staff had to evacuate for the UNOSOM withdrawal to Nairobi, Kenya, and eventual shutdown.

I paid our local staff from large boxes of inflated Somali cash and moved the balance of our program cash (in about fifteen rice bags) to the UNOSOM cashier office at Mogadishu Airport. The trip involved armed SUVs, maneuvering around roadblocks, burning vehicles, agitated militiamen, and the development of new skills, among which was being able to distinguish the different sounds made by the variety of live-fire rounds whizzing overhead while en route to the airport.

On February 11, 1995, as US Marine hovercraft were landing on the beach a few hundred yards away to evacuate remaining military personnel and equipment, all remaining Humanitarian Division staff (four of us) boarded a UN-contracted Russian commercial jet. On departure, after receiving our Russian-accented seatbacks and table trays-up pre-take-off briefing, the pilot perfectly performed the standard precautionary missile-evasion maneuver.

One week before, I had moderated the last UNOSOM situation report/security briefing in Mogadishu for the joint UNOSOM/nongovernmental organization daily briefing, apparently a privilege reserved for whoever was still around and available before final evacuation.

My contract with the UN ended March 31, 1995, with the expiration of UNOSOM's mandate. But I was still in the IDP resettlement business for the time being. The temporary IOM representative went back to Bangkok, and I was hired by IOM to continue doing the same job I had been doing for UNOSOM, except that now I would be managing my Somali national staff, still in Mogadishu, from Nairobi.

This was accommodated by periodic, unannounced flights to a remote airport not far from Mogadishu in order to meet with my Somali staff and finish up several remaining IDP operations already underway, and also carry out a countrywide survey of IDP camps.

I was running the IOM-Somalia office from Nairobi until we (international staff) got clearance from the UN Undersecretary General for Security to move back to Mogadishu. Such clearance basically depended on General Aideed and his primary rival warlord Ali Mahdi coming up with an agreement on who got to be the new president first.

The presidency is significant in a place where, traditionally, the clan that controls (by virtue of holding all the important ministerial and military command posts) is the clan that gets the power and resources. Basically, the political and human dynamics in Somalia are no different than anywhere else, except that they arrived at the adversarial extreme, therefore involving actual survival, not just advantage.

Teach Them Peace

Concerning the UN's intervention in Somalia, it was a case that the doctor was not competent for the situation and the patient was uncooperative. In the 1990s, the UN, contrary to what one might imagine, had very limited shooting-war conflict-management understanding or capability, particularly involving ethnic-conflict situations. For example, the UN military force arrangement in Somalia of contingents from more than two dozen different countries was utterly self-defeating, effectiveness-wise.

There were small skirmishes all over the country. Distrust and accusations of intrigue seemed as impervious to the passage of time as ever. There were Somalis seeking healing and reconciliation, and, if given sufficient support, could gain in influence to help turn things around.

The Somali Joint Peace Committee, made up of different clans and officially charged with working for national reconciliation, was sponsoring an all-clan food-for-work clean-up Mogadishu project. A chief and member of the committee told one of my Somali staff that, as he supervised the volunteers, "teach them peace, because they are ill inside and need hope." This chief knew where the problem lay and knew a treatment.

Some individual Somalis and UN staff tried to address this inner illness, this trauma, and teach peace, reminding people of their common humanness and conscience, and consequently did touch on core elements of the conflict. And I suspect, for those willing to listen, did stimulate some broader awareness, some memories of positive inter-clan relationships prior the civil war, some feeling of hope—planting seeds of peace for the future.

However, as a whole, UNOSOM's focus, resources, and efforts were devoted largely to political catering to the warlords—"entertainment for UNOSOM" as local residents sometimes referred to it.

Intervention Dilemmas—Human Rights

Generally speaking, despite ample mistakes and misunderstandings generated in international interventions—on the part of all involved—important tasks are often accomplished and needed aid rendered to affected populations. However, there is, often enough, a price to pay.

Michael Smith provides this observation:

> One can hardly talk about Bosnia, Rwanda, Haiti, Somalia, or other cases of possible outside intervention, without recognizing that ethical dilemmas abound in the way we define our goals, our interests, and the means we use to pursue them. Even Samuel P. Huntington, not usually known to be a moralist, has asserted that "it is morally unjustifiable and politically indefensible that members of the [US] armed forces should be killed to prevent Somalis from killing one another."
>
> (M. Smith, qtd. in Hayden 2001, 478–501)

Smith (in Hayden 2001) and Samuel Huntington (2011) touch on two important, if not overriding, factors concerning interventions, humanitarian or otherwise: (1) ethical dilemmas and (2) a willingness to put oneself or others in harm's way. Humanitarian or stabilization interventions often involve messy arrangements with questionable local authorities and warlords.

Such arrangements often involve dubious warlord or militia "protection services" or "logistical assistance" or "consent" for the distribution of relief and development goods and services, or turning a blind eye to the systematic theft of portions of the same goods or services—or, standing back when warlords and militias ethnically cleanse, or otherwise abuse, the very people that the international community (IC) is trying to help.

Sometimes, turning a blind eye is due to the inability to do anything about it. Sometimes, it is due to political expediency. There are, often enough, only poor options.

I witnessed occasions in Somalia, Rwanda, Zaire (now the Democratic Republic of Congo), and Kosovo in which civilian and military-intervention authorities were compelled to exercise dilemma-immersed decisions. In almost every instance, civil and human-rights issues were involved. Such decisions often ended in stress, anger, regret, and anxiety for those involved—internationals, and local representatives and citizens.

In the case of Somalia, UNOSOM I and II were essentially humanitarian-relief operations and police-action interventions calling for the use of necessary force to protect life and property in much the same sense as understood by law enforcement and first-responder agencies worldwide. The practical realities of Somalia, however, induced intervention authorities to take increasingly passive stances in regard to threats and attacks.

There was at least one instance in which a UN civilian zone headquarters (Mercka) was overrun by a local militia. International staff were held hostage. The UN military contingent across the road declined to intervene. I believe that the political impetus by the force commander and unit commanders to not risk casualties was so strong in the mission that the consistent practice of passivity, unless UNOSOM military peacekeepers were directly targeted, eventually led to the total routing of UNOSOM from the country, and the necessity for US Marines to evacuate remaining UNOSOM staff and troops from the country.

To intervene or not, to avert continued massive human-rights atrocities and save civilian lives or not, to do business with killers or not, to risk casualties or not—there are no easy answers.

The enforcement of human rights protections also impinges on state sovereignty. This issue is more of a problem concerning interventions involving a strong regime (not necessarily a strong state). Smith (in Hayden 2001, 482) discusses the delicate balance between nation-state prohibitions against intervention in the internal affairs of other states (Westphalia Conference Protocols of 1648), and, in contrast, compelling calls for intervention in response to massive human-rights violations, for example, genocide.

Smith, referring to Michael Waltzer's (1977) evolving attitude on "just wars," explains that Waltzer was previously an ardent advocate of "quick in and quick out" interventions, but after years of observing intervention failures, Waltzer became more circumspect and now argues for what is today referred to as a thought-through exit strategy: "There is an obligation to make sure the conditions that require the intervention in the first place do not simply resume once you leave" (Waltzer, cited in Hayden 2001, 483). Implications, of course, resonate with ongoing conflicts in Afghanistan, Syria, and Iraq.

Another factor is that the lion's share of attention and funding is given to structural elements (technical, economic, institutional, legal, and political) for planning, policy, and resource allotment in connection with stabilization, reconstruction, and development tasks. That is to say, in contrast with much less attention and resources that are typically dedicated to relationship improvement.

Smith (in Hayden 2001) and Wayne Sandholtz (2002) concur that a kind of balancing "tension" has been arrived at. It should be pointed out, however, that political expediency usually prevails. Recall the decision by the White House to not intervene in the Rwandan genocide in 1994 or sincere efforts at genocide in Dar Fur, Sudan on the basis of framing the conflict as technically not genocide. Otherwise, intervention action would have been mandated by the international convention on genocide signed by the United States.

George Kennan, a stalwart of Cold War international-relations thought, as quoted by Donnelly (2003, 158), more-or-less sums up the nation-state perspective still largely in effect (Kennan 1985): "There are no internationally accepted standards of morality to which the U.S. government could appeal if it wished to act in the name of moral principles" (207).

Although Kennan (1985) expresses the legalistic/nation-state perspective by taking no notice of the UN's (1948a) Universal Declaration of Human Rights, or the "Convention on the Prevention and Punishment of the Crime of Genocide" (1948b), he does advocate the still-prevailing nation-state philosophy of nonintervention into the internal affairs of other nation states—the "CNN effect" notwithstanding. Nevertheless, the IC does continue to experience periodic fits of conscience and demands for taking "responsibility to protect" (Evans 2008).

The exception to the statists' tradition of noninterference in the sovereign affairs of other states was, of course, flexible in the cause of the Cold War containment of Communism—that is to say, armed interventions to ensure that Communist-backed proxy dictators were not tolerated in the abuse of their own citizens, as opposed to US-backed proxy dictators being tolerated in the abuse of their citizens.

Although many countries advocate for the legitimacy of human rights-based interventions (citing international conventions, declarations, and moral duty to act in response to massive human-rights violations), it still seems to be a matter of whether the troubling abuses are politically convenient, or not, at the time to actually take action.

Based on the Organization for Security and Cooperation in Europe's (OSCE) declaration that its basic texts (instruments of legitimacy) are of a political nature, and that it is not an enforcement agency, it begs the question of what options are available when the moment of truth arrives in an intervention scenario to take action or not (see OSCE 1998). The OSCE must call on sponsoring bodies such as the UN Security Council, the North Atlantic Treaty Organization (NATO), the UN international police, or an international criminal tribunal—in sum, a "coalition of the willing"—to do the heavy lifting on enforcement.

In the case of a recalcitrant Serbia on massive abuses in Kosovo, the Security Council obliged with UN Resolution 1244, resulting in the expulsion of Serbian authorities, troops, and militias from Kosovo, and the creation of the United Nations Interim Administration Kosovo (UNMIK) to administer the establishment of democracy-based political and infrastructure systems in the province until a final political status and protections could be established.

The 1995 Dayton Accords for Bosnia were a similar response aimed at stopping ethnic cleansing and other massive human-rights atrocities brought to the world's attention by international media (the CNN affect). As Marianne Hanson (2001) says, the future of human rights as an intervention rationale was set (at least for the time being).

What remedy should be suggested for abusive regimes in conflict zones in which the leadership argues in absolute terms that national sovereignty is absolute and that an intervention violates a peoples' right to choose their own destiny?—from that perspective, it might be said that an uninvited intervention violates a peoples' right to choose to be murdered and to be ethnically cleansed by their leadership.

I believe that, ultimately, whether agreed-upon legal instruments and laws exist or not, and whether natural rights versus human rights, or statist-legalist versus relativist philosophical arguments can be made convincing or not, the matter comes down to a personal, or national, moral decision to intervene or not.

10

Rwanda

My experience of Rwanda is limited to two short trips: one, in 1995 for a week, to visit our International Organization for Migration (IOM) chief of mission in Kigali and get an orientation on the work of the mission there; then again in 1997, to respond to an emergency situation at our IOM office in Kigali. I should mention again that the IOM is a sister organization to the United Nations High Commissioner for Refugees (UNHCR), and is not a religious organization. A "Mission" is the customary term for an office and operation of the United Nations in any country.

Refugees and Hostages

The IOM transferred me to its Geneva headquarters in 1996 to fill a desk officer slot in its Bureau for Africa and the Middle East. My new responsibilities included support for budgeting, reporting, and occasionally back-stopping (filling in for) chiefs of mission at IOM offices in Africa when they went on leave.

My focus on my first trip to Rwanda was the workings of the mission in general, and the circumstances of Rwandan refugees in particular. The IOM was assisting the UNHCR with tracking and aiding refugees, most of whom were in refugee camps across the border in Zaire (now the Democratic Republic of the Congo)—the primary objective being to help prepare conditions for the return of refugees to Rwanda and to facilitate their return when conditions allowed. The IOM coordinated closely, through weekly coordination meetings, with the UN, Rwandan, donor government officials (military and civilian), and NGO representatives. The safety and welfare of returning refugees comprised the central question. National normalization was the broader context.

Issues involved food supply, housing, healthcare, schools, jobs, civil society normalization, discrimination, and the very sensitive matter of justice for victims. This is a typical list of problems facing intervenors, leaders, and citizens in most "post"-conflict zones, especially if the conflict is interethnic or interracial at its core—or can be made to seem so.

I qualify the "post"-conflict above with quotation marks to emphasize my opinion that, although a war might be over (the shooting war), often the conflict is not. In other words, the original causes, conditions, and sentiments underlying the conflict are often untouched.

Although the episode of genocide in 1994 was relatively short, as conflicts go (April 1994 through July 1994), it was extremely intense, and, not surprisingly, embedded in a long history of prior low-intensity conflict interspersed with periodic violent flare-ups between the Tutsi and Hutu ethnicities. The modern-era conflict spans many decades, pre- and post-independence (1962), and includes the involvement of numerous outside actors, African and colonial (Prunier 2009).

Major historical markers include numerous conflicts among various indigenous kingdoms in Central Africa and associated population movements in the seventeenth, eighteenth, and nineteenth centuries, followed by colonial control by Germany (1884–1917) and Belgium (1917–62).

Belgium introduced mandatory ethnic identity cards in 1935 for the Hutu (84 percent of the population), Tutsi (15 percent), and Twa (1 percent) ethnic groups. Prior to that, there had been a significant crossing of ethnic identities between Tutsi and Hutu. Generally, colonial powers supported Tutsi (cattle herders) political domination over Hutu (farmers). In the early 1960s, Belgium switched its political support to favor Hutu-majority rule, which precipitated retaliatory mass killings and discrimination toward Tutsi by Hutu, and mass Tutsi refugee movements into Zaire and Uganda.

From 1990 to 1993, amid continued killings and discrimination, exiled Tutsi initiated guerrilla-warfare incursions into Rwanda as the Rwanda Patriotic Front (RPF) from inside Uganda, culminating in the Arusha Peace Accords political settlement of August 1993. The settlement called for Tutsi representation in a Hutu-majority transitional government, integration of RPF forces into the national army, and the establishment of a United Nations Assistance Mission for Rwanda (UNAMIR).

The turbulent national normalization process was cut short. On April 6, 1994, the aircraft carrying President Agathe Habyarimana of Rwanda and President Cyprien Ntaryamira of Burundi (both Hutu) was shot down as it approached Kigali Airport.

The assumed assassinations were followed the next day by the start of the Rwandan genocide in which 500,000 to 1 million Tutsi (approximately 70 percent of the Tutsi population), and Tutsi sympathizers among the Hutu, were murdered over the following three months. Most Hutu moderates opposing the genocide were killed or fled into hiding.

Hutu soldiers, police units, militias, neighbors, friends, and family members methodically carried out the killings according to instructions from Hutu governmental leaders. It is believed that the genocide was planned and prepared by Hutu extremists long before, through a campaign of dehumanizing rhetoric and weapons stockpiling—machetes in particular—followed by telephone instructions and radio broadcasts beginning April 6 to "cut down the tall trees"— the code to start killing Tutsi.

UNAMIR was not authorized to use force to intervene. The United States and European countries evacuated their own citizens but otherwise declined to intervene. The Rwandan Civil War picked up where it had left off in 1993.

Hutu government military units attacked recently integrated Tutsi military units. The former Tutsi RPF, under the leadership of Paul Kagame, re-initiated its civil war campaign, and over the next several months, through the end of July 1994, pushed the Hutu government, army, and most of the Hutu population across the border into Zaire, yielding approximately 2 million Hutu refugees in camps along the Rwanda–Zaire border.

Some Hutu refugees fled to Tanzania or elsewhere. Hutu leadership established themselves as unofficial managers of most of the refugee camps in Zaire and supported subsequent Hutu insurgent militias into Rwanda.

Paul Kagame became president of Rwanda and established an interim government in Kigali. The Rwandan Civil War then morphed into a general "African civil war" or "Congo war" involving Rwandan RPF troops and various proxy militias in pursuit of Hutu "genocidaire" leadership, militias, and perpetrators in Zaire who had the support of Zairian President Mobutu and Zairian troops.

Troops and proxy militias from various African Great Lakes-region countries became involved in varying combinations of allies and enemies fighting each other throughout Zaire from 1996 through 2006, while Hutu militias continued incursions into Rwanda.

Around 1997, the Kagame regime in Kigali began accommodating the return of Hutu refugees back home and into the government. New identity cards were issued to all Rwandans, but without their ethnic identity indicated.

In the following decades, hundreds of thousands of "genocidaires" were imprisoned, tried, and sentenced for their participation in the genocide. Rwandan courts handled lesser criminal cases. The UN International Criminal Tribunal for Rwanda tried principal Hutu government civilian and military leaders who instigated and managed the genocide.

As I mentioned above, my first trip to Rwanda was a basic orientation trip. It involved meetings with international and Rwandan officials and staff, and visits to refugee camps across the border in Zaire, north of Goma. The camps were numerous and very large. Hundreds of thousands of Hutu refugees populated blue-tarped or stick-covered huts crowded onto the hillsides for miles in every direction along the border. UN agencies, the IOM, and international and local NGOs did the best they could to provide food, shelter, medical care, and other services to the refugees.

Given the large numbers of people and the problem of Hutu genocidaire leadership often being involved in the management of the camps (officially and unofficially), with insurgent warfare underway all around, the task was immense, very complex, and rife with the kind of intervention moral dilemmas that I described earlier in the Somalia essay. Trauma and violence saturated the atmosphere.

During the night I spent in Goma, I awoke about every twenty minutes from extremely violent dreams. I had never experienced that before, nor anywhere else since. I am not a psychic. I can only say that it felt like a great disturbance in the psychic atmosphere, if such a thing exists.

My second trip to Rwanda, in 1997, was in response to a hostile takeover of our IOM office and compound in Kigali by contract truck drivers hired to transport Rwandan refugees from camps in Zaire back into Rwanda. About fifty of our local IOM staff were taken hostage. The newly reconstituted Rwandan Army freed the hostages after a couple of days.

Our IOM legal officer and I were flown from Geneva to Kigali to deal with the crisis. Our legal officer was tasked with negotiating with the transport driver-contractors. The IOM chief of mission position was vacant at the time, so I was tasked with working with our IOM-Kigali national officers and staff to get the IOM-Rwanda operation going again.

We were installed in the Hotel des Mille Collines where our legal officer met with the driver-contractor representatives over the course of the next week. I do not recall the details of the driver-contractor grievances or negotiations beyond their demand for more money due to encountering greater risks than originally expected.

The day after we arrived, we were driven with armed guards to the IOM compound to meet with our Rwandan national staff. The best way I can describe our meeting is that it was a long heart-to-heart decompression meeting with about forty local staff members and several international staff. The meeting went well enough. We agreed to work together over the coming weeks to resolve outstanding issues and concerns as best we could, given the difficult circumstances of Rwanda at the time.

Our legal officer and the driver-contractor representatives reached an agreement on revised transport contracts. He then headed back to Geneva. I stayed behind, meeting with staff and other international and Rwandan officials over the next few weeks. My task was to help get communications, logistics, and administrative systems going again, including payroll, and to generally calm things down and help restore a functional level of mutual trust on the part of all concerned.

One of IOM's personnel officers back at IOM Headquarters in Geneva shared her concern for me and their support by informing me that they had given me a "beaucoup increase in life insurance" before my trip to Kigali.

Chosen Traumas

I am not a psychiatrist, nor a psychic, as already confessed, but it is worthwhile mentioning here some thinking on psychological dynamics associated with overlapping traumatic events. First, the concept of "chosen trauma" was developed by Vamik Volkan (1999), a psychiatrist who has studied ethnic conflict in depth. Second and third are violence and the ancient human ailment of humiliation.

To elaborate on Volkan's concept of chosen trauma from his book *Bloodlines: From Ethnic Pride to Ethnic Terrorism* (1999), he describes the phenomenon this way:

> I use the term to describe the collective memory of a calamity that once befell a group's ancestors. It is, of course, more than a simple recollection; it is a shared mental representation of the event, which includes realistic information, fantasized expectations, intense feelings, and defenses against unacceptable thoughts ... I maintain that the word *chosen* fittingly reflects a large group unconsciously defining its identity by the transgenerational transmission of injured selves infused with the memory of the ancestors' trauma.
>
> (Volkan 1999, 48)

Clearly, unresolved past traumas are a core complicating factor in reconciling conflict parties, or, perhaps more accurately, reconciling differing perceptions of past traumas.

Beyond conflict-resolution scholars, only a small group of people such as psychiatrist Vamik D. Volkan, former diplomat Joseph V. Montville, and Demetrios A. Julius (Volkan et al. 1991), and sociologist Johan Galtung (1969) have long advocated for direct use of psychology and sociopsychology to better understand conflict and violence intervention analysis and tasking.

In recent years, however, a growing number of psychiatrists, social psychologists, and political psychologists have taken up the challenge to study the problem of large-scale conflict. For example, the Society for the Study of Peace, Conflict, and Violence, a division of the American Psychological Association, established the journal *Peace and Conflict: Journal of Peace Psychology*.

Collectively, mental health professionals have contributed much to the subject of psychology and conflict dynamics. Following the lead of astute leadership such as that of Nelson Mandela and Archbishop Desmond Tutu (South Africa's Truth and Reconciliation Commission), perhaps the involvement of well-trained international and local NGO staff could prevent or mitigate excesses of violence. Of course, it would be helpful to have the support of enlightened diplomats, politicians, military leadership, and political and civil affairs personnel before matters get out of control.

One question is whether relevant approaches can be conducted without openly advocating or even using the term "reconciliation," which often does little but further anger traumatized people if they are not ready for it, that is, if they have not yet effectively mourned their losses—an essential step insisted on by Volkan (1999)—or if victims have not received at least an acknowledgment of remorse on the part of perceived perpetrators (Chapter 3 of Volkan 1999).

In the context of anguish, Lonnie H. Athens (1992 or 1997 or 2017) uses the term "psychological disorganization." In connection with this point of psychological theory, the name Malcom X probably does not immediately come to mind. But since the subject here is chronic violence—essentially a state of anguish, an experience well known to those who have been subjected to serious racism—a discussion of psychology is relevant.

Malcom X would presumably disagree with Athens on the point of taking responsibility for all of one's actions. Malcom X once explained: "I'm nonviolent with those who are nonviolent with me. But when you drop that violence on me, then you've made me go insane, and I'm not responsible for what I do" (excerpt from Malcom X speech: "Ballot or The Bullet", April 3, 1964) https://www.gilderlehrman.org/sites/default/files/inline-pdfs/ballot_or_bullet.pdf.

Along those lines, I often heard the phrase "It drives me crazy" from local nationals in discussions about enemies and conflict, including those involving International Community (IC) policies, practices, and prejudices brought to an intervention.

Conversely, Malcom X and Athens may well concur on Athens' description of the violentization process itself. Malcom X describes his own observation of what Athens would later call the brutalization stage of violentization:

> They'd all had the same look in their eyes, the same distancing of themselves from what was happening around them. In time I thought, this boy, too, would go on to acquire the same wariness, a quality of disguised hurt, a quality of removal and disavowal. In some important way he, like them, would cease to care. It wasn't just that these boys had come to expect to be blamed when they really had done nothing, although that was part of it. No, what was really important was that they'd made it so that it didn't matter anymore. Because they'd long ago discovered that the way to survive was to hide their real selves from the world. And no matter what happened, they would never, ever, let anything touch them.
>
> (Malcom X, qtd. in Steger and Lind 1999, 176)

In so many words, the above is a good description of violentization as shared with me by a number of local staff, citizens, and leadership, and my own layman's observations, in Somalia, Rwanda, and elsewhere.

The Matter of Humiliation

Humiliation is another significant factor in the violentization process. I believe that it is a major factor in Rwanda's history. Humiliation is a principal factor in the initiation, escalation, intensity, and intractability of conflict, particularly humiliation of the sort perpetrated by those who profess to be superior to those being dominated.

Evelin Gerda Lindner (2002) conducted extensive research into the phenomenon of humiliation in connection with the First World War, and with the recent conflicts in Somalia, Rwanda, and Burundi, and refers to the ongoing dynamics as "cycles of humiliation."

She defines humiliation as

> enforced lowering of a person or group, a process of subjugation that damages or strips away their pride, or dignity. To be humiliated is to be placed, against your will and often in a deeply hurtful way, in a situation that is greatly inferior to what you feel you should expect.
>
> (Lindner 2002, 125–38)

...

> Humiliation entails demeaning treatment that transgresses established expectations. It often involves acts of force, including violent force ... the idea of pinning down, putting down or holding to the ground. Indeed, one of the defining characteristics of humiliation as a process is that the victim is forced into passivity, acted upon, made helpless.
>
> (Lindner 2002, 6)

Lindner also describes a dynamic that she calls "humiliation entrepreneurship":

> Feelings of humiliation provide a highly potent element that may be appropriated by leaders. Hitler and the extremist Hutu leaders engaged in what may be called "humiliation entrepreneurship" – the deliberate activation and manipulation of feelings of humiliation in others for the purpose of achieving personal, social, or political objectives.
>
> Humiliation entrepreneurship may be a very cost-effective method of undermining or eliminating rivals or victims ... The Hutu elite succeeded in inciting their population to buy their own weapons and take up arms against those they believed to be their would-be humiliators ... Such excessive degrees of mobilization are possible because of the virulence of the feelings of humiliation experienced by the perpetrator in the past and feared in the future, and the subsequent urge to retaliate against or preempt such feelings by committing acts of humiliation.
>
> (Lindner 2002, 128–9)

Lindner's (2002) description of humiliation processes in effect in Nazi Germany and Africa has clear resonance with Athens' violentization dynamics. Acts of humiliation were also deliberate strategic objectives in the conduct of war in Bosnia and Kosovo, as evidenced by widespread calculated rape and mutilations, and the destruction of religious and cultural facilities and artifacts of ethnic groups.

Using Lindner's (2002) perspective, one would conclude that the perpetrators of the atrocities were acting out predictable manifestations of prior humiliations and violentization processes.

The key points that Athens (1992 or 1997 or 2017) puts forth in this context are the assumptions of "domination" and "subordination," and the need for "institutionalizing" such perspectives as defense mechanisms following prolonged exposure to a "special form of socialization" and dramatic social change, characteristic of the violentization process at any level.

The insidiousness of the violentization process, as Athens (1992 or 1997 or 2017) argues, is that the conditions of being subjected to violence and subjecting others to violence in an ongoing pattern of domination and exacting subordination become desirable and second nature to those caught up in the cycle.

The Balkans has for centuries been a labyrinth of mutual offenders and mutual victimhood. Several Bosnians of different ethnicities told me that family members of their great-grandfathers were tortured and killed by families of an "enemy" ethnic group (families that knew each other) in their village or the next one over.

They made clear that the cycle is repeated every two or three generations, with each opposing ethnic family taking turns killing members of the other ethnic family, and, as a matter of course, expecting revenge in-kind by the same families in subsequent generations.

They described this practice as a life-and-death cycle and had no expectation of seeing its end. This is a profound expression of experiential humiliation (Lindner 2002) and, in my opinion, indication of Athens' perspective on the virulency stage of the violentization process (2003, 8).

The notion of a role for psychology in peace operations is captured and summarized by Harvey J. Langholtz (1998) in *The Psychology of Peacekeeping*:

> "War represents the failure of diplomacy." This attributable quote is well known within diplomatic circles. But in today's wars, characterized by ethnopolitical conflict and chaos, war represents not just the failure of diplomacy, but also the failure of psychology. It is the premise of this book that there are emerging roles for psychologists and other social scientists to play in peacekeeping before, during, and after conflict.
>
> (xi)

I think that it is safe to say that empires and inter-tribal warfare have all effectively employed humiliation and violentization in reaching vengeance, power, political, and nationalists' objectives and have, knowingly or unknowingly, generated chosen traumas.

The task now is to educate all concerned about the consequences of humiliation and violentization in connection with chosen traumas and conflict cycles, whether in Africa, the Balkans, Russia, Ukraine, the United States, or anywhere else.

11

Kosovo

There is a saying that "all politics are local." So, it seems, is murder.

The Kosovo War (1998–9) shares many commonalities with the other "Yugoslavia wars" during the breakup of the Socialist Federal Republic of Yugoslavia (FRY) in the 1990s. I will give a brief description here in the Kosovo section and elaborate further in Part III in connection with my doctoral field research in Bosnia in 2009.

In the summer of 2000, I traveled to Kosovo to explore the possibility of working for the United Nations (UN) again, this time armed with a newly minted master's degree in Conflict Analysis and Resolution (CAR). I had taken two years off to work on the degree program full time.

Although my time with the International Organization for Migration (IOM) had been very productive and rewarding, I was operating under the notion that I might be able to more directly apply my newly acquired knowledge, skills, and abilities to conflict assessment and peacebuilding tasks as a UN field officer again.

Over the course of two weeks, I did informational interviews with UN and other international organization (IO) personnel in Kosovo to better understand the situation there and how I might fit in professionally, post-graduation. Subsequently, I applied for a civil affairs officer vacancy with the United Nations Interim Administration in Kosovo (UNMIK), which was an operation of the UN Department of Peacekeeping. I was hired and assigned in-country as a local communities officer. I returned to Kosovo in November 2000 to begin work.

But, before I comment on my on-the-ground observations and experience in Kosovo, I will elaborate on the context below.

All Politics Are Local

Whether noble call for a common humanity or shouts to inspire crimes against your neighbor, messages proclaimed on capitol steps are meant to resonate on the doorsteps of citizens back home, and, eventually, to inspire action at the local level. This tradition is an ancient and still effective practice for good or ill. It is a tradition well known in the Balkans, as is ethnic cleansing. The uncertain existence of mixed-ethnicity nation states is part of this story—the United States included.

In an effort to bring order out of the endless chaos of warring European kingdoms and principalities of the Middle Ages—essentially, ethnic or clan-based city-states—protocols for the newly emerging nation-state system were established at the Conference of Westphalia in 1648 to resolve sovereignty questions and territorial disputes. This arrangement for defining the nation-state and for employing protocols for state-sanctioned violence lasted, with dubious success, until the end of the Cold War (1991).

It was about this time that the arrangement finally lost its elasticity to cover the multitude of nation-state proxy wars (intrastate wars) in other countries, often generated by and on behalf of empires and want-to-be empires comprised of armies, commercial interests, ideologues, and religious groups.

The imperial impulse for certain political and commercial advantages, competitive geopolitical security, and appeasing internal interests back home with external proliferation was often accommodated by supporting or starting conflicts in the territories of other nation-states or continents.

Although many conflicts are evidence of the pushing and shoving of empires and superpowers, there have also been ample indigenous groups inclined, coerced, or otherwise desperate to take advantage of outside commercial or military offerings to undermine, murder, or assimilate their neighbors. The strongest prevailed. Innocence was less of a concern.

Imperial elbowing in near and far lands was effective in instructing locals in evermore advanced ways of warfare and ethnic cleansing if such instruction and arming were needed. The legacy is a lasting one. In this new-old era of intrastate conflict, nine out of ten conflicts worldwide are essentially internal conflicts within nation-states (Hewitt et al. 2010). Intrastate conflicts are often induced along ethnic or race fault lines in ethnically or racially mixed states, cities, towns, and villages. Hence, murder by neighbor.

The only real difference now is that multinational corporations, globalizing terrorist organizations, and transnational organized crime syndicates are more effectively enabled by globalizing communications technology, such as the cell phone and internet, and are less and less bothered by the sanctity of national boundaries.

At the same time, there are more organizations and globalized citizen initiatives (post-Second World War and post-Cold War) that advocate for greater attention to civil rights, human rights, and peacebuilding, along with institutions to provide associated legal instruments such as the Convention for the Protection of Human Rights and Freedoms, the Helsinki Final Act (OSCE 1975a,b), the Organization for Security and Cooperation in Europe (OSCE) (1998; 2003), the UN Commission on Human Rights, and the International Criminal Tribunal in The Hague.

The establishment of the European Union (EU) and North Atlantic Treaty Organization (NATO) has successfully deterred war between European states since the Second World War, with the exception of the breakup of Communist Yugoslavia and the recent invasion of Russia into Ukraine (Yugoslavia was not, and Russia and Ukraine are not members of NATO or the EU). Nevertheless, there has been a swing in recent years back toward authoritarianism in some countries, which has, in turn, stirred fascistic impulses in certain ideological or race supremacists' groups.

Kosovo, like other states or provinces connected to the breakup of Yugoslavia, suffered badly. Yugoslavia (literally meaning Southern Slavic Land) itself was a remnant of geopolitical bargaining between Soviet and Allied leadership at the end of the Second World War, briefly falling under the Soviet Eastern Bloc sphere of influence until 1948 when it split from Soviet dominance, solidifying its place in the nonalignment movement.

The dissolution of the Soviet Union (1991) and lapse of the moderating influence of Yugoslavia's founding President Josip Broz Tito, who died in 1980, proved too much for the tenuous hope of a common humanity that Tito had promoted in his multiethnic federation. Increasingly, ethnic-Serb nationalist hardliners in the largest Yugoslav state, Serbia, pushed for a pan-Serbian state that would encompass Serb populations residing in the other Yugoslav states.

Slovenia had few Serbs. Serbian hardliners assumed that Montenegro, with a 29 percent Serb population, would support Serbian nationalistic initiatives within a Yugoslav federation. So, the primary focus for incorporating additional Serb populations into a Greater Serbia was the Serb-majority towns and villages of Croatia (12 percent Serbs), and Bosnia (31 percent Serbs).

A dominant Greater Serbia in a Yugoslav federation was not an attractive proposition to the mostly non-Serb states (Croatia, Slovenia, Bosnia, Macedonia). Nevertheless, as Serbian nationalist hardliners gained political control in Serbia through the rise of increasingly Serb-hardliner, Slobodan Milosevic (eventual

Serbia and Yugoslavia president), Serbia worked diligently to realize Greater Serbia objectives.

Serbian right-wing hardliners simultaneously used federation institutions to their benefit while undermining those same institutions through their "Anti-bureaucratic Revolution"—an initiative similar in tone and intent to President Trump's war on the "Deep State" (taken to mean America's governmental institutions and professional civil service).

Also similarly, American extremists attempted a mob takeover of the Capitol Building in Washington, DC, on January 6, 2020, encouraged by a collection of right-wing hardliners and extremist-leaning media personalities to stop the 2020 presidential electoral vote count and overturn President Joe Biden's election in favor of Trump.

Incidentally, undermining an election in this way, as promoted by President Trump, would constitute a failure to meet a key UN benchmark of responsible governance, and would likely result in disqualification from governance if it had taken place in a peacekeeping mission scenario.

Serb nationalist's insistence on partitioning Yugoslavia according to ethnicity, yet keeping the federation intact, was based on federal authority and an assumption of Serbia being the greater among equals in the federation.

Belgrade, the capital of Serbia, was also the capital of the Yugoslav federation and seat of the federal presidency, which contained the Federal Executive Council, which controlled the federal armed forces and federal police throughout Yugoslavia. One by one, the other Yugoslav states declined partition, declared independence, and left the federation.

One by one, Serbian/federation forces attacked Croatia, Slovenia, and Bosnia (1991–5). Gradually, Yugoslavia federal forces and federal police and militias came under total Serbian control and were decisively attached to Serbian nationalist objectives.

Milosevic, as commander-in-chief of Yugoslavia federal forces, placed 80,000 Serbian federal troops under the command of Yugoslav Army colonel and Bosnian-Serb Ratko Mladic, who executed Bosnian-Serb and Greater Serbia war objectives, which included the ethnic cleansing of non-Serb populations in Serb-majority areas of Croatia and Bosnia.

The entire scenario was exceptionally complicated, with many episodes of intrigue, provocation, and political maneuvering, involving various federal forces, police units, militias, and political and religious leaders at all levels. A further complicating factor was the fact that all of the Yugoslav states contained ethnically mixed populations, including two autonomous provinces in Serbia, Vojvodina and Kosovo.

At various times, President Franjo Tudman of Croatia and President Milosevic of Serbia discussed partitioning Bosnia between them with the objective of creating a Greater Croatia as well as a Greater Serbia. Bosnian-Muslims (Bosniaks) rejected this idea. At the time, Bosnia contained about 44 percent Bosniaks, 31 percent Bosnian-Serbs, and 17 percent Bosnian-Croats.

The ensuing wars resulted in over 100,000 dead, about 4 million refugees and internally displaced, the complete breakup of the FRY, economically devastated populations, and widespread political instability. The stage was set for the war in Kosovo.

The Kosovo Conflict

The war in Kosovo, a province of Serbia, was the last of the "Yugoslavia wars." Although armed conflict had not yet arrived in Kosovo by 1989, its precursors had. Civil unrest was increasing. Serbia rescinded Kosovo's autonomous provincial rule in 1989. Suppression of Kosovo-Albanians by Serbian authorities was deepening.

Structural violence (institutionally and legally sanctioned measures) included revocation of constitutional rights and freedoms of Kosovo-Albanians, and the removal of Kosovo-Albanian governmental officials, institutional administrators, business and industry leaders, and university professors from their jobs. Serbs in Kosovo, and Serb refugees from Serbia's other wars who needed housing and employment were installed in the resulting forced vacancies.

Ethnic-Albanian universities in Kosovo were closed and the use of the Albanian language in government offices and schools was prohibited. It appears that, by 1999, institutional discrimination (structural violence) and direct violence and repression against Kosovo-Albanians were similar to that employed in South Africa's system of apartheid.

Ethnic Albanians made up about 92 percent of the population in Kosovo, Kosovo-Serbs approximately 5 percent, and Roma, Bosnians, and other minorities comprised the remaining percentage. I should qualify here that many Kosovo-Albanians told me that "things were OK" for them in Kosovo before the resurgence of aggressive Serb nationalism, and the rescinding of Kosovo provincial autonomy in 1989.

In 1990, in response to a decade of civil unrest and progressively repressive measures and violence against them, the Kosovo-Albanian majority in the Kosovo National Assembly passed a declaration of independence of Kosovo from Serbia. This first declaration of independence was only recognized by Albania. Eventually, Kosovo-Albanians established armed militias known as the Kosovo Liberation Army (KLA) to conduct a guerrilla-warfare rebellion. Serbian authorities considered the declaration to be an illegal separatist movement to be put down by any means.

Serbs deem Kosovo to be a sacred Serbian-origin land. The centuries-old Serbian Eastern Orthodox Patriarchy is traditionally located in Kosovo. It is also the location of the single most important event in the Serbian narrative—the Battle of Kosovo Polje (Field of Blackbirds). The battle, which took place on June 15, 1389, symbolizes simultaneously two principal aspects of Serbian national identity—"chosen glory" and "chosen trauma"—to use Volkan's (1999) terms for significant socio-psychological events in a peoples' historical memory.

The chosen trauma refers to the defeat of the Serbian forces, led by Serbian Prince Lazar Hrebeljanovic, by Ottoman Empire forces led by Sultan Murad Hudavendigar. The battle was essentially a stalemate, with heavy casualties on both sides, and the deaths of the prince and the sultan. The following year, the vastly larger Ottoman army regrouped and overwhelmed opposing forces in Southeastern Europe, establishing Ottoman-Muslim control of the area for about the next five hundred years.

The same battle represents a chosen glory in that it signifies Serbian sacrifice on behalf of a Christian Europe. The sacrifice narrative is reinforced by the Serbian defeat of Ottoman forces in the First World War and removal of Ottoman control in 1912. Also connected to the sacrifice narrative is the fight of Serbian guerrilla forces (Chetniks) in the Second World War against Nazi and Fascist forces, which included Nazi-backed Croatian militias (Ustase) and Ustase ethnic cleansing and massacres of Serb civilians.

I point out all of this to highlight the profound historical complexities of interethnic cultural and national memories and identities in Kosovo, and the Balkans in general—a history of mutual victimization and mutual victimhood.

It is in this context that Milosevic declared to Serbs at a rally in Kosovo on the 600th anniversary of the Battle of Kosovo Polje that no Serbs would be harmed again.

Following the decade of increasingly severe repression and violence against Kosovo-Albanians by Yugoslav forces and Kosovo-Serb authorities, the UN Security Council issued United Nations Security Council Resolution (UNSCR) 1160, on March 31, 1998, under Chapter VII authority—that is to say, enforcement authority to maintain or restore international peace and security. Specifically, the Security Council called on the FRY to stop the violence against Kosovo-Albanians and resolve the conflict through political dialogue.

Further, Yugoslav and Serb authorities were called on to adhere to the principles of the Helsinki Final Act of the Conference on Security and Cooperation in Europe of 1975 as shown on OSCE's website accessed in October 2020.

i. Sovereign equality, respect for the rights inherent in sovereignty
ii. Refraining from the threat or use of force
iii. Inviolability of frontiers
iv. Territorial integrity of states
v. Peaceful settlement of disputes
vi. Nonintervention in internal affairs
vii. Respect for human rights and fundamental freedoms, including the freedom of thought, conscience, religion, or belief
viii. Equal rights and self-determination of peoples
ix. Co-operation among States
x. Fulfillment in good faith of obligations under international law.
(OSCE 1975a,b)

The Helsinki Final Act (1975a,b) articles are intended as updated guidance for assumed more morally conscious nation-states, compensating for such deficiencies in the Westphalian Conference rules of 1648. However, as the United Nations and all concerned discovered in Somalia, Bosnia, and Kosovo, reconciling Articles VI and VII is not easy—that is to say, reconciling the principle of nonintervention into the internal affairs of a sovereign state with the principle of intervention on behalf of war-crimes victims without the consent of the sovereign state in question. Family interventions are problematic—a family of nations included.

Humanitarian-protection intervention without consent was not particularly a diplomatic problem in Somalia. Somalia was a completely failed state without central or local governments, and under assault by dozens of competing clan militias in the middle of a famine and civil war.

The wars in Croatia and Bosnia involved limited intervention in those individual sovereign states with consent, but without the consent of the Yugoslav federation—meaning Serbia and the Serb areas of Bosnia and Croatia.

UNSCR 1160 established an arms embargo on all parties in Kosovo the same way the earlier UN arms embargo had frozen all rearming in the earlier Bosnian war resulting in all non-Serb forces being vastly outmatched in military capacity in both wars; in effect, UNSCR 1160 froze military capacities in the Kosovo conflict at a vastly asymmetrical status in favor of Serbia.

The UN Security Council also demanded that Serbian authorities be guided by the counsel of Contact Group representatives, an informal advisory group of major power representatives (the United Kingdom, the United States, Russia, France, Germany, and Italy) who had an interest in Southeastern European affairs.

Unlike Bosnia, the UN Security Council requested that the OSCE provide on-the-ground verification of the status of conflict-party compliance in Kosovo with Security Council resolutions and measures passed to mitigate violence in the Serbian province, particularly concerning the treatment of Kosovo-Albanians. The OSCE Kosovo Verification Mission agreement was signed by Yugoslavia on October 16, 1998, and the mission began its work (as shown on OSCE's website accessed in October 2020; OSCE 1975a,b).

While the Verification Mission carried out its work, negotiations in Belgrade and elsewhere involving Contact Group representatives and US Ambassador Richard Holbrooke (who had shifted the focus from Bosnia to Kosovo) continued as violence against Kosovo-Albanians increased. Additional UN Security Council resolutions were issued condemning Serbian military, police, and militia violence against Kosovo-Albanians.

On March 20, 1999, the OSCE Verification Mission pulled out of Kosovo citing a lack of cooperation by Belgrade and Kosovo-Serb authorities and determined that it was too dangerous for verification teams to continue their work.

What followed on March 23, 1999, was a decidedly different approach from that taken earlier with the UN peacekeeping mission in Bosnia (United Nations Protection Force [UNPROFOR]).

Following the intervention disaster in Somalia, the decision to not intervene in the genocide in Rwanda, and the complete failure in Bosnia to protect Bosnian-Muslims from Serb atrocities in UN "Safe Havens," the United Nations and NATO coalition partners decided on a different approach to the conflict in Kosovo.

Based on prior UN Security Council resolutions and consultations with the Contact Group and OSCE, and the determination of noncompliance by Yugoslav and Kosovo-Serb authorities with those resolutions, NATO Secretary General Javier Solana authorized NATO airstrikes against Yugoslav and Kosovo-Serb targets in Kosovo and in Serbia. NATO bombing began on March 24, 1999, ending June 10.

Subsequently, Yugoslav President Milosevic signed the Rambouillet Agreement (a peace agreement) (US Dept. of State 1999) and the associated Military Technical Agreement with NATO (1999), consenting to NATO security forces in Kosovo.

On June 10, 1999, UNSCR 1244 authorized the expulsion of Serbian authorities, troops, and militias from Kosovo. UNSCR 1244 established the UNMIK to initiate stabilization and reconstruction measures and administer the establishment of democracy-based political and institutional systems in the province until a final political status and protections could be determined.

The Kosovo conflict resulted in the ethnic cleansing of over 1 million Kosovo-Albanians from Kosovo by Serbian and Yugoslav troops and militias, and Kosovo-Serb authorities. About 8,600 non-Serbs were killed and many thousands were missing. Approximately 1,700 Serbs were killed, and approximately 200,000 Serbs and Romani left Kosovo toward the end of the conflict. Large quantities of Kosovo-Albanian vehicles, machinery, household furnishings, musical instruments, and animals were taken by Serbs and moved out of Kosovo.

Complicating factors: Roma ethnic-minority communities were subject to widespread discrimination in Kosovo by Kosovo-Albanians. Unsurprisingly, many Roma were accused of helping Serb authorities with information used in the ethnic cleansing of Kosovo-Albanian families.

Post-Conflict Intervention

I believe that the NATO intervention in Kosovo saved many thousands of lives and shortened the war by years. Overall, the use of NATO military force to bring about compliance with Security Council resolutions was effective, enabling emergency relief, stabilization, reconstruction, and refugee and internally displaced person returns to be carried out unencumbered by a protracted war.

UNMIK, a variation on peacekeeping, was charged with responsibility for managing the civilian aspects of emergency relief, stabilization, security, reconstruction, and the return of refugees and IDPs. NATO was tasked with establishing the Kosovo Force (KFOR) to provide the military-security protection and stabilization component.

Kosovo has been stabilized and reconstructed and is functioning reasonably well. Essentially, the infrastructure, governance, justice system, banking, and economic institutions had to be rebuilt from the ground up. The economy was transferred to the European Euro. Nonrepresented ethnicities (minority groups) were supported in establishing political representation. UNMIK supported the creation of transparent nongovernmental civil-society organizations.

There were significant obstacles (drivers of conflict) to peace and the establishment of transparent institutions due to organized crime and widespread corruption in the governance, economic, and justice sectors—legacies of Communist authoritarian and Balkan traditions (Dziedzic 2016). Additionally, there were numerous property disputes related to socially owned factories, businesses, and housing properties involving labor and business groups, organized crime, and private citizens.

There was widespread discrimination along ethnic lines preventing fair access to jobs, schools, housing, healthcare, and other public services. Post-conflict discrimination fell along ethnic-majority/minority fault lines in Serb- or Kosovo-Albanian-dominated districts, respectively.

As I mentioned above, Kosovo-Albanian professionals and leadership had been removed by Serb authorities over the previous decade or so from their positions in the province—in effect, an involuntary "braindrain." Not only did institutions have to be established or re-established, but also the many people who were required to run them had to be trained or retrained. The reconstruction of Kosovo was indeed an exercise in nation building from the ground up.

For a time, Kosovo was a desolate place. Literally a lawless land. Hundreds of thousands of homes and businesses were destroyed. Factories were shut down and hundreds of thousands of people were homeless. Over 70 percent unemployment. No government. No police. No fire protection. No courts. No banks. No schools. Barely functioning hospitals. No social services. No pensions. No electricity. Little water.

People, especially children, were driving without a driver's license or the benefit of driver training with an unsurprising spike in traffic fatalities. Mafia gangs were extorting most businesses for "protection services." All in all, an anarchist's dream.

Early on, the tasks were focused on emergency relief (food convoys, emergency shelter, water, emergency healthcare, imposed security by NATO troops and UNMIK international police). Progressively, as security conditions and essential services improved, the focus shifted to supporting conditions for the return of refugees and internally displaced persons, followed by the re-establishment of municipal and central government offices, rule of law, and economic and social welfare systems.

Generally, work toward these objectives was initiated at the central level, and district by district, as KFOR troops and UMMIK security officers established security and a presence throughout Kosovo. Initially, the United Nations High Commissioner for Refugees (UNHCR) and UN World Food Program (WFP) handled emergency relief (food, shelter, water) and housing reconstruction for the most vulnerable, and refugee/IDP return tasks. The OSCE monitored human-rights issues and violations.

The EU focused on re-establishing banking and monetary systems and project funding. UNMIK re-established municipal and central government offices and services, and served as the principal coordinator.

UNMIK international officials performed all political and civil-governmental management duties until such time as Kosovo officials were in place. Initially, UNMIK appointed the officials. Gradually, governmental authority was transitioned to Kosovo officials as Provisional Institutions of Self-Governance (PISG) criteria were met—essentially, fair, legal, and transparent management of the institutions and resources of governance. Public-office elections were initiated at the local level first, then later for central government offices.

Figure 11.1 is my graphic based on KFOR Military Liaison Officer Major Andy Baud's original graphic from 2001. It lays out the intervention division of responsibilities and authority following the emergency response phase. The Reserved Powers of the Special Representative to the Secretary General (UN) refers to UNMIK retaining oversight authority for police powers, court decisions, and monetary control.

UNMIK and KFOR levels of authority are shown on the left side of the chart. The levels of responsibilities and authority of elected Kosovo officials are shown on the right side of the chart.

Eventually, UNMIK transitioned from direct governance and administration roles to representation and support. Full transfer of authorities transpired over a roughly six-year period.

	KFOR	UNMIK	KOSOVO
KOSOVO	Commander Security Main Force	SRSG Reserved Powers Police / Civil Affairs / OSCE / EU	President Kosovo Assembly Prime Minister + 9
REGIONAL	Multinational Brigade	Regional Administrator	
MUNICIPAL	Task Force	Municipal Administrator Civil Administration Political / Legal / Economics / Social Welfare / Technical / Local Communities	President Municipal Assembly CEO + Department Heads

Figure 11.1 Sample Intervention Structure: Kosovo.
Source: Diagram by James R. Adams, 2023.

There are no regional levels in Serbia, only municipal districts and a central government structure. The UN designation of regions in Kosovo was purely for UNMIK administrative purposes to oversee stabilization and reconstruction more efficiently.

About Dialogue and Community Affairs

"There will be no talk here about anything controversial." That statement by a Spanish KFOR colonel at an interethnic community meeting that I witnessed shortly after I arrived in Kosovo reflects the style of mediation or discussion facilitation typically used by UNMIK and KFOR officials in Kosovo—that is to say, a traditional diplomatic, political, or arbitration approach. Some referred to it as a dialogue, but it was not a dialogue at all.

The purpose of the meeting was to address the lack of cooperation on municipal governance matters between Kosovo-Serb and Kosovo-Albanian refugees who had returned to their hometown—the same hometown—which traditionally had a Serb majority.

At the center of the confrontation was Kosovo-Serb insistence on flying the national flag of Serbia in front of the municipal building, and Kosovo-Albanian insistence on flying the national flag of Albania. Fundamentally, the problem was deep ethnic hostilities and mistrust and the inability to develop a shared understanding of how to move forward for mutual benefit.

Harold H. Saunders (1999), a retired American diplomat turned conflict-resolution scholar, argues that a different kind of process is needed in such circumstances:

> Relationships across borders today are facts of life. We cannot ignore them. If we look at these relationships in the context of changes in how nations interact, we may see not only the dangers of improper intervention; we may see that some cross-border interaction can offer opportunities for peaceful change with full respect for others. A sensible approach today might be neither to denounce this interaction nor to apply the principle of nonintervention in internal affairs in pure and rigid ways, but to build relationships in which mutual respect might keep that interaction within limits that define and protect the integrity of each party. Understanding the interaction more fully might even suggest imaginative approaches to common problems in an interdependent world.
>
> (Saunders 1999, 155)

I believe that such a perspective applies to inter-community as well as international interactions. The KFOR colonel's approach mentioned above was to impose a decision, much as an arbitrator or judge might—fly a UN flag, or no flag.

No confrontational discussion was allowed, nor the suggestion of a deeper ongoing dialogue, so there was no opportunity for people to air their underlying perspectives, grievances, or emotions in a safe environment. In effect, a town cold-war was established—a negative peace, without anticipation of a transition to a process for mutually working out problems.

Generally, true dialogue facilitation (nonpolitical settlement-driven relationship work) was not attempted in Kosovo by UNMIK or KFOR officials. I understand the security necessity for an imposed decision during an interim political status, but the blockage of all confrontational discussion precluded the airing of perspectives and the development of genuine dialogue. It precluded trust-building and mutual problem-solving experiences in a safe, respectful, controlled environment.

A command to adversaries to cooperate with each other is usually not productive but does encourage the perpetuation of shouting the same position demands. It leaves little room for creative exploration. Essentially, sole reliance on an imposed, coercive, negative-peace approach is of little use in creating anything beyond itself.

From my perspective, it was a missed opportunity for facilitating constructive relationship-building experiences and mutual problem solving (constructive conflict), and for establishing the possibility of better interethnic relations and cooperation in Kosovo and elsewhere.

To be clear, neither should the initial objective be reconciliation, in my opinion. In fact, it is best, initially, not to mention reconciliation as an objective at all. That is typically only inflammatory and counterproductive for deeply injured individuals or groups with nerves on edge. I suggest using reconciliation-intended processes but refraining from using the term reconciliation. I am talking about establishing functional working relationships. Reconciliation will follow in its own good time.

Concerning community affairs, I had arrived in Kosovo in November 2000 on a fixed-term contract as a UN Department of Peacekeeping Operations civil-affairs officer. I was assigned in-country as a local communities officer attached to the UNMIK Office of Community Affairs. Initially, I was posted in the Pec/Peja UNMIK office from which I was dispatched to the community meeting mentioned above.

The Office of Community Affairs was created by UNMIK in response to a particular problem—the lack of cooperation between Kosovo-Serbs and Kosovo-Albanians. Although basic security was largely accomplished and the technical reconstruction of Kosovo was underway, Kosovo-Albanian and Kosovo-Serb interethnic hostilities ran deep, thereby seriously inhibiting progress on political and institutional normalization in Kosovo, as well as further refugee and internally displaced-person return efforts.

Kosovo, like most areas in the former Yugoslavia, consists of mixed-ethnicity towns and villages requiring interethnic cooperation for day-to-day living, working, and basic civic tasks. However, interethnic tolerance and cooperation had become nearly nonexistent after the war.

Discrimination was serious and widespread between the ethnicities. Violence and civil unrest were common enough. Cooperation was needed for progress in all areas of central and municipal governance; therefore, the UNMIK Office of Community Affairs was established in the Capitol in Prishtina and an international UNMIK Local Communities Officer (LCO) placed in every municipality to work on community relations, cooperation, and minority protection and advocacy.

There are about thirty municipalities in Kosovo. The idea was to have one UNMIK international LCO in each municipality to facilitate functional inter-community relations, and to ensure fair treatment for all residents—Serbs in Albanian majority areas, and Albanians in Serb majority areas—in addition to fair treatment for the smaller ethnic minorities in Kosovo.

This effort would culminate in the creation of a Communities Mediation Committee of the municipal council in each municipality and a Municipal Communities Office (MCO) in each municipality under the direction of the mayor. The MCO would have an interethnic staff of local professionals.

In the meantime, UNMIK LCOs handled issues related to minority protection, inter-community grievances, discrimination, access to public services, housing, jobs, schools, healthcare, property disputes, social services, etc. They also coordinated with international and local legal, finance, economic, political, social welfare, and security officers as needed. Coordination with international and local police, military, and civilian officials (KFOR, OSCE, EU, UNHCR, and the International Committee of the Red Cross (ICRC), etc.) was routine.

The duties and responsibilities of each LCO would eventually be handed over to a duly established MCO with a trained interethnic local staff. In effect, the process was the creation of governmental responsibility for ensuring the fair and equal treatment of all ethnic communities.

Although LCOs were free to engage meetings to address individual cases, convening broader interethnic negotiations and conferences was reserved for UNMIK/KFOR administrators, political officers, and commanders. Essentially, LCOs were dedicated case workers. A crucial role without question, but a major gap in mission capability and intent remained.

That gap lay between the roles of the UN administrator/political officer/commander (civilian or military) and the LCO; it was the critical role of trained mediation and dialogue facilitators *not focused on political settlements but dedicated to the development of real dialogue processes and relationship improvement.*

Someone needed to explain the fundamentals of peace and conflict dynamics so that people could better understand the situation they were in and maybe how to get out of it.

As I noted earlier, the UN has since established a Mediation Support Unit (2006) within the Policy and Mediation Division of the UN Department of Political and Peacebuilding Affairs (the term "peacebuilding" in the departmental name is also a recent addition). The unit contains professional staff and consultants trained and specializing in CAR principles and practices, a capacity complementary to traditional political affairs practice in my opinion.

Most facilitated dialogues follow a similar pattern of four or five stages. By way of examples, I cite three dialogue-facilitation formats as follows: (1) Saunders' (1999) *Public Peace Process*; (2) Howard Zehr's (1990) Victim-Offender Conferencing model; and (3) Volkan's (1999) Tree Model of Dialogue.

Saunders' (1999) S*ustained Dialogue* is a facilitated five-stage interaction that brings conflict parties together to change the nature of their relationships, and not to negotiate for assets or political settlements (253).

It is intended to probe the dynamics of contentious relationships that underlie the causes and conditions of a conflict and gradually develop a capacity to jointly design solutions and change relationships for the better. Then, participants go on to decide how to take those insights and steps to the wider community.

Stage one: deciding to engage in dialogue
Stage two: mapping and naming problems and relationships
Stage three: probing problems and relationships to choose a direction
Stage four: scenario-building—experiencing a changing relationship
Stage five: acting together to make change happen

The *tree model of dialogue* was used successfully by Volkan (1999, 202–24) and the Center for the Study of Mind and Human Interaction in Estonia. Volkan's model (1999, 151), like the others, takes conflict parties through various stages of interaction. A primary distinction, however, is that the psychological dynamics that are inherent in the process are openly spoken of and guided, whereas in most other models such things are not mentioned openly:

Stage one: facilitating team diagnoses of the conflict situation
Stage two: facilitation of psychopolitical dialogues between opposing groups
Stage three: expanding psychopolitical dialogues to larger groups at the community, governmental, and societal levels
Stage four: reducing poisonous emotions and resistance to change (conscious and unconscious), thus allowing for more realistic discussions and strategy planning (with regard to cognitive blindness and resistance)
Stage five: implementing practical projects and building institutions together

Victim-offender conferencing, a restorative justice approach, which has evolved as a subset of the field of conflict resolution, contains a core focus on restitution by the offender to the victim. Zehr (1990), a pioneer of and authority on the approach, describes various elements of the process whereby the offender and victim meet face to face, after the offender has admitted the offense:

> In these meetings, emphasis is upon three elements: facts, feelings, and agreements. The meeting is facilitated and chaired by a trained mediator, preferably a community volunteer ... Both parties are encouraged to tell their stories. Both get a chance to ask questions ... They also talk about the impact and implication of this experience. When they have done this, they decide together what will be done about it. Once they come to agreement, they sign a written contract. Often this takes the form of financial restitution, but that is not the only possibility ... These encounters can be important experiences for both victims and offenders. Victims receive a unique opportunity to "get the facts," to ask the questions that bother them. They can talk about what the offense meant to them and to the one who did it.
>
> (Zehr 1990, chap. 9)

Zehr goes on to describe how, in most instances, victims are able to get closure, resolve damaging emotional issues, and move on with their lives:

> Offenders are able to see the impact of their actions firsthand and take emotional responsibility. Often offenders are put on a reflective empathetic path that would not otherwise have occurred. Usually, both victim and offender are healed in some way by the reduction in fear and anger that the breaking of stereotyping affords and the taking back of control of one's emotional life. Also, real justice is experienced, not simply a distant and lingering pain felt by the victim, and a prison sentence experienced by the offender that often does nothing to change his or her assumptions or feelings about anything in a constructive sense; although, in fact, a victim-offender conference sometimes occurs in a prison in which an offender has been placed to carry out a related sentence.
>
> (Zehr 1990, chap. 9)

My purpose in mentioning victim-offender reconciliation approaches is that the steps of initial airing/sharing of experiences, asking questions, coming to understand what happened and why, reduction of fear and anger, and coming to agreement on forms of making things right again are all specific or implicit elements of third-party-facilitated conflict resolution. Additionally, and perhaps more importantly, this approach allows for emotional release and closure.

In cases of generational mutual-victimization histories, it might be useful to explore how the process can be adapted for *mutual victimhood-mutual offender reconciliation*.

In which case, it might be better to not use victim-offender terminology, but instead, establish a context of, perhaps, a co-existence dialogue or community problem-solving dialogue with the parties being participants.

The following sets out the stages of Zehr's (1990) victim/offender conferencing and restorative justice approach:

Stage one: both parties are encouraged to tell their stories
Stage two: both get a chance to ask questions
Stage three: both parties talk about the impact and implications of the experience
Stage four: parties decide together what will be done about it
Stage five: parties sign a written contract for restitution. (Zehr 1990, chap. 9)

Why?

Over the course of my time in Kosovo—a little over three years—I had many discussions with Kosovo-Albanians and non-Serb minorities since most of my time was in a Kosovo-Albanian majority area. I had some conversations with Kosovo-Serbs also. The grievances shared with me were essentially the same, regardless of ethnicity.

Victims had been verbally or physically abused, or their property stolen, or were blocked from employment, the use of public services, or returning to their homes. They would sometimes state that it was because Serbs or Albanians "are just that way," and "I don't know why they did that me."

I recall a young Kosovo-Albanian woman, I will call her Mirdita, telling me of her conversation after the war with her former roommate, a Kosovo-Serb. Her roommate had sold all of Mirdita's possessions while Mirdita was a refugee in Albania. When Mirdita returned, she asked her roommate, "Why did you do that?" She said her roommate thought a moment and, not really having an answer, simply shrugged her shoulders.

This is the insidious nature of protracted conflict. After a while, after many years or generations of mutual victimizations and victimhood, the rationale is lost. It's habitual. It's just the way it is.

Two young people told me that they were in medical school when ethnic cleansing forced them to leave. When they returned, they and their families, being financially ruined, saw no hope of finishing their training.

Most Kosovo-Albanians were forced to make do with underground house-schools when, in 1991, the Albanian language was outlawed in schools and government offices. Thousands of Kosovo-Albanian teachers lost their jobs. All state support was stopped for Albanian schools. Albanian-language radio, TV, and press sources were outlawed.

Another young man, who had been forced out of university, said: "Maybe in ten years they [Serbs] will understand what they have done." He was now trying to get by with a job as a security guard for UNMIK. Many were now working as guards, interpreters, drivers, and administrative help with IOs, a lifeline for extended families.

Tough Place

People came to me with many different issues. A particularly difficult case involved a single mother with children. She had lived with her husband in a house they owned on the edge of a small village in the district. Her husband was dying of cancer. They were of a non-Albanian, non-Serb ethnic minority. There were a handful of Kosovo-Albanian neighbors nearby. They, like many thousands of others, were forced from their home and became refugees in the ethnic cleansing.

I do not recall if her husband died before or after refugees returned to the area. In any case, her neighbors refused to allow her to return to her house, accusing her husband of having collaborated with Serbs in ethnic cleansing, which she denied. She was told that, if she returned, her children would be killed. I gathered two local municipal officials, one being from the municipal clerk's office and my interpreter and went to the village.

The neighbors confirmed the mother's residence. They repeated the accusation that her husband collaborated with "the enemy" [Kosovo-Serbs]. However, in typical Balkan fashion, they claimed that they had no problem with her returning, but that they could not guarantee her safety if "outsiders" wanted to kill her children. They assumed the threats to be real.

I held discussions with police, the mayor, and other local officials. In the end, it was decided that the municipality would give her the deed to a comparable piece of land near another village in exchange for her property, and request that an IO build her a comparable house with refugee-resettlement funds. And that is what was done. The new house was built, and she moved in with her children. It so happens that her new neighbors were of the same ethnic minority as her.

When returning to town after talking with the neighbors that day, our little delegation talked about the woman's situation. The municipal officials expressed regret that she had to go through so much. I said, "Tough place." One of them replied, "You have a clean spirit, it's good that you're here."

Maybe. The result was OK. The mother was able to get herself and her children back into a house on a comparable piece of land. They were safe. Nevertheless, it felt a little bit like ethnic cleansing.

Another case involved looking after six elderly Serbian women living in the priest's house at a local Serbian Orthodox church in town. The priests were evacuated earlier. Several of the women ran to the church during the war. One of the nuns had worked at the church for many years. Kosovo-Albanians stated it as fact that Serbian Orthodox priests had participated in ethnic cleansing in Kosovo.

The women, at least two of whom were nuns, had been staying in the centuries-old church compound for a couple of years by the time I arrived. They were the only Serbs remaining in the district of about 90,000 after the war. There had been about 3,000 Serb residents before the war. Armed KFOR troops from the Italian contingent guarded the church compound twenty-four hours a day, seven days a week. Protection included high walls, concertina wire, sandbags, and guard towers.

A Serbian Orthodox priest from the Patriarchy in Decani or Pec/Peja would come in a KFOR armored personnel carrier to visit them occasionally. One of the ladies would walk from her house to the church with a KFOR escort. Adults would yell insults at her. Children would throw eggs and rocks. After a while, the ladies rarely left the compound. When they did, it was in a fully enclosed armored KFOR vehicle.

I accompanied them on two occasions—once so that one of the women could be driven by her house in town, which was occupied by a Kosovo-Albanian, to see if it was OK; the other time, following vandalism at a Serbian cemetery outside of town, to see if the headstones on their deceased relatives' graves had been damaged.

After the social welfare office in town opened for business again, I would go there and pick up the women's pension payments (similar to social security) and deliver it to them. I delivered extra food and gifts on Christmas and Easter; otherwise, the Italian military contingent took care of them.

I asked the women if they wanted to go live with relatives elsewhere in Kosovo or Serbia. They declined, saying that Gjakova/Djakovica was their home and that they were staying. It seems that they had encouragement on this count from the Serbian Orthodox Church, which had an interest in maintaining a Serb presence in the church building and the district.

A few weeks after I left Kosovo (February 2004), riots broke out across the province after the media reported that three young Kosovo-Albanian boys had been chased by Kosovo-Serbs into a river, where they drowned.

In the civil unrest that followed, hundreds were injured and seventeen killed in rioting that lasted several days. Thousands of Serb houses were burned and many Serbian Orthodox churches destroyed, including the one in Gjakova/Djakovica where the Serbian ladies were staying. After retreating to the church building, which came under assault, they were evacuated to the Serbian Orthodox monastery in Decani where they remained. The church has since been leveled and a parking lot put in.

UNMIK, KFOR, and Kosovo Police, with a few exceptions, failed to act, or act sufficiently, in this instance to protect Kosovo-Serbs or Roma minority groups—the great majority of the victims of the riots.

The cycles of violence were fortified once again.

Other Business

First, occasionally, we were asked to fill in for our supervisor, the UNMIK Municipal Administrator, while he was on vacation. At such times, I would facilitate meetings on problems outside of my usual type. One occasion involved a meeting with local authorities and a contractor who had submitted a bid for a supply contract to the municipality. The complication was that the bid was proposing decidedly illegal contract stipulations.

When this problem was explained, the contractor was hesitant to proceed. At that moment, one of the other local participants in the meeting asked our UNMIK legal officer, through our interpreter, what the penalty for submitting an illegal contract was. It was made clear that it was thirty days in jail.

The one who asked that question followed up with another question, this time to the distressed contractor: "It's only thirty days in jail, so what's the problem?" he asked with some exasperation. There is a different take on corruption in some places.

Second, sometimes, community relations can be tricky. On one occasion, I was driving down the street in town with my interpreter in my white UN-labeled Toyota 4-Runner. It was a pleasant sunny day and I—as a conscientious driver, mindful of my surroundings—glanced over at a young woman pushing a baby carriage away from us on the sidewalk ahead.

It so happens that I perhaps glanced for too long. My interpreter, a respectable young woman, asked me, "Oh, do you think that she's attractive?" Or words to that effect, referring to the lady pushing the carriage, who we had not yet passed. My interpreter then declared that she was her sister. I replied, "Is that right?" Or words to that effect. After momentary contemplation, I said, "She looks like a very nice person from behind."

Transitions

In the little over three years that I was in Kosovo, I handled hundreds of cases and issues. Most were resolved to some degree of satisfaction, at least temporarily. Beyond immediate relief for those needing protection and advocacy, UNMIK's broader objective was interethic cooperation, which included the establishment of Municipal Council Mediation Committees and MCOs, and support for civil society building in general.

A central strategy was to establish governmental responsibility for inter-community cooperation and problem solving, with particular attention given to the protection and fair treatment of ethnic minorities.

An Office of Community Affairs was similarly established at the central government level in Pristina. One of my main tasks as an LCO was to interview, hire, and train MCO local professional staff to replace me, which I did. Five were hired and trained. Given that there were no Serbs in the district at that time, a sixth slot was reserved for a Kosovo-Serb.

The new MCO staff were already skilled in their respective professions. The training involved an orientation on transparency in governance, and casework and advocacy in a multiethnic community context. Particular attention was given to fundamental elements of civil and human rights, and civic participation.

In nearly all MCOs in Kosovo, or perhaps all, only ethnic-minority individuals were hired. An overriding reason for this was that it provided jobs for minorities who were typically frozen out of government jobs. I argued that an ethnic majority person should be hired also (Kosovo-Albanian) for the MCO staff (my district was an ethnic Kosovo-Albanian majority area). My argument was that, in the long run, it was important to have a mixed ethnic-majority, ethnic-minority staff to demonstrate interethnic cooperation on real problems.

My superiors ultimately agreed, and a mixed majority-minority staff was established. One was a lawyer, one a social services specialist, one an administration and finance officer, one a technical officer/engineer, one a community development officer, and one head of office. All dedicated themselves to interethnic cooperation among themselves and in the communities.

My primary task being completed, I transferred to the UNMIK Office of Community Affairs in Pristina for my final two months in Kosovo before heading back to the United States to start my doctoral program to sort out unfinished conceptual work.

In conjunction with the Office of Community Affairs, I gave two presentations in Pristina on "Briefings on Select Third Party Processes for Peace Operations." Not coincidentally, my focus was on the mission-capability gap that I described earlier; that is, advising and training related to mediation efforts and interethnic dialogues not driven by a political settlement expectation. The presentations were pitched as a basic orientation/briefing for interested international and local officials and staff.

My practical field background and academic preparation (master's thesis: "Peace Operations & Peace Building: Integrating Positive Peace Processes") enabled me to integrate the subject matter into a peace and stabilization operation context, which made the presentation and material meaningful to the audience.

The Head of Office for the UNMIK Office of Community Affairs made this observation following the briefings:

> It seems to me that more focused, skilled, and coordinated efforts to initiate and/or support genuine dialogue and informed mediation by local and international officials, groups, and communities would be valuable as an aid in changing

attitudes toward problem solving, and engaging in constructive rather than purely confrontational dialogue. Specific to Kosovo, my hope is that our efforts will prove useful in stimulating relevant debate, interests, and initiatives in the mission for the benefit of all communities, civil-society building, and more timely realization of overall standards based on cooperation.

I believe that the need is clear, and the concept is practical enough, whether for this mission or others, now or later.

Parting Thoughts

Was the earlier international intervention in Bosnia a lesson learned for Kosovo? Yes and no. Wishing to be better prepared for major crisis situations, two years after the Bosnian War, US President Bill Clinton issued Presidential Decision Directive 56 (PDD 56, May 1997): "Managing Complex Contingency Operations." It was a comprehensive civilian agency and US Department of Defense (DOD) outline for future coordinated interventions. The subsequent Bush Administration rescinded PDD 56.

Nevertheless, conceptually, protection of civilians across borders has taken on greater resonance, as is reflected in what has come to be known as the *Responsibility to Protect (R2P)* concept that was adopted by the UN World Summit in December of 2005 (A/RES/60/1), which "endorsed the principle that State sovereignty carried with it the obligation of the State to protect its own people, and that if the State was unwilling or unable to do so, the responsibility shifted to the International Community (IC) to use diplomatic, humanitarian and other means to protect them" (United Nations website for The Office of Genocide Prevention and The Responsibility to Protect [United Nations 2005]).

On the one hand, repeated attacks on civilians in Darfur by government-backed militias did not trigger an R2P IC response. On the other hand, the Kosovo intervention was essentially unfinished business in the Yugoslav wars, and the intervention capitalized on the momentum of a compelling sense of guilt associated with the failure to protect Bosnian civilians from genocide in the middle of Europe just a few years earlier.

The Kosovo National Assembly declared independence on February 17, 2008, as the Republic of Kosova, which was subsequently recognized by about ninety-five countries and the UN. Serbia has not recognized the independence of Kosovo.

There are still profound hostile sentiments and interethnic discrimination among the ethnic groups in Kosova, which is essentially unchanged, as it is essentially unchanged in post-war Bosnia.

Michael Smith (1999) exemplifies the robust policy and scholastic commentary of the 1990s and 2000s, which argued for or against an ethics-based rationale, from realist and idealist perspectives, for humanitarian intervention, without the consent of the country in question—a robust debate that continues to this day.

A distinction of the Kosovo intervention is that it constituted the final push toward decisive post-Westphalian action to intervene, on behalf of victims, with the use of force in the internal affairs of a sovereign state—without consent.

Kosovo embodied a critical-mass convergence of rapid communication and global-humanity awareness that had been building for decades, if not centuries. It constituted a critical mass to reconcile the Westphalian-paradigm dilemma of respect for another state's sovereignty, no matter the consequences to victims within its borders, with a growing compelling sense of obligation to intervene in the name of humanity and civil society to save victims of mass human rights atrocities within those borders.

The EU, NATO, OSCE, and UNMIK each maintain a small presence in Kosova today.

12

Afghanistan

The situation in Afghanistan is significantly different from those in the former Yugoslavia and African countries that I have discussed so far. The breakup of Yugoslavia was fundamentally ethnic identity driven by hardline nationalists with side bets by organized crime. Afghanistan has been, historically, a circumstance of Afghans versus foreign invaders.

So Many Wars, So Little Time

Islam became a dominant factor in Afghan identity after an Arab push into Afghan territories in the seventh, eighth, and ninth centuries. Since the ascension of the Taliban, after the Russian Army pulled out in 1989, conflict circumstances include a dynamic of Islamist extremism versus modernism. Modernism-modernization initiatives were pushed from time to time in the twentieth century by outsiders and Afghan leaders with varying degrees of effect.

All of the conflicts were/are subject to superpower interests and influences. Afghanistan's "recent" wars in the nineteenth and twentieth centuries are directly grounded in a barrage of attempted superpower/imperial occupations and interventions, with maneuvering by smaller southwest Asian regional powers in the mix.

Specifically: (1) three British military occupation efforts in the 1800s ostensibly to deter the Russian Empire from moving south into Afghan territories and thereby threatening British colonial interests in British India and Pakistan (The Great Game); (2) the Russian nine-year military occupation/war in Afghanistan in the 1980s to prop up their preferred Soviet-friendly regime against an Afghan tribal insurgency with United States covert backing; and (3) following the attack on the World Trade Center on September 11, 2001, the American/NATO intervention to capture Osama bin Laden, degrade al-Qaeda, and remove the

Taliban from power; and, in the summer of 2022, the exit of American forces and return of the Taliban to power.

The search-and-destroy mission aimed at bin Laden, who had been given sanctuary by the Taliban, turned into a war to overthrow the Taliban. The Taliban, one of the jihadist insurgency groups (Mujahedeen) fighting the Russians, had come out on top in the five-year civil war that followed the withdrawal of an exhausted Russian Army in 1989. Approximately 14,000 Russian soldiers and 500,000 Afghans died in the war against the Russians: estimates of Afghan civilians killed among the 500,000 are about 80 percent.

A so-called post-civil war status continues. Initially, prior to the total collapse of Afghan government military forces in the face of a rapid Taliban resurgence in the summer of 2021, and the withdrawal of all US troops in August 2022, there were periodic attempts at ceasefires and a political settlement between the Taliban and the re-established Afghan government with US/EU/NATO political and military support.

The planned American/NATO withdrawal was already well underway in the summer of 2021. US troop strength had been drawn down from a peak of about 100,000 in 2010 to 2,500 in July 2021 to complete the total withdrawal by August 31, 2021. Casualties for the US-Taliban War Era are US troops killed in action: 1,833; Afghan civilians killed from 2009 through 2019 approximately 35,000.

Additional complications now are the presence of al-Qaeda and ISIS Islamist extremist elements out of the Iraq and Syria wars who seek bases of operation in Afghanistan. Further complications include tribal organized crime militias supported by extremist elements and organized crime in Pakistan and elsewhere. There are regional destabilization pressures on Pakistan, which holds nuclear weapons. Currently, the Taliban, enforcing Islamic fundamentalist principles, have total control of Afghanistan and its government with relatively minor resistance.

The above recent wars are scripts written on top of countless invasions, occupations, evictions, and reordering of populations, governments, and territories going back thousands of years—back to Alexander the Great and before. The history of Afghanistan involves as much tribal conflict from within as invaders from without.

Attempts at modernization by internal or external actors in the last one hundred years or so have not been well received by much of the mostly rural and very conservative population, which had a literacy rate below 20 percent in 1980, and which is currently, according to UNESCO, estimated at 55 percent for men and 30 percent for women. It seems that the only conflict circumstances that might be more complicated and difficult are those of Israel-Palestine and Bosnia.

In my view, the recent US/EU/NATO/UN effort to stabilize Afghanistan with a viable Afghan coalition government and reconstruction would have had a much better chance of lasting success early on if the United States had not engaged in the second war in Iraq in 2003 in the same timeframe.

The second US-Iraq war, based on a false premise about Iraq's nuclear capability and state support for al-Qaeda, was started with especially ill-considered post-war planning and inexperienced international civilian post-war management. Even lower-level UN staff familiar with basic stabilization practices saw major problems coming for Iraq in that operation. The most obvious error was the US decision to remove all experienced Sunni Iraqi government civilian and military leaders and managers, leaving huge national competence gaps.

The second war in Iraq was not only counterproductive in terms of having destroyed a functional state, but also created very fertile ground for the rise of Islamist extremism, particularly ISIS, while pushing al-Qaeda into Afghanistan and northern Africa. Beyond the immense problems created for Iraq and the immediate region, the second Iraq war was a debilitating and unnecessary distraction from the international effort in Afghanistan.

Before continuing with Afghanistan specifically, I think elaboration on some related issues is warranted.

Conflict of Perceptions—Clash of Paradigms

Conflict and intervention decision-making relies in part on the historical narrative and perceptions of reality that guide it. This is a crucial point, given that there are inevitably differing interpretations of the same event, positions taken, or statements made, and considering that many interventions involve massive resources and lethal force capability.

Intervention officials routinely encounter the problem of differing interpretations of the same events by different groups at all levels among intervenors, conflict parties, and constituencies back home. At best, this leads to annoying or stressful delays and an inefficient use of energies while intervenors re-explain or re-argue the same points with each other and the conflict parties.

Sometimes, after a perception-fight, things are clearer, trust is higher, and relationships are stronger. Sometimes, though, under highly stressed circumstances, different perspectives lead to serious distrust, violence, and bloodshed. What drives this difference of perceptions?

Perhaps it is better to characterize perceptions and paradigms as misperceptions and opposing paradigms. In any case, contrary to Descartes' "naturalist" position that people may have different interpretations but the same basic recognition of events (Sandole 1999, chap. 6), Thomas S. Kuhn argued that the problem of contradictory perceptions can be due to different internalized paradigms resulting in a different recognition as well as a different interpretation of the same event (Kuhn 1996).

There is plenty of cynical realpolitik and opportunists' representation on both the conflict party and international intervention sides, but I think that, for the most part, relief aid officials and workers are genuinely certain that they are delivering compassionate aid and are just in their cause.

I make three points here: (1) clashes of paradigm and perception might well be the driving force in many ethnic and identity conflicts; (2) some conflict theorists seem to use definitions of conflict that are not cognizant of "internalized" paradigms; and (3) some theorists' definitions imply a human-realism perspective. However, conflict can be as simple as wanting someone else's oil fields.

Cultural Considerations

William W. Wilmot and Joyce L. Hocker (1998) make distinctions between *high-context* and *low-context* cultures (23). High-context cultures generally pertain to traditional cultures that are socially characterized by collectivism, such as Asia, the Middle East, and Africa. Low-context cultures generally pertain to Western cultures, which is to say Europe, the United States, Canada, and Australia that place a higher value on individualism.

Wilmot and Hocker (1998) list the associated characteristics of each group in terms of values, beliefs, and styles, and how they believe each group would be expected to view and manage a problem. For example, a high-context culture would typically be expected to approach a conflict in an "indirect" manner with a "non-confrontational attitude," whereas a low-context culture would be expected to typically approach a conflict, or intervention, in a "direct" manner with a "confrontational attitude." I believe that there is a mixing of styles depending on circumstances and personalities involved.

The point here is that if the track 1 (governmental) or track 2 (nongovernmental) intervenor is not sufficiently aware of the cultural differences, trouble is not far off. I think it is safe to say that a general lack of awareness of the problem by conflict parties and intervention officials and staff is a contributing factor to clash-of-paradigm problems. This is especially true for officials and staff, military or civilian, who are new to conflict and stabilization environments.

Concerning the theoretical high-context, indirect, nonconfrontational culture of, say, Afghanistan, my impression is that it is indirect and nonconfrontational until the shooting starts.

Another perspective on cultural conflict is captured by the concept of ethnocentrism or "local knowledge" to use Clifford Geertz's (2000) perspective, which incorporates the psychology, beliefs, meanings, and common-sense assumptions of a people. Such dynamics are fully relevant to any intervenor/conflict party engagement, which, often as not, is a negotiation of perceptions, regardless of the actual point of discussion.

Kevin Avruch (1998) writes specifically on culture, conflict, and conflict resolution. He stresses that "culture" has a wide variety of applications; that it can apply to assumptions (often dubious) about culture, ethnocentrism, types of culture, culture and negotiation, culture and third-party roles, individual and family culture, organizational culture, military culture, diplomacy culture, realism culture, idealism culture, and the variety of ways that cultural misassumptions and misinterpretations can get us into trouble.

I add humanitarian and stabilization intervention cultures to the list.

Relevant to the resolution or at least mitigation of conflict among intervenors, Avruch (1998) adds, "One strategy for conflict resolution immediately presents itself: the proactive deconstruction, in the sense of debunking or unmasking, of these inadequate ideas" (16).

He further points out, while referring to disciplines such as international relations, "Older, dominant paradigms of the discipline—realism and neorealism—have silenced or misappropriated cultural accounts in striking ways" (Avruch 1998, 23). In other words, "Any one of the major assumptions of realist thinking can render culture invisible" (28).

I agree with Avruch's (1998) conclusion, "In the end, we argue that in any sort of intercultural conflict resolution, a cultural analysis is an irreducible part of the problem-solving process" (74).

This principle certainly applies to intervenors vs. local conflict parties, and intervenors quarreling among themselves over intervention policies.

Avruch's (1998) points apply well enough to the current rhetoric of resurgent white supremacists and left and right extremists' ideologies in the United States—our current "culture wars."

Primary Conflict—Intervention Conflict

Stabilization and peacebuilding interventions come with their own set of issues, but before getting into that, some basic definitions. Dave Davis, former director of George Mason University's Peace Operations Policy Program, offers the following broad definitions specific to peace and stabilization operations (from classroom lectures):

- *Peacemaking: general peace operation decision-making and coordination* involving diplomacy, international law (treaties), negotiation, mediation, fact finding, sanctions, and direction of stabilization efforts by international militaries, police, and administration units in support of peacebuilding.
- *Peacebuilding: (1) delivery of short-term humanitarian relief goods and services, and (2) longer-term institutional rehabilitation and development* involving good governance, infrastructure, economics, healthcare, return and reintegration of refugees and internally displaced persons, and the establishment of ongoing conflict prevention, management, and resolution mechanisms—all in support of sustainable recovery and stabilization.
- *Peace Support: entails tasks generally carried out by international military and international police units involving observation, use of force, liaison work, logistics, presence, security, and command and control* (Davis 2008b).

Conflicts and interventions include tasks and problems decision-makers must deal with on a daily basis. To better understand this, it's necessary to distinguish more clearly the different types of conflict associated with humanitarian, stabilization, and peacebuilding operations. There are dynamics common to all types of conflict, considering that *basic human interaction is the common denominator*. I distinguish two general types of conflict in the intervention environment.

I refer to the first type as *Primary Conflict*, meaning the conflict between the primary conflict parties that precipitated an international intervention. A secondary type is *intervention conflict*, which can in turn be divided into two sub-types: (1) conflict between intervenors and conflict parties and (2) conflict among the intervenors themselves (in-house conflict).

All three types become highly interrelated and reactive to each other. I believe that intervention conflict is no small factor in frustrating primary conflict peacemaking and peacebuilding.

Primary conflicts are highly resistant to the use of force, or to mediation and negotiation diplomacy based on a very high conflict resurgency rate (thirty-one out of thirty-nine from 2000 to 2010 [Hewitt et al. 2010]). This problem is compounded by intervention conflict. Some factors common to these types of conflicts are conflicting self-interests, conflicting mandates and policies, conflicting training and intervention approaches, external pressures, and, often enough, just the lack of coordination. I also highlight personality clashes since it is difficult to over-emphasize the impact of that problem.

Add to this the many complexities injected by encounters of groups unprepared for interaction with each other, and the numerous conflicts around the world given life by the lifting of US/Soviet Cold War geopolitical suppression of populations intent on self-determination.

In short, we (humanity) find ourselves face to face with each other with all our shortcomings in a tightly wound world, in adversarial-based systems, with minimal understanding of our conflicts or reactions, and a minimal sense of practical ways for coping constructively with each other. Such dynamics are concentrated and pressurized in a peace and stabilization intervention scenario.

Something else—there have been conflicts and various societal stresses for a very long time. However, until recently we (humanity) were able to take turns being isolated from each other in terms of total global impact. That is no longer the case. New technologies, population growth, massive population movements, global environmental impacts, and political and economic interdependence are now such that a thump on one side of our now highly interconnected world will, with certainty, reverberate to the other side and back again in the blink of an internet eye.

Fewer and fewer can escape some manner of impact. Consequently, peacebuilding in today's more complex world requires a more sophisticated understanding of conflict and possible solutions to help us get beyond temporary fixes or mere delaying tactics in dealing with each other, as individuals, groups, nations, and as humanity.

In-House Conflict

John A. Vasquez's (1993) description of conflict escalation driven by rivalry among primary conflict parties can also easily describe many interactions among International Community (IC) actors on almost any given day.

Most track 1 and track 2 representatives are subject to the stresses and strains of a simple reality—internal organizational conflict and conflict between organizations since much organizational conflict revolves around workplace rivalries and interpersonal conflict (personality clashes)—again, human fundamentals.

I think it is safe to say that hostile rivalry of any kind negatively impacts interventions, including the problem of simply not being able to work together. I cannot count the number of times I have noticed intervention activities somehow negatively impacted by competition-driven or personality clash-driven negative rivalry.

Personality clashes and stress-based clashes are a significant issue in undermining mission performance and unity of effort. In Afghanistan, the personality clash issue was serious to the point of being a known mission-wide problem. Another significant problem is that, often, agencies and NGOs try to perform tasks that they are not trained for or structured to take on. I have little doubt that this is an insidious factor in conflict escalation.

Such circumstances have improved somewhat with the passage of time. But, despite best efforts at pre-deployment orientation and training, immersion into a conflict zone always entails a steep learning curve for the uninitiated.

Given the availability of much larger budgets for military and police units, there is usually adequate pre-deployment training for military and police units in connection with interventions, as well as for track 1 governmental field staff.

Training small NGO staff or local professionals to run counterpart humanitarian and civil society organizations is typically under-supported. However, training and civil society organizations are crucial for medium- to long-term mitigation of protracted conflict issues.

Just the same, such support puts pressure on local and national governments to be more transparent and to take more responsibility for looking after the welfare of their own citizens. Long-term, on-the-ground international support is essential to provide moral support and institutional backup for threatened local organizations and individuals trying to improve governmental and societal circumstances.

What all of this means is that track 1 (government representatives and agencies) and track 2 officials (nongovernmental representatives and organizations), being subject to human inadequacies like everyone else, are subject to virtually all the mental, physical, and multicultural complications that one can name, including PTSD. This, of course, applies to conflict parties as well.

Add to this the challenge of operating within differing paradigm worlds of realism and idealism, hardliners and moderates.

And add to this, trying to keep up with a rapid shift from a comfortably known nation-state world to a simultaneously internal and globalized reality. Transnational groups such as terrorist organizations, insurgency groups, and organized crime pay little attention to nation-state boundaries.

Bad Strategies—Bad Habits

See the above.
Also:

In terms of conflict and interventions, few are without sin—me included. My time in Afghanistan as a US Agency for International Development (USAID) Crisis, Stabilization, and Governance Officer had its ups and downs, meaning that sometimes I was productive and sometimes not. I arrived in Afghanistan in 2011 at the peak of the US military and civilian surge for the stabilization and reconstruction of the country.

At the time, the Taliban were waging a guerrilla war against the Afghan government to try to get back into power. Their hope was, as events later proved out, to wear the Afghan government down until they got tired and gave up, and to wear the US/NATO forces (and associated constituents back home) down until they left.

The Soviet Union and the United States, in their respective time periods, both set deadlines for withdrawal from Afghanistan preceded by last-try troop and civilian surges. Both followed the impulse to create an Afghanistan in their own image. Both have been dismayed by substantial investments in blood, treasure, pride, and unexpectedly poor results. The Russians lost their brutal war against Afghan tribes. The US/NATO coalition won the initial war against the Taliban but were having a very tough time winning the peace.

Is there a balance to be had for the safety and happiness of Afghans, and international security for the rest of us? That is the question.

Taking extra care to minimize outsider arrogance and the lack of knowledge of Afghan history and culture is always a good idea. In that spirit, taking more time to ask Afghans what they want as opposed to explaining what we are delivering is always a good idea. That, I think, is a good approach anywhere.

Actually, the Foreign Service Institute, USAID, and the US Department of Defense (DOD) do provide orientation trainings on Afghanistan and other conflict zones. However, difficulties arise due to unrealistic expectations on implementation timeframes aggravated by rapidly changing or conflicting policy directives, particularly during US presidential administration turnovers.

There is also, often, a distinct difference between civilian and military approaches to a problem (although this is very gradually improving due to further development of military civil affairs unit training), and different perspectives on short-term versus long-term solutions that are not fully appreciated.

The problem of what to do about the Taliban—or any extremist group/regime determined to murder large numbers of noncompliant citizens—is a more difficult one, as is that of other extremist groups given safe haven by the Taliban, or otherwise taking advantage of instability.

My job in Afghanistan was, essentially, to encourage transparency and cooperation in governance at the local district level. The need for this was due to a long tradition of little or no interaction or trust between central, provincial, and local government, which was induced by disruptive decades and centuries of war, insurgencies, and the presence of extremists, and tribal rivalries. This same dynamic also gives rise to deeply embedded organized crime and corruption at all levels.

Due to these circumstances, governance in Afghanistan was/is a hybrid of state authority and traditional tribal authority (councils) based on *Pashtunwali* (tribal law)—that is to say, community-level Shuras, tribal-level Jirgas, and country-level Loya Jirgas.

Most of my time was spent in Shinwar District, Nangahar Province, near the Khyber Pass, a Pashtun tribal area. I was embedded in a US Army forward operating base (FOB) joint military-civilian District Reconstruction Team (DRT). A typical week involved security and tasks briefings, studying Afghan government and tribal law (*Pashtunwali*) processes, and reviewing and inspecting US government/military assistance projects. USAID and US Department of State officers coordinated daily with US military civil affairs staff. USAID is the foreign aid agency specializing in nonlethal aid within the US Department of State.

The rest of my time was spent meeting with local authorities to discuss political, rule of law, economic, and social issues, and coordinating with my civilian and military counterparts about various concerns and projects.

A particular focus of mine was educating local authorities and staff on the expectations of "internationals," and vice versa. Another primary task was liaising with US and Afghan officials with regard to orienting district officials and staff on transparent budget and finance administration (initially US/EU funds).

Usually, I caught a ride with a US Army armored vehicle convoy. Occasionally, I accompanied a foot patrol if a meeting was nearby. Typically, each civilian and military interlocutor would take turns in the meeting or shura to "state their piece." The exchange was usually a concise briefing and question-and-answer format. A genuine dialogue was rare due to security time constraints and the military briefing approach.

One of my more useful accomplishments was facilitating Afghan inter-district cooperation on transparent budget and finance administration and training. One of my least useful accomplishments was to stop talking to a colleague that I had a personality clash with. Such behavior tends to lead to unfounded assumptions on everyone's part and inefficiency. I do not recommend it.

What is the answer for Afghanistan beyond the basic suggestions above? I am not sure. But that is the wrong question. A better question is: What is the answer from Afghans? In any case, I would need a couple of years on the ground in Afghanistan to survey opinions and facilitate dialogues to get at a process that might be helpful.

Ultimately, a nonviolent, nonthreatening Afghanistan status is a long-term undertaking, whether by Afghans or by outsiders.

A final thought—something about know-thy-enemy—and do not forget to know thy friends also.

Part Three

The Conceptual Perspective

My journey, at least in terms of countries in which I have worked, terminates here. So, at this point, I offer forgiveness to anyone wanting to run to the nearest bar or tea shop to assuage sensitivities that I have surely abused. My speculations only get bolder from here on. I start talking about scientific methodology.

But for those who are agitated to see where this whole thing goes, I welcome you to the remainder of my explanations.

Note: For this *Citizens Edition*, I make the questionable promise of minimizing academic explanations.... In any case, I believe that what remains is worthwhile considering; take what is useful to you.

For those who are seeking another civil war in America, or who are advocating for the breakup of the United States into Red and Blue states, as some proud politicians and militias are suggesting, it would be helpful for you to know what to expect in the ensuing chaos because the following will inevitably apply—destruction, stabilization, and reconstruction.

As appealing as this might sound to some, efforts to separate interspersed, interethnic, politically and culturally diverse populations have been tried many times before elsewhere and rarely are the results what was expected, or kind. Typically, the results are mass atrocities, ethnic-cleansing, attempts at genocide, devastated economies and infrastructures, a major surge in organized crime, one or two or more lost generations educationally and financially, and inevitable violent repetitions of the same.

Actually, all concerned citizens, regardless of one's opinion on the matter, would do well to be at least minimally informed on how stabilization and reconstruction works, since everyone will be feeling the impact for many years—the initial civil strife, violent conflict, and its decades-long, if not generations-long, aftermath. The following essays provide descriptions of what it looks like and some words of advice on how to avoid the worst effects.

13

Who Would Manage an Intervention in the United States?

There is a large well-educated, well-trained body of professionals in the United States, with supporting institutions and organizations (governmental, nongovernmental, civil society, military, academic, professional, and community-based) capable of managing the tasks of a large-scale in-house intervention in the United States should it be necessary.

I think that an intervention task force from outside the United States is not needed and would probably be counterproductive. However, some groups would likely consider humanitarian aid or mediation intervention efforts by other "internal" groups to be meddling if not outright enemy actions. Such a scenario could get very sticky and is best avoided entirely of course.

Ideally, sufficient preventative measures would be carried out precluding the need for a post-conflict intervention. There is time yet. The core task is to prevent a violent, total political, and societal breakdown, although Polarization-Phase 1, to call it that, is already well underway in the United States and elsewhere.

But by way of hopeful news, there are people and organizations working on the problem. I will have more to say on this.

For now, there are some conceptual factors to highlight. One is a distinction to be aware of with regard to governmental and nongovernmental decision-makers (generally speaking); there is a kind of conceptual parallel universe with regard to the interpretation of *conflict transformation*.

Track 1 (governments) typically proceed according to political imperatives accompanied by structural/technical solution strategies, followed by policy and planning implementation (planning and execution if military).

Track 2+ (I am thinking of scholar-practitioners and civil society organizations) typically proceed according to narrative and to relationship change imperatives conditioned by peer-reviewed discourse, followed in turn by applied theory and practice in the field by trained facilitators.

Different conceptualizations of conflict transformation imply different responses and possible cross-purposed actions. This can also mean an implementation void or implementation imbalance—*essentially, it is a matter of structural/technical solutions versus relationship and narrative change.*

Policy for the reconstruction, or construction, of transparent democratic institutions (structural elements) is fairly well understood and receives the predominate share of planning, funding, and resources. *Generally speaking, policy and funding for relationship work is missing, and is a significant gap in the overall intervention picture.*

The conceptualization of approaches, whether policy or theory derived, is a definable distinction between track 1 and track 2+ interventions, and perhaps a meeting ground between the two, as there is overlap.

A reality factor is that there is precious little time for operations' administrators and commanders to do relationship work even if they were inclined to, and far too little time and resources are allotted to scholar-practitioners to carry out meaningful relationship studies and relationship or narrative change facilitation.

In any case, many would, hopefully, have an interest in, if not a stake, knowing more about the approaches of their various intervention counterparts across governmental and nongovernmental, and political and societal divides.

I should point out here that a difficulty in providing helpful assistance with establishing democracy in post-conflict zones is a less-than-optimal understanding of or practice of honest democracy here in the United States of late.

A Problem

Many conflicts in our post-Cold War era reignite—with all of the accompanying tragedies—after a peace settlement has been signed.

Often, the war is over, but the conflict is not. This is the case despite intense military and diplomatic stabilization and reconstruction efforts. It is due to the fact that (the war in Ukraine being an exception) most conflicts (nine out of ten) in recent decades are internal to nation-states and not between nation-states, although covertly supported by nation-states in some cases.

Internal conflicts are highly resistant to the use of force, or to diplomacy mediation and negotiation efforts (a recurrence rate of thirty-one out of thirty-nine conflicts between 2000 and 2010; Hewitt et al. 2010). That trend has not changed much since although there is more saber-rattling lately between nation-states in connection with Ukraine, Taiwan, and Israel/Gaza.

Another way to look at the problem is to ask why stabilization and peacebuilding interventions often get stalled in a negative peace status, for example, Bosnia. My analysis of the problem evolved out of my field experience, doctoral studies, and field research pertaining to international peacebuilding and stabilization interventions and environments. I think that I have figured out a useful way to *efficiently track and explain the status of conflict, stabilization, and peacebuilding elements, and to direct attention to intervention gaps and possible solutions.*

Negative peace (coercion) puts a temporary lid on civil unrest and violence. Positive peace is a search for fairness and balance. This takes place in a conflict zone. A conflict zone is a field of saints, the corrupt, opportunists, murderers, and all in between. That is why I developed a concept I call *human realism* to account for this reality.

My human realism perspective and *operationalized negative- and positive-peace framework* lay a different foundation for understanding realism and idealism assumptions—assumptions that can lead to tragedy when pursued to their logical extreme and the exclusion of one from the other.

In my approach, I separate interview-based field research data into *structural elements* (institutions/infrastructure) and *relationship elements* (conflict parties/ethnic groups) to take this important perception dichotomy into account.

For orientation and briefing purposes, I run real-time survey data through my *War to Sustainable Positive Peace Continuum* analysis model to associate the perceived status (as perceived by interviewees) of structural and relationship elements in relation to conflict and peacebuilding thresholds (the associations are inferred) (see Figure 19.1).

This enables all concerned to see a situation more clearly and to better track peace and conflict dynamics (see related graphic models). The model also provides a common perspective and language that can be shared and therefore facilitates more informed, joint considerations and responses. It enables all concerned to see the same picture for situational awareness purposes.

The pressing problem now is what to do when a political settlement, and stabilization and reconstruction as we know it—all essentially accomplished in Bosnia, for example—are not enough to break a deep-rooted, protracted conflict cycle. As one diplomat in Bosnia told me, "A mistaken assumption is that the

Dayton Accords [peace agreement for Bosnia] was a reconciliation process" (see Hanson 2001).

It was not. I argue that it was—is—a negative peace mandate. Negative peace (use of force to stop violence), although sometimes necessary early on, inevitably erupts into violent conflict again if not transitioned to positive-peace status in due course.

Essentially, *negative peace* is the imposed suppression of hostilities. I define *sustainable positive peace* as the successful establishment of ongoing mechanisms and relationships among conflict parties to address contentious issues locally, and to get at underlying causes and conditions—without violence or outsider-imposed stabilization or arbitration.

When considering a conflict endgame, I have come to prefer the concept of conflict transformation over conflict management, conflict settlement, or conflict resolution, although timing plays a part in each. These terms are well-known general concepts in Conflict Analysis and Resolution (CAR) that I consider helpful as basic framework markers.

The descriptions below are my adaptations of the ideas for my purposes as applied to peace and conflict circumstances whether small or large, domestic or international.

Conflict Management alone implies repetitive cycles of conflict and fragile periods of stability interrupted by periodic (often desperate) negotiations and ceasefires with little serious attention given to the underlying causes and conditions.

A *Conflict Settlement* (meaning a political settlement/peace agreement) can stop the killing and work out a political arrangement, but if the core underlying causes and conditions are not addressed, the settlement needs to be characterized as transitional. Put another way, reignition of violent conflict is inevitable—sooner or later—if underlying injustices, resentments, and hostile sentiments are not adequately addressed, along with reforming or eliminating institutions that support discrimination and indirectly feed violence (structural violence).

Conflict Resolution is sufficient if it indeed accounts for primary structural and relationship issues and sentiments that drive the conflict, and it leaves in place a viable mechanism by which capable local and national representatives and citizens can resolve future differences. Also, other key drivers of conflict such as corruption and organized crime have been taken into account.

Conflict Transformation, for me, better captures a deliberate intent from the beginning to transform a dispute or conflict from an unhealthy destructive process into a healthy constructive conflict process, which includes resolving *structural violence* drivers of conflict (discriminatory institutions and laws) and *cultural violence* issues (prejudice/personal direct violence), and transforming dysfunctional relationships for the better. Structural violence and cultural violence are concepts developed by Johan Galtung (1969).

Continuing my adaptation of the concept: *A conflict transformation approach simultaneously allows for the recognition of conflict as involving realism and idealism*. In other words, an opportunity to put obvious tangibles (political demands and positions) and not so obvious intangibles (non-negotiable values and identity) on the table together, early on, as mutual problems to be solved and a mutual failure of relationship to be remedied.

Building on John Burton's *basic human needs theory* and the more recent *human security* conceptualization (a recent framework for an ancient problem), I explain my concept of human realism and why I believe that its insertion into the discourse on war and peace, or conflict on any scale, is needed (see Burton 1990a,b).

Today's international interventions often involve robust military actions (stabilization) in conjunction with complex reconstruction and peacebuilding initiatives. I explain why understanding human realism and negative and positive peace dynamics provide greater clarity on war and peace circumstances.

Although a veteran, and at times a liaison to military contingents in the field, I make no claim to be an expert on military affairs. And there are others who are more proficient as specialists in peacebuilding, development, and governance. What I profess to contribute to stabilization and peacebuilding, and humanity's discourse around peace and conflict, is a composite framework that I refer to as my War to Sustainable Positive Peace Continuum model utilized for:

1. assessing the perceived status of structural and relationship elements,
2. in notional association with negative and positive-peace parameters,
3. along a War to Sustainable Positive Peace Continuum,
4. based on a human realism perspective (see Figure 19.1).

In short, this means the assessment of structural and relationship elements within negative and positive peace parameters. I assure you that it is a carefully thought-through process intended as an efficient analysis and briefing tool. I designed the approach for busy decision-makers, planners, analysts, policymakers, military and civilian implementers, conflict parties and citizens, and concerned others (academics, students, the general public).

As I have mentioned, the purpose of this *Citizens Edition* is to reach a wider audience of concerned citizens with a less academic message and an affordable book.

The framework and models guide situational analysis, intervention selection, and conflict, stabilization, and peacebuilding threshold tracking. The approach and models accommodate general conflict and peacebuilding discussions and training. I believe that, with minimal adjustment for local adaptation, the concepts and models can be applied to differing scales of conflict—community, national, and international.

My War to Sustainable Positive Peace Continuum model (Figure 19.1) showing a continuum of peace and conflict indicators/thresholds can be used for general orientation and discussion whether or not data is gathered on a particular conflict.

I was told by a number of Bosnians and international representatives (my dissertation field research location) that my models and graphics are intuitive, that they can be used with just a little guidance, and that the resulting survey data, analysis, and modeling reflect on-the-ground reality reasonably well.

I clarify here again that the statistical data that I collected in the Bosnia analysis, and ran through my War to Sustainable Positive Peace Continuum model, is to be inferred with the indicated conflict, stabilization, and peacebuilding thresholds because statistical significance has not been completely established. That step remains to be concluded. Nevertheless, the results and modeling seem to come close enough to be useful for working-group discussions and basic situational awareness.

I concur that a primary focus on positive-peace is essential. At the same time, I believe that it is important to recognize and understand negative peace in order to preclude confusion and misunderstandings about what is or is not positive peace, and *to better ensure that authoritarian-inclined leaders cannot easily pass off negative peace as positive peace.*

My framework, model, and methodology were field tested on the ground in Bosnia and Herzegovina over a four-and-a-half-month period. My assessment of that conflict is an on-the-ground applied example of the approach.

I personally interviewed and surveyed fifty international and fifty local-national representatives from a variety of societal and professional levels. I interviewed and surveyed Bosnian-Muslim (Bosniak), Bosnian-Serb, and Bosnian-Croat ethnicities. They expressed clear opinions about war and peacebuilding. I pass on their sentiments and wisdom, as well as that of others that I encountered elsewhere.

I would have interviewed many more to increase the statistical validity of my model but I was paying for this research and my time in Bosnia out of my own pocket, so I only claim it as an initial proof-of-concept effort. Hopefully, others will take it further.

The following sections provide an overview of key components of stabilization and peacebuilding scenarios. This is followed by a deeper look at the Bosnia conflict using my negative and positive peace framework and War to Sustainable Positive Peace Continuum. Comments from intervenors and local citizens are included.

Finally, means are explored by which to integrate positive peace processes into a conflict environment based on human realism principles (an acknowledgment of humanity's dual capacity for constructive and destructive interaction).

I believe that the following models and explanations can be used for basic peace and conflict situational awareness purposes regardless of scale. Think of your community and societal or global scenario when reading these explanations; picture the scenario in your mind when looking at a model. Although most readers will not be directly involved in case analysis or intervention actions, I believe that it is essential for the health of a democracy for the general public to have some familiarity with the basic elements of peace and conflict, and certain realities.

The different models highlight different aspects of peace and conflict. The intent is to draw a picture of what is going on, what is needed, and what is possible, both good and bad.

The important thing to understand is the difference between negative peace and positive peace, and that a negative peace status that is not eventually transitioned to a positive peace status is likely to erupt in violence again at some point perpetuating conflict cycles.

14

Stabilization and Peacebuilding Operations Basics

There are several ways to look at basic intervention tasks in stabilization and peacebuilding/peacekeeping operations. I primarily focus on concepts used by the UN. In this essay, I also elaborate a little further on the conceptual dichotomy between track 1 actors and track 2 actors as to what constitutes peacebuilding, and, in fact, what constitutes a status of peace. This distinction centers on the use of the term *conflict transformation* as defined previously.

Having described the chronic problem of conflict reignition earlier, and that many conflicts stall in negative peace—I briefly outline my composite framework below, which builds on the ideas and experience of others who have come before me. I attempt a brief discussion of the connection between theory and practice, or, in stabilization operation terms, between planning and execution.

I begin with a peace operation framework developed by David Davis (2008b) (classroom lectures) that is keyed to the implementation of primary objectives and tasks in humanitarian and peace operations. Primary tasks derived from former UN Secretary General Boutros Boutros-Ghali's (1992) *An Agenda for Peace* are contained within the framework. I modify the model slightly.

Readers acquainted with the framework will see familiar terms and ideas in this section. The concepts addressed in Boutros-Ghali (1992) *An Agenda for Peace* (preventive diplomacy, peacemaking, peacekeeping, peace support) retain their essential meanings (see also Boutros-Ghali 1995, 2nd ed.).

In short, the vastly more complex operational demands driven by post-Cold War realities—that is to say, the trend toward increasing nation state internal conflicts, and the greatly increased number of intervention participants (governmental and nongovernmental)—called for a more complex operational framework for the understanding, management, coordination, and fine-tuning of intervention approaches.

Figure 14.1 The War Is Over, But the Peace Has Yet to Be Won.
Source: Photo by James R. Adams.

In other words, interventions had to become more informed and flexible beyond simply keeping the conflict parties apart (the classic peacekeeping model) until a political settlement could be had, then maintaining a presence on the ground for years (monitoring) since the settlement was likely an inherently unstable negative-peace arrangement.

For me, the photo (Figure 14.1) above captures the negative peace nature (armed and armored personnel carrier on the left) and positive peace nature (UN staff vehicle on the right) of the more recent understanding of intervention dynamics.

In any case, I begin with Robert Oakley's (1998) basic model of Core Components of Peace Operations in Figure 14.2.

Oakley (the UN's first Special Envoy in Somalia), with substantial international experience in peacekeeping operations and environments, indicates that three core components comprise peace operations: diplomacy, aid, and the military.

David Davis (2008a), US Army-Retired, builds on this framework through his Conceptual Model of Peace Operations (CMPO) model below, in which *An Agenda for Peace* tasks are expanded upon. This framework incorporates primary task areas: peacemaking, peacebuilding, and peacekeeping/security, with peace support providing general support to the other three components, as indicated in Table 14.1.

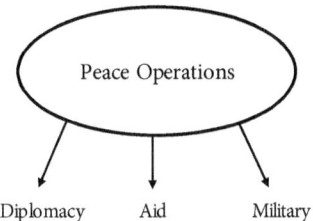

Figure 14.2 Core Components of Peace Operations.
Source: Robert B. Oakley's (1998) basic model.

Table 14.1 Conceptual Model of Peace Operations (CMPO).

Peacemaking	Peacekeeping/ Security	Peacebuilding	Peace Support
Fact Finding	Observation	Human Rights	Situation Awareness/Decision Support
Diplomacy	Force Presence	Humanitarian Aid	Supervision/Synchronization
Negotiation	Security	Disaster Relief Aid	Information: Awareness Operations and Logistics Liaison
Mediation	Military Force/Unit Movements	Refugee Relief Aid	
Facilitation	Law and Order	Development Aid	
Coercion (Sanctions/ Rewards)	Demining Demobilization/Disarmament	Good Governance	
Information		Institution Building	
Agreements/Treaties		Infrastructure	
		Democratization	
		Economics	

Source: US Army, retired David Davis, 2008a CMPO framework model, *An Agenda for Peace* (Fairfax, VA: George Mason University).

Increased *Peacebuilding*, shown on the line from lower left to upper right, yields increased justice by virtue of national reconstruction and humanitarian assistance (physical and institutional, X axis).

Peacemaking, ideally, moves a complex emergency situation toward stabilization and a peaceful environment by making strategic political and coordination decisions in support of peacebuilding efforts overall (pushing both X and Y elements toward a stable and peaceful environment overall ("Peace and Stability")).

Peace support provides logistical, liaison, and other types of mission support to the other three primary tasks/operational components. Davis stresses that peacekeeping, security, and social justice do not function independently—an increase in civil order encourages an increase in social justice, and an increase in social justice increases civil order. Security (stabilization) initiatives usually dominate in the early stages.

Overall mission coordination is a core function of intervention executive management (peacemaking). Also indicated (think of Bosnia and Kosovo) are the primary roles of the UN and security coalitions (such as NATO) in peace support activities as well as participation of other international and intergovernmental organizations and NGOs in peacebuilding activities.

The goal is that the primary components (peacekeeping/security, peacebuilding, and peacemaking (facilitated by peace support)) work in a coordinated and synergistic fashion through track 1 and track 2+ actors/intervenors.

Diamond and McDonald's (1996) Multi-track Diplomacy model indicates nine tracks: track 1 through track 9 (see Figure 16.1, in the Body Politic section)—that is to say, government, NGO, professional, business, private citizen, research-training-education, activism, religious, funding, communications, and media organizations.

Of course, this is easier said than done. The zig-zag line in the middle for peacemaking indicates that diplomatic efforts are usually subject to a series of advances and setbacks calling for alternating and judicious use of peace support and peacebuilding elements (Davis 2008a). Note that this is an intervention model, not a conflict model.

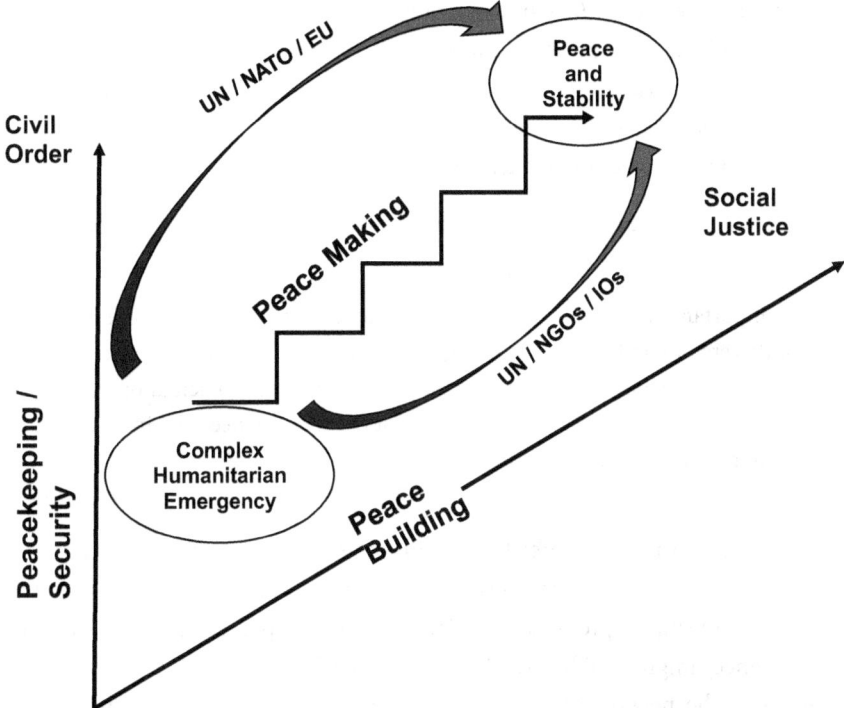

Figure 14.3 Conceptual Model of Peace Operations: Civil Order—Social Justice.
Source: David Davis. 1999. CMPO: Civil Order and Social Justice in Peace Operations. Referencing an unpublished classroom handout. Peace Operations Policy Program. Arlington, VA: George Mason University. Adapted by James Adams, 2010. With permission from David Davis.

Davis (2008a) conveys several other important ideas associated with the CMPO framework (see below and Figure 14.3):

- Peace operations: an impartial intervention for the purpose of maintaining or restoring civil order and social justice.
- It is apparent from historical experience that, during an intervention, the *Order* component is determined by the intervenor, yet the *Justice* component is measured by the people involved in the conflict.
- Peace, according to the CMPO, is the concurrent state of civil order and social justice, implying the presence of both negative- and positive peace dynamics.
- The peacemaking process can only function where the root causes of the conflict are being addressed. In many cases, these root causes are more than the simple power politics on the surface. Poverty, human-rights abuses, displaced populations, ineffective government, corruption—all of these

contribute to the conflict and are counter to the work of the peacemaker. If the violence is stopped by a negotiated settlement, but no attempt to address the causes of the violence is made, the settlement is extremely fragile. The process of addressing these underlying root causes and conditions is that of longer-term peacebuilding.

Referring to the *quest for viable-peace* framework (Covey et al. 2005), which I discuss below, Davis observes:

> An important observation is that 22 of the actions are directed at diminishing the drivers of conflict (peacekeeping/security) and 31 are directed at capacity building (peacebuilding). This 2:3 ratio is often not seen in actual operations, where the conflict drivers are the narrow focus and the need for institutional building is given a lower priority.
>
> (Davis 2008a)

This means that the lion's share of funding and attention goes to negative peace political/technical/structural/security tasks. Much less goes to positive peace relationship improvement initiatives. Negative peace measures (stopping the violence) might well be crucial early on, but I do not think that I can over-emphasize the necessity to transition to positive peace measures as soon as possible wherever possible, even district by district.

Leaving the basic structure model, I say a little about how I operationalized the concepts of negative peace and positive peace in relation to peace and stabilization operations. Then I move on to peacebuilding and intent.

15

Operationalized Negative and Positive Peace

I add negative and positive peace to the conflict management range. I have adapted Johan Galtung's (1969) concepts for practical insertion into my peacebuilding and stabilization operation framework described in previous sections. I take full responsibility for taking the liberty to do so.

Readers might have noticed that, under positive peace, I qualify structural violence to read as "minimal" (essentially, structural violence means institutional and legal prejudice and discrimination), in contrast to Galtung's "absence" of structural violence for positive peace. The simple reason for this is that I am reluctant to view human systems, political or otherwise, in absolute terms (Table 15.1).

Linkage of a Positive Peace Process to the Conflict Management Range

Below is a graphic model to illustrate how a positive-peace process can be applied to conflicts within a peace operation framework (see Figure 15.1). The Conflict Management Range model reflects various elements associated with deep-rooted protracted conflict, such as *destructive interaction*, a *protracted conflict cycle*, *latent or open conflict*, *strong suppression*, and too often a *complex emergency*. It also contains *constructive interaction* and *functional/considerate relationships*—elements known to be indicators of successful prevention, management, or resolution of conflict.

I have taken Adam Curle's (1971) basic conflict progression structure and superimposed it over David Davis' (2008a) order and justice in peace operations model (see Table 15.1).

The general idea is to highlight measures known to aid conflict parties in moving out of a negative peace mode into a positive peace mode. Ideally, the

Table 15.1 Operationalized Negative and Positive Peace.

Positive Peace
• The underlying root causes and conditions of conflict are effectively addressed. • Structural violence is minimal, and measures are in place for its control. • There is legitimate functioning governance and a civil system that ensures sufficient political, rule of law, economic, and social-welfare, security, recognition, and identity for all groups. • There are effective constructive-conflict processes for sustained governmental and civil collaborative dialogues. • Peace enforcement or assisted stabilization by outsiders is not needed.
Negative Peace
• War and widespread violence/civil disorder are suppressed by coercion. • The underlying root causes and conditions of conflict are not effectively addressed. • Structural violence is prevalent. • There is no legitimate functioning government and civil system that ensures sufficient political, rule of law, economic, and social-welfare, security, recognition, and identity for all groups. • There are no effective constructive-conflict processes for sustained governmental and civil collaborative dialogues. • Peace enforcement or assisted stabilization by outsiders is needed.

Source: Table design and content by James R. Adams, 2021.

violent conflict stage in the conflict management range (lower left to upper right) would be avoided entirely.

Just the same, positive peace processes are designed to move parties beyond protracted conflict cycles where they are caught up in a vicious cycle of fighting and periodic bouts of desperate negotiations which break down, or result in, agreements which are signed but predictably fall apart and the violence cycle starts again.

As indicated, a strong push for order can result in no open conflict, but conflict is present all the same (latent conflict) underneath the tip of the iceberg. In such a scenario, *latent conflict* exists whereby conflict parties are biding their time until conditions are advantageous for them to try to overthrow, or re-overthrow (often violently), the incumbent group.

Routinely, in post-Cold War scenarios, in which superpower support is withdrawn, neither the "in" nor the "out" group(s) are strong enough to decisively overcome their opponent(s) to maintain a status quo for very long. And they have little understanding of conflict transformation principles and practices, or value, and therefore most likely cross the confrontation threshold into violent conflict multiple times.

Destructive interaction escalates and conditions are ripe for a complex emergency in which there is a catastrophic convergence of political, social, economic, environmental, and infrastructural disasters—all while even well-intended negotiations and mediation efforts are taking place.

Often, the nature of the social conflict (culture wars?) is ethnic/identity based. It is at this stage that conflict parties become mired in what I refer to as the *critical zone* (note the hyphenated circle in Figure 15.1).

Conflict parties find themselves bouncing back and forth across the horizontal critical zone line—that is, between fighting and periodic bouts of desperate negotiations (with or without third-party mediation). They are unable to move further across the conflict management range into the positive peace/constructive interaction domain in the upper-right corner of the model. They are caught in a protracted conflict cycle.

It is in this situation that most major, and costly, international emergency interventions take place. The stronger party might have sufficient strength to suppress their opposition into a temporary latent conflict status, in which case it is often only a matter of time before the opposition recovers and the conflict parties again cross the confrontation threshold entering into the critical zone, and again are at high risk of renewing the protracted conflict for another cycle.

Again, I suggest that these dynamics are active regardless of the scale involved, that is to say, group, community, society, nation, globally, since fundamental human dynamics apply at all levels—the primary difference being scale, number of resources involved, and intensity.

Why are many current conflicts highly resistant to mediation and negotiation diplomacy by local authorities, nation-states, the United Nations (UN), or regional political bodies? Why are many negotiations (mediated or otherwise) failing? The nature of position-based negotiations (win/lose bargaining) of non-negotiable cultural, security, religious, and identity needs and values by conflict parties is fundamentally a futile exercise (Burton and Dukes 1990; Burton 1997).

It accounts for much of the perpetuation of conflict cycles in many instances, despite enormous political and financial resources being brought to bear on the parties by third-party coercive mediation (power mediation) (Ronald J. Fisher 1997, 165).

Considering the non-negotiable nature of many basic human values and needs, alternatives to position-based negotiation and mediation are needed. It is in this context that sustained dialogues and other positive peace-oriented approaches are of particular use, the key distinction being that *positive-peace approaches are aimed at changing the underlying assumptions, perceptions, and relationships that drive conflicts.*

There is little doubt that potent forces of greed, corruption, power, ambition, hatred, prejudice, indifference, and even apparent evil are evident in chronic conflict zones. However, the likelihood of coerced or purchased peace settlements lasting very long is not good.

Also associated with negative peace is the lack of forums for sustained collaborative governmental and civil dialogues and constructive relationship change.

The order and justice frame remains in place along with all other elements previously introduced. The distinction here is that the primary components of peace operations—peacemaking, peacebuilding, and peacekeeping/security (outlined with the Conceptual Model of Peace Operations in Table 14.1 in the prior essay)—are now taking responsibility for:

- *Order* (military, police, peacekeeping/security).
- *Justice* (institutional reconstruction, courts, peacebuilding).
- *Conflict Management* (executive decision making, general management, and coordination).

Now we can look at how a positive-peace process, for example, a sustained problem-solving dialogue, fits within a peace operations scenario (see Figure 15.1).

I have chosen Harold H. Saunders' (1999) *sustained dialogue* model for this illustration since, for me, it captures the essence of interactive mutual problem-solving approaches aimed at working on fundamental issues and relationships—not simply getting a political deal (which is often tenuous, at best). The sustained dialogue process supports civil society capacity building and institutional reconstruction at different levels.

Ideally, conflict parties could avoid the open conflict/destructive interaction entirely (following the arrow from the lower-left corner to the upper-right corner of the model in Figure 15.1).

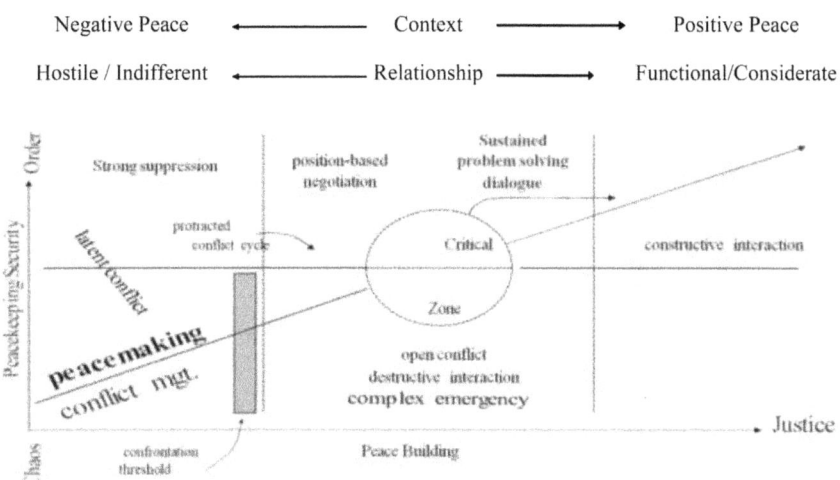

Figure 15.1 Conflict-Management Range, Positive-Peace Process Added.
Source: Diagram designed by James R. Adams, 2012.

Just the same, positive peace processes are designed to move conflict parties toward constructive interaction from wherever they happen to be at the time in the conflict.

To reiterate, the sustained dialogue process is a specific process within a broader multilevel *public peace process approach*. It originally evolved during the *Dartmouth Conference* as a joint de-escalation and relationship and options improvement process over many years within the US–Soviet semi-official, *bilateral effort to get the nuclear arms race under control*.

I point out that the nuclear non-proliferation agreement between the United States and the Soviet Union/Russia did put a lid on the likelihood of nuclear war for many decades.

Sustained problem-solving dialogues have proven helpful in broadening the perspectives of high-level conflict-party influentials, mid-level influentials, and grassroots representatives with regard to their situation and each other (Saunders [1999] on Tajikistan, Kelman [1990] on the Israeli/Palestinian conflict; and Volkan [1999] on Estonia).

Sustained dialogues can be accomplished by establishing relevant guided processes for sustained collaborative governmental and civil dialogues and constructive relationship change at several societal levels simultaneously, and within different sectors.

16

Peacebuilding and Intent

There are a wide range of views on the exact meaning of various terms, including those defined in the United Nations (UN) publication, *An Agenda for Peace*, and exactly what peace operations do, or should do (see Boutros-Ghali 1992; 1995).

Broadly speaking, this is a debate about intent and imperatives. A. B. Fetherston (2000) complains that peace operations are operating under a conflict management framework, contrasted with those who push for a more proactive emancipatory transformation (192). Fetherston advocates intervention in order to "disrupt destructive local hegemonic mindsets" to accommodate more broad-based constructive democratic and human rights-friendly narratives, and thereby sustainable peace (Fetherston 2000, 190–218).

Oliver Ramsbotham and Tom Woodhouse (2000), who have considered conflict transformation extensively, make a number of points about the evolution of stabilization/peacebuilding operations and conflict transformation:

> All of this has been brought together within the conflict resolution field in John Paul Lederach's characterization of *peacebuilding* as the attempt to address the underlying structural, relationship and cultural roots of conflict: "I am suggesting that '*peacebuilding*' be understood as a comprehensive term that encompasses the full array of stages and approaches needed to transform conflict towards sustainable peaceful relations and outcomes."
>
> (Lederach, qtd. in Ramsbotham and Woodhouse 2000, 171)

Since then, a development component has been added to get at root causes and to enhance sustainable peace objectives.

Ramsbotham and Woodhouse (2000) also take pains to make a distinction between post-settlement and post-conflict peacebuilding—a settlement being, usually, only the beginning of a peacebuilding process. They make distinctions between negative peace, which they describe as "Task A"—"preventing relapse into war"; and positive peace, described as "Task B"—"constructing a self-sustaining peace" (172–4).

Concerning the intent to achieve long-term sustainable peace, they argue that post-settlement peacebuilding should be a "composite process" in which a political settlement is underwritten by "constitutional and institutional reform, social reconstruction and reconciliation, and the rebuilding of shattered polities, economies, and communities."

Ramsbotham elaborates much more, but suffice it to say that they add a kind of final-stage measure of positive-peace attainment—"More broadly, Task A can only be said to have been finally secured when an incumbent government voluntarily and peacefully relinquishes power after losing an election" (Ramsbotham and Woodhouse 2000, 180).

The reluctance of US President Donald J. Trump to clearly state before the 2020 election that he there will be a peaceful transfer of power to the next administration, presented an insidious possibility that the country could be placed in a pre-negative peace status of civil disorder. A clear and traditional declaration that a peaceful transfer of power must be assumed is a sustainable positive-peace prerequisite. The phrase "playing with fire" comes to mind.

A Sample Positive Peace-Oriented Process

I have also chosen the highly experienced diplomat and author Harold H. Saunders's (1999) sustained dialogue model for this next illustration since, for me, it captures well the essence of interactive problem-solving approaches designed with deliberate positive peace-oriented intent. It is aimed at working on fundamental issues and relationships to better create conditions for a more durable political settlement, an easier stabilization, and the implementation of sustainable positive peace-oriented measures beyond the initial dialogue.

The Sustained Problem-Solving Dialogue model (Figure 16.1) supports civil-society capacity building and institutional reconstruction at multiple scales/levels.

Familiarity with realpolitik and human realism, as described earlier, is helpful for understanding the positive peace framework since such a dialogue proceeds under the influence of both paradigms simultaneously (realpolitik and human realism).

This is particularly true early on in the process, then less so for different participants as time goes on and as positive peace dynamics gradually take hold. An additional distinction between realpolitik governmental relations (realism in the usual sense) and human realism is that, using Saunders, (1999) perspective on civil society involvement in peacebuilding efforts, government officials tend to focus on narrow technical solutions while citizens tend to focus on values and relationship improvement (47–68).

My perspective on human realism is also reflected in Saunders, "human dimension": *"The human dimension of conflict must become central to peacemaking and building peaceful societies. Only governments can write peace treaties, but only human beings—citizens outside governments—can transform conflictual relationships between people into peaceful relationships"* (Saunders 1999, xvii; italics are Saunders').

Considering that many, if not most, conflicts today are essentially values-driven, it is helpful to analyze issues and facilitate interactions with that in mind.

I created the model in Figure 16.1 to better illustrate the symbiotic relationships involved in an *interactive multilevel/multisector sustained dialogue process*.

I have taken the liberty of linking three different models by three different interactive process-oriented scholar practitioners (John Paul Lederach's [1997] three-tiered society leadership model on the left; Saunders's [1999] sustained dialogue stages in the middle; and Louise Diamond and John McDonald's [1996] multitrack diplomacy model on the right). The combined models reflect the overall sustained dialogue structure and dynamics.

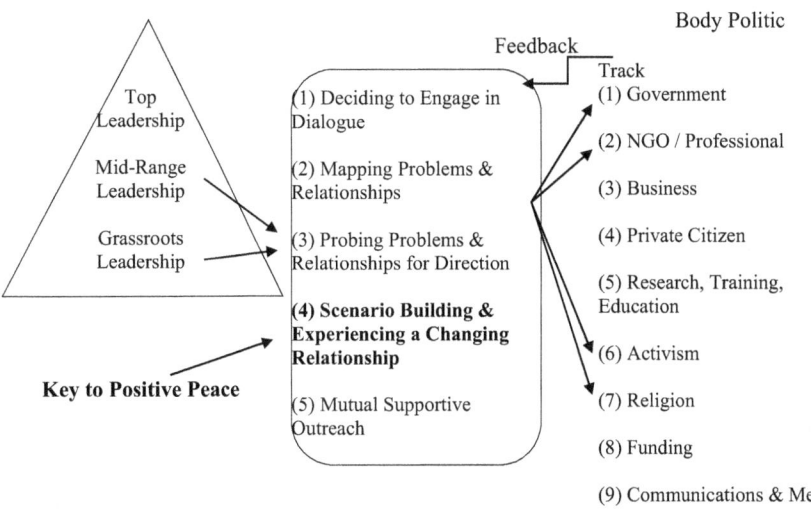

Figure 16.1 Sustained Problem-Solving Dialogue.
Source: Diagram designed by James R. Adams, 2012.

As mentioned earlier, sustained dialogue is embedded within a broader *multilevel public peace process* (Saunders 1999, 39) which aims at generating needed political will and momentum within and between interacting civil society levels and sectors; similar in principle to Lederach's (1997) *integrated framework* for establishing "an infrastructure for sustaining the dynamic transformation of conflict and the construction of peace ... a process-structure ... a peace-system characterized by just and interdependent relationships with the capacity to find nonviolent mechanisms for expressing and handling conflict" (Lederach 1997, 84).

As indicated on the left side of Figure 16.1, mid-range leadership (usually in consultation with top leadership) and grassroots leadership participate in joint interaction problem-solving (hopefully relationship/perception-changing). Participants typically include near-top influential and official leadership and top or near-top opposition leadership, as well as key private influential persons from diverse sectors of society.

The five stages within the sustained problem-solving dialogue reflect the general pattern used by most dialogue processes. Typically, there is revisiting of stages as new problems are selected for consideration and jointly worked through.

Once the participants arrive at a place where they are functioning as a collaborative problem-solving team and have developed options or steps for peaceful interactions and solutions, they take these insights and options back to their respective superiors or communities for consideration, input, and action.

The civil society body politic is well captured by Diamond and McDonald's (1996) Multitrack Diplomacy framework containing nine tracks. The resulting feedback is directed from the body politic back to the sustained dialogue group (Morton Deutsch, Peter T. Coleman, and Eric C. Marcus [2006] refer to this as a virtuous cycle, in contrast to a vicious cycle), establishing a positive cycle of joint deliberation, feedback, and adjustments.

Note: when I used the term "track 2" previously in this book, I did so in the way that governments, diplomats, and intervenors traditionally use it, meaning that the term refers to all nongovernmental actors, as opposed to governmental actors (track 1).

Diamond and McDonald (1996) have simply broken down nongovernmental actors into tracks 2–9 (multitrack diplomacy), which I sometimes refer to as track 2+. The United Nations is a track 1 entity since it is an organization comprised of nation-state governments.

Sustained dialogues have resulted in positive movement in otherwise paralyzed official positions. One reason is that this enables top leadership to discretely encourage unofficial dialogues behind the scenes with the "enemy" while maintaining an official position against such contact.

A common practice at Stage Five is that having taken on a joint problem-solving mindset, representatives from opposing conflict parties mutually support each other in their "re-entry" consultations with their own governments or groups. In connection with these phenomena, most scholar-practitioners stress that problem-solving processes eventually need to be institutionalized—meaning transitioned into law and policy.

The insights, constructive treatment of issues, options for movement ahead, and changed relationships eventually generated in the dialogues can be expected to slowly transfer to key decision-makers and groups outside of the immediate dialogue group.

In some cases, the outcomes of previous dialogues have evolved into acceptable negotiation points, agreements, and processes that were eventually adopted by official governmental and faction entities as well as broader social movements, all representing important steps toward sustainable solutions (Saunders [1999] on Tajikistan; and Volkan [1999] on Estonia).

Note that I highlight stage four of the sustained problem-solving dialogue (Figure 16.1). This is a crucial stage. Most participants from opposing conflict parties in a sustained dialogue eventually find themselves working together productively to explore problems and solutions from a joint problem-solving perspective.

This does not usually happen unless the representatives have, with the help of knowledgeable facilitators, effectively moved beyond their earlier realpolitik position-based demands, assumptions, and perceptions with regard to the conflict and each other. In essence, they find a third perspective beyond their initial hardened positions. Saunders' five-stage sustained dialogue public peace process is fully outlined and explained in Chapter 6 (1999, 97–145).

The paragraphs below, directly from Saunders (1999), are offered as reinforcement of the concept. At the end of each paragraph, I have added (within brackets) a specific comment on how the dynamics or content described in the respective paragraph applies to conflict resolution capability and an indication of its value in civil society restructuring and capacity building:

Beyond diplomatic exchanges, there can be a depth of communication among human beings that reveals deep-rooted interests, perceptions and misperceptions, priorities, identity, purpose and political dynamics. Now we are beginning to see the possibility of adding to governmental channels nonofficial dialogues that can broaden the range of interaction, sharpen understanding, deepen communication and partly replace adversarial interaction and contests of force as a means of resolving differences ... In a process of sustained dialogue, participants can actually design a scenario of interactive steps that will gradually make bodies politic aware of a changing pattern of interaction. (Saunders 1999, 39) [This statement describes a potent and likely trickle-up and trickle-down effect]

...

Above all, I argue that the multilevel peace process is the context for peacemaking in which all parts of a society can interact. (Saunders 1999, 249) [Versatility, public support and ownership]

In the back of his book, Saunders (1999) includes a thorough organizers' and moderators' manual for sustained dialogues (253–303). Although Saunders' book was published over twenty years ago, I believe that the tried-and-tested concept and format remains viable given that human-interaction fundamentals remain much the same.

17

The Case of Bosnia and Herzegovina

"We have more than one truth"—that statement to me from a Bosnian Serb reporter in Bosnia captures well the complexities and sensitivities of a mixed-ethnicity country that has experienced the tragedies of political and social extremism and civil war.

I elaborate at some length on Bosnia in this *Citizens Edition* to emphasize, for those in the United States who are toying with the idea of a breakup of the United States into Red or Blue states and all that implies, what they might look forward to in terms of political, civil, and cultural strife. Put another way—chaos, war, refugees, internally displaced persons, economic devastation, and a multitude of inconveniences.

Again, I suggest that you imagine such conflict consequences in your own backyard by getting familiarized with how such scenarios played out in the real world in Bosnia and the former Federal Republic of Yugoslavia (FRY)— conflicting political and ethnic perceptions, values, and narratives similar in many ways to the American experience today when pushed to extremes.

The complexities of ethnically interspersed populations, historical events, and current affairs in the Balkans, and Bosnia and Herzegovina (BiH) in particular, are almost limitless. Much of this is due to the seemingly never-ending ebb and flow of populations, civilizations, religions, and marching armies over millennia as emperors, local kings, warlords, and nationalist extremists of varying sorts intrigue and contest for influence or control of the same landscape.

Complexity is deepened by claims of superior ethnic legitimacy based on conflicting claims as to what history says about who got where first, or who is or was in the majority on a given day, and therefore, what group is presumably entitled to control the land and associated political, economic, and cultural prerogatives. Conflict-intractability in this regard has been deepened by unspeakable brutality and injury.

All of this is further complicated by confusion or by contrivance in connection with which perspective is to be used in adjudicating or enforcing claims—that is to say, which measurement of legitimacy and entitlement is to be used: ethnicity, religion, or nation-state authority?

Nearly all Bosnians—to use the term uncharacteristically all-inclusive by local standards—agree on one thing, that traditionally there is no distinction to be made between ethnicity and religion, that they are exactly interchangeable. Based on my interviews, nearly every interviewee stated that, in Bosnia, all Bosnian-Croats are presumed Roman Catholic, all Bosnian-Serbs are Serbian Orthodox Christian, and all others are Bosnian-Muslims (Bosniaks)—with the exception of a few tiny minorities, and that religion and ethnicity are inseparable. I did talk with some individuals who did not subscribe to this presumption.

Many Bosnian-Serbs vigorously argue that state nationality should be separate according to ethnicity/religion—Croats somewhat less so, and Bosnian-Muslims much less so.

Another confounding factor is the often-discussed argument that multiethnicity does not apply in BiH (concerning Bosniaks, Croats, and Serbs) since modern-day Bosniaks are deemed to be of Slavic descent but adopted or were coerced into Islam during the roughly 500 years of Ottoman rule. The term "Bosniak" was first introduced in the nineteenth century by the Austro-Hungarian Empire, after the end of Ottoman rule, to distinguish Muslims in Bosnia from Croatians and Serbs since Austro-Hungarian authorities (the new rulers of Bosnia at the time) did not want to recognize citizenship according to religious affiliation.

The term went out of use during the FRY era in favor of the more universal "Yugoslav" (Southern Slav) pertaining to all ethnic groups as per the wish of Marshal Josip Broz Tito. But "Bosniak" was brought back into use by international intervention authorities after the 1992–5 war for largely the same reason it was introduced the first time by the Austro-Hungarian rulers (Malcom 2002).

All primary sources for current BiH population statistics start with the 1991 census. The most commonly cited total population estimate for BiH (roughly the size of West Virginia) currently is about 3.8 million (CIA World Factbook [online 2024]). Additional BIH population demographics from the Factbook are as follows:

Nationality/ethnicity: Bosniak (Muslim) (50.1%), Serb (34.8%), Croat (15.4%), others

(2.7%).

Religion: Muslim (50.7%), Serbian Orthodox Christian (30.7%), Roman Catholic (15.2%), Protestant (4%), other

(1.2%).

Language: Currently described as Bosnian, Serbian, or Croatian by the respective ethnic groups. All are essentially the same language described as Serbo-Croatian prior to the 1992–5 war, with slight local dialectic differences. Serbians use Cyrillic script; Croatians and Bosnians use the Latin alphabet.

Two other basic perspective statistics are those concerning refugees and internally displaced persons. These particular numbers are and have been extremely sensitive and politically charged points of discussion and contention in the Balkans. This is especially true for BiH since it has the most ethnically diverse population and is seen historically as the melting pot of the Yugoslav people in relation to the surrounding, more homogeneous nations, principally Croatia and Serbia.

In fact, some Croatians and Serbs, particularly those in Croatia or Serbia, have argued that Bosnia has no nationhood of its own at all since Bosniaks are simply Slavic Croatians or Slavic Serbs who converted to Islam during Ottoman rule.

There are distinct categories of refugees and internally displaced persons. There are those who have been pushed by conflict across international borders (refugees) or displaced internally within a country (internally displaced persons [IDPs]), or those that find themselves back in their country of origin but not specifically the villages or homes that they were forced to leave (also IDPs). I cite two statistics for BiH provided by the UN High Commissioner for Refugees (UNHCR) Refugee Data Finder. 2018 (accessed October 30, 2024):

Refugees: forced displacement to outside of Bosnia as of 2018—16,956.
Asylum Seekers: As of 2018—1,619.

When the war ended in 1995, refugees numbered 900,000 and IDPs 1.3 million (UNHCR Working Paper No. 8, May 1999, 1). My point here is that the consequences of civil wars last many decades and beyond. Ethnic rivalries might be the most intractable.

Any discussion of the Balkans and Bosnia and Herzegovina (BIH) must contain references to coerced population movements (ethnic cleansing) since such is the core of common experience and complaint of the Bosnian people, currently and historically.

The history of the Balkans and BiH in particular is one of migration, population displacements, conquests, subjugation, intrigue, ethnic conflict, and struggles for independence and identity. Put another way, invasions, settlements, ethnic cleansing, civil and imperial wars, shifting boundaries, and shifting rule and allegiances—internally and externally.

The same can probably be said of the entirety of human affairs and of all civilizations throughout human history, but I conveniently set aside that detail for now and focus on Bosnia, with relevance to an imagined conflict scenario in the United States should it come to that—the basic human fundamentals are similar if one looks close enough.

In any case, there is little doubt that Bosnia's place as a literal crossroads of history has, over millennia, reliably concentrated acute competition among warring civilizations, religions, ethnicities, and authoritarian or democratic passions.

The First World War facilitated repetitions of long-familiar Balkan war patterns of atrocities, ethnic cleansing, and refugee movements between empires and between Serb, Croat, and Bosniak factions in various configurations. Once again, empires and Croatia and Serbia worked to carve up Bosnia among themselves.

Post-First World War agreements led to the establishment of the Kingdom of Slovenes, Croats, and Serbs and, separately, Bosnia and Herzegovina (BiH). The various ethnic groupings, and increasingly politicized religious leaders, pursued a variety of peaceful and violent efforts to further their respective causes until the advent of the Second World War when, in April 1941, Germany, Italy, Bulgaria, and Hungary, in a collective axis, invaded Yugoslavia.

Croatia, which had developed a potent nationalist-fascist component, split off to the Nazis; Serbia, also with a potent nationalist core, sided with the Allies (the United States, the United Kingdom, France, Union of Soviet Socialist Republics [USSR]). Bosnia, as usual, was annexed entirely by another power, in this case Croatia with Nazi Germany military backing, and Italy, which got a large part of the Dalmatian coast for its participation. Croatia's paramilitary Ustase, Serbia's paramilitary Chetniks, and Tito's paramilitary Communist Partisans fought each other in a three-way war while simultaneously fighting alongside their great power Axis or Allied partners, respectively.

Ultranationalists in Croatia and Serbia worked diligently with extreme violence to take advantage of the chaos generated by the Second World War to realize a Greater Croatia and a Greater Serbia at each other's expense, and especially at the expense of multiethnic Bosnia.

In February 1942, Serbian ultranationalist Stevan Moljevic argued for the "cleansing" (*čišćenje*) of the land of all non-Serb elements (Malcom 2002, 178). Bosnians, especially Bosnian-Muslims, again having no country of their own, fought on all sides against all sides, but primarily against Croatia.

As with previous wars in the Balkans, and Bosnia in particular, the Second World War facilitated unspeakable atrocities and massacres and the generation of hundreds of thousands of refugees and internally displaced persons. Approximately 1 million people were killed in the Balkans during the Second World War.

I take time to mention these historical details because the United States is headed toward historic ethnic/racial population transitions in the coming decades. There is much to learn from the people of the former Yugoslavia about enthusiasm for divisions and ethnic and nationalist purity. Hopefully, we will take to heart the hard-earned lessons of Balkan tragedies.

While Tito was alive, the FRY enjoyed a relatively prosperous and stable period with Tito's non-alignment stance, which held ultranationalists' ambitions in check. But this phase was short-lived. After Tito's death in May 1980, the 1980s and 1990s were characterized by escalating confrontations between hardline nationalists in Serbia for dominance in Yugoslav affairs, and hardline nationalists in Croatia reacting in kind, with Bosnians again caught in between.

The problem of ethnic and national identity for Bosnians and Bosnian-Muslims (the term in use during this period) in particular remained a challenging dilemma, even within the all-encompassing identity of Tito's Yugoslav brotherhood. This is reflected in ongoing debates about the proper categorization of nationalities, ethnicities, and religious groups in national census exercises in the decades following the Second World War.

Malcom (2002) describes the fluid nature of the identity debates revealed in the national census exercises of 1948, 1953, 1961, and 1971:

> In the 1948 census the Muslims had three options: they could call themselves Muslim Serbs, Muslim Croats or "Muslims, nationally undeclared" (or "undetermined"). This gave the Bosnian-Muslims a chance to demonstrate just how reluctant they were to be either Serbified or Croaticized: 72,000 declared themselves as Serbs and 25,000 as Croats, but 778,000 registered as "undeclared."
>
> (Malcom 2002, 197-8)

Malcom (2002), pointing to the many centuries of absorption and mixing of different races and ethnic groups in the Bosnian lands, concludes about Bosnian ethnicity that "all that one can sensibly say about the ethnic identity of the Bosnians is this: they were Slavs who lived in Bosnia" (12).

With regard to the impact of Tito's constitutional trending toward decentralization and greater local autonomy (meaning *de facto* ethnic autonomy), Malcom (2002) concludes that *"federations of different national entities can work successfully only if they are based on a genuinely democratic political system*; but this was not the case in Communist Yugoslavia" (202; emphasis mine or emphasis in the original).

Consequently, it is not surprising that the otherwise well-intended gesture of decentralization did not work out in a politically and economically corrupt and dysfunctional Communist system, nor that subsequent ethnocentric pressures contributed to the simultaneous rise of ultra-nationalism and the fall of the FRY.

Ironically, allowing greater autonomy and representation (*de facto* ethnocentrism) facilitated a direct line of increasingly potent hardline nationalist reaction through media, academic, and political mechanisms, culminating in arrival at the logical extremes of nationalist agitation and reaction. Further changes to the constitution in 1974 created the autonomous province of Vojvodina (Hungarian and Croatian majorities) in the north of Serbia, and the autonomous region of Kosovo in the south (Albanian majority).

But ultimately, the creation of autonomous non-Serb ethnic regions in Yugoslavia was too much to bear for determined Greater-Serbia and Greater-Croatia hardline nationalists—along with the temptations of power and territorial gains.

A rapid acceleration of ultranationalist actions and statements characterized 1990 and 1991. Tactics to radicalize Serbs were employed by militant Serb nationalists with the use of incitements through the media and staged armed attacks on villages and local police stations to induce calls for armed defense by local police and villagers and demands for Yugoslav Army intervention and protection. These tried-and-true population-radicalization and country-destabilization tactics long used by guerrilla movements around the world were refined and repeated often and successfully in Bosnia.

This fact should serve as a particularly poignant point of cautionary tale for American readers.

Eventually, the levels of agitation and violence reached critical mass, leading to declarations of independence, first by Slovenia and Croatia, then shortly after by Bosnia and Macedonia. The full weight of Yugoslav Serbian and Bosnian-Serb army, security, and paramilitary units was pressed into full-scale war against Croatians and Muslims in Croatia and Bosnia, presumably to save the Federation.

But as the conflict intensified, Serb police and Yugoslav Army units became instruments more of Serb or Croatian nationalism than of Yugoslav federalism. The centuries-old fight was on again for a Greater Serbia, a Greater Croatia, and the ever-tempting division of Bosnia between the two. The FRY was not to survive.

Renewed age-old calls by pan-Serbia and pan-Croatia ultranationalists to incorporate all Serbian and Croatian populations into their respective motherlands resurfaced forcefully once again during the simultaneous rise of Serbian nationalist Slobodan Milosevic and the notcoincidental fall of the Yugoslav federation.

A few proud American politicians have recently called for Texas and Georgia secession from the United States. They should very carefully consider the hard lessons learned in the Yugoslav wars. How will the status of Texan or Georgian be decided? Who decides who stays and who goes? Who arbitrates the breakup of families and their property and businesses, and who can use state and county public services?

Ethnic, race, religious, and ideological firestorms burn everyone for a very, very long time.

I should mention here that a seriously dysfunctional and divided America is a weak America, and like a fractured Yugoslavia or Bosnia, will not do well in an unstable world while contributing to its instability.

The overriding concern then is, will Americans be able to resist the temptation of signing on with a willing authoritarian claiming to save us from ourselves and abandon notions of democracy and a free society? Can US citizens take to heart the lessons available from the Yugoslav wars?—particularly, those about the dissemination of false narratives and disinformation.

Memory and Conflict

What linkages can be made between historical memory-related points discussed so far and FRY conflict particulars—or current American particulars for that matter? There are obvious connections to blocked memory (widespread denial), intellectual and politicized semantic memory or memory consciousness. A concrete example of applied historical memory manipulation is examined at length by Cohen (*Serbia's Secret War: Propaganda and the Deceit of History* 1996) in which he details a well-oiled and systematic historical memory development and manipulation machine managed by Serbian authorities and intelligentsia since the Second World War—a review of memory manipulation from the communist era through to recent years. Cohen cites Serbian sociologist Dinko Tomasic who "observed in 1948 that the ruling Communists in Yugoslavia had successfully institutionalized a pattern of deceit" (134). Cohen adds a revealing 1988 comment by former Yugoslav politician and dissident Milovan Djilas reflecting on the confounding nature of the practice: "The hardest thing about being a Communist is trying to predict the past" (134).

Cohen elaborates:

> Within postwar Yugoslavia, much of the documentation that would reveal the sequence of historical events was suppressed, while the interpretation of history was tailored to suit contemporary ideologies.
>
> (134)

Given the profound meaning attached by each of the conflicting groups in the former Republic of Yugoslavia to their respective national narratives, a discussion dedicated to the subject of memory and conflict is warranted.

Avishai Margalit (2004) ponders the ethics of memory, which is appropriate for inclusion in a study of conflict involving ethnic cleansing and genocide. Margalit contends that historic relations develop "thick" relations between friends, relatives, and like-kind tribal or ethnic group members, which accounts for better mutual understanding, compassion, and treatment. Margalit also contends that historic relations develop "thin" relations between strangers and those who have little in common. The thin status leads to selective application of positive attributes assigned to the "other."

Another example of thinking on collective memory and ethics is provided by Paul Ricoeur (2004), who tries to explain why some historical events remain fresh in "memory-consciousness" and others do not, for example, the holocaust versus the Armenian genocide or colonialization genocides.

Ana Douglass and Thomas A. Vogler (2003) explore the effects of mental and physical shocks on witnesses to serious violence, as compared to those who have not personally witnessed or experienced such violence (similar to Athens' description of the violentization process). Douglass and Vogler stress that witnesses and nonwitnesses alike contribute distinctive collective memories.

Branimir Anzulovic (1998) looks at dominant Serbian myths and psychological-sociological factors to explain rationalizations for genocide in the region. Philip J. Cohen (1996) looks at the role of propaganda and the "deceit of history" in the conflict. Other authors examine factors such as the inadvertent or deliberate contributions of the international media, academics, and intervenors of all sorts to the creation of or perpetuation of myths or their distortions.

Maurice Halbwachs (1992) contends that memory is not an individual function but one taking place only within the collective context, and that collective memory is selective, it influences behavior, and reconstructs the past accordingly: "As soon as we locate people in society it is no longer possible to distinguish two types of observations: one exterior, the other interior" (169).

The idea of individual selective memory is not new to popular understanding—"So and so only remembers what he wants to." What Halbwachs (1992) introduces is a framework for explaining living social memory processes and social construction. In the context of the Balkan conflicts, this can translate into a concept that societies, as well as individuals, can become "fused" with the past and "have the illusion of reliving it," a collective freezing in the past.

I suggest that such a phenomenon afflicts all societies everywhere.

Yaacov Y. I. Vertzberger (1986) discusses a concept he refers to as "practical-intuitive historians applied history" in connection with poor foreign-policy decisions. In other words, there can be a problematic reliance on individual intuition or faulty collective memory (false mental construction) that is divorced from the fact that political leaders, as well as historians, often enough, and perhaps more so, operate on false assumptions.

Ricoeur (2004) has much to say about memory, history, and forgetting. Helpful to this discussion are his comments on "blocked memory," "manipulated memory," and "obligated memory." Ricoeur speaks of manipulated memory as being a "passive" acceptance of memory "abuses" by people "resulting from a concerted manipulation of memory and of forgetting by those who hold power" (80).

This idea also has clear resonance with Lonnie H. Athens' description of what he calls the violentization process (Athens and Ulmer 2003) in which those further along in the violentization process try to intimidate, coerce, manipulate, and "teach" their subordinates in the ways of the world while trying to force submission; then, the abuser conveniently forgets that they have abused the subordinate (blocked memory).

Ricoeur (2004) then links the memory question to that of identity: "The problem is therefore carried back a step, from the fragility of memory to that of identity (manipulated memory)" (81).

Catherine Newbury (2002), in her work on history and memory pertaining to the Rwandan genocide, would be familiar conceptual territory to a student of—or, for that matter, a participant in—the Balkan conflicts. She states with regard to the Rwandan case:

> It is these competing visions of the past—the politics of history—that I explore here ... The debate about the nature of the country's history is central to the process of political reconstruction; the postgenocide government in Kigali has not only to deal with the trauma of a whole people and society, but it also has to consider how its policies will be interpreted within the context of various conceptions of Rwanda's past.
>
> (67)

> ....
>
> A key element in politicizing ethnic cleavages in the recent history of Rwanda has been the development and propagation of a corporate view of ethnicity. The generalization of blame was dramatically evident ...
>
> (67)

What further linkages can be made between the historical memory-related points discussed so far and former Yugoslavia conflict particulars? There are obvious connections to blocked memory (widespread denial) and politicized memory.

A concrete example of historical memory manipulation is examined at length by Cohen (1996) in which he details an historical memory-generating machine managed by Serbian authorities and intelligentsia after the Second World War—a review of memory manipulation from the Communist era through to recent years.

> In the 1990s, in order to influence Western policy makers and blunt international outrage, Serbia's information campaign has promoted its war effort as justifiable. One essential feature of Serbian propaganda has been to portray Serbia's

enemies, especially the Muslims and Croats, as a threat not only to the Serbs, but to European civilization. Thus, Belgrade has claimed an "Islamic threat" in Bosnia-Herzegovina, where religious fundamentalism has never existed, and has accused Croatia of fascism, when in truth the resistance movement against Nazi's during World War II was strongest in Croatia.

(Cohen 1996, 135)

There are "episodic memory" elements that Volkan would describe in terms of chosen trauma—that is, the Serbian defeat at the 1389 Battle of Kosovo Polje to the Ottomans, and the subsequent "semantic memory" exercise by the defeated Serbian leader Knez Lazar (and subsequent Serbian generations) to choose heaven (meaning death) over military victory, as the national imperative, in order to bear the unbearable.

Such a historical memory-coping mechanism has been continuously relied upon and manipulated for centuries in response to a perception of ultimate national humiliation.

Wolfgang Schivelbusch (2004) focuses his sociological-psychological lens on the American South after the Civil War, France following the Franco-Prussian War, and Germany at the end of the Second World War. His description of reactions to total defeat and perceived national humiliation could just as well describe the Serbian experience. An important distinction, however, is that the Serbian experience, or acting out, of national trauma and mourning is still at the forefront of Serbian consciousness, and, consequently, still central to the mindfulness of Serbia's neighbors.

Schivelbusch (2004) characterizes the kind of total defeat that can be associated with early Serbian experience, and for that matter with the experience of all Balkan entities at various times, as "crushing" to national self-confidence. Such experiences are purported to eventually induce mental and physical reactions such as heroic self-characterization, a sense of superiority, and quests for security and revenge.

The question now is how can this kind of reality, once deeply internalized and spread far and wide, be changed in light of general retreats to hardened nationalism and centuries of repetition? And to what extent is a culture-of-defeat a factor in historical memory on the part of all Balkan conflict parties as they retreat to bastions of nationalism, as Schivelbusch puts it? These are largely unanswered questions at this point.

Perhaps some extremists or political groups in the United States are reacting to various historical memory-based culture-of-defeat feelings (unresolved grievances)?

Since the 1992–5 Bosnian War and intervention dynamics are closely interwoven, I sequence points on that war with the intervention discussion next.

18

Interventions into the Recent Bosnian War

Although I highlighted a variety of perspectives on peacebuilding and stabilization operations earlier, the descriptions were generic in nature. Now I provide an overview of the Bosnian intervention circumstances specifically. However, as I pointed out earlier, an intervention into a post-conflict United States would likely be carried out internally, not by an outside intervention force.

General Considerations

In any case, it would likely involve many of the same resolutions, operations, motivations, and harsh intervention realities that the Bosnian case reveals. An international intervention coalition would likely be generated to respond to other serious conflicts elsewhere involving nations having much less in the way of internal material and human resources than the United States.

For this *Citizens Edition*, I abbreviate this essay; for my complete analysis of the interventions in Bosnia, see my *Analytic Reflections from Conflict Zones: A Cautionary Tale for A Polarizing America and World* (Adams 2021).

The Bosnian case presents a particularly complex scenario given the multiple, largely reactionary interventions involved and a timespan of nearly twenty-eight years and still counting since there is still some outside intervener presence in the country (European Union [EU], North Atlantic Treaty Organization [NATO]).

To begin, I stress a point concerning political will and interventions—Bosnia being a tragic case in point. Generally speaking, when political, military, and humanitarian imperatives clash, and facts on the ground present an inconvenient reality, political imperatives win. This clash of imperatives is central to understanding the Bosnia intervention, its failures, and the current negative peace stalemate.

For the purpose of wading through complexities, I shift to a field-based perspective on intervention. I divide tasks into stabilization and reconstruction—the bedrock divisions of responsibility in the new intervention era. In this context, civilians tend to think in terms of conceptualization and implementation. The military thinks in terms of planning and execution.

Traditional United Nations (UN) peacekeeping missions that involve neutral mediation and nonintervention unless there is local consent—even for emergency humanitarian relief or the mitigation of genocide—fare badly in the middle of a shooting war or violent civil disorder involving uncooperative conflict parties.

Some lessons have been learned following disastrous or nearly disastrous intervention episodes in Somalia, Angola, Rwanda, and Bosnia, hence revised mandates and policies paving the way for more comprehensive, sometimes nonconsent-based interventions leading off with a robust stabilization phase, then, in due course, an all-fronts reconstruction phase—for example, Kosovo and East Timor.

The United Nations, and a substantial number of member states, understand intervention limitations a little better now, and the need for a comprehensive approach to stabilization and reconstruction.

As I stated previously, *the pressing problem now is what to do when a political settlement, and stabilization and reconstruction as we know it, are not enough to break a deep-rooted protracted conflict cycle.*

Stabilization

Resolutions, Peace Conferences, Operations, Protection

Comprehensive, ground-up state building, essentially comprising reconstruction tasks, was fairly well identified and refined by the time of the Kosovo intervention five years after the Bosnian War ended. However, just to be clear, the tone and parameters set in a stabilization phase significantly impact what reconstruction and peacebuilding initiatives are possible, as well as the medium to long-term outcome.

As shown on the UN's website in November 2024, ninety-one UN Security Council resolutions were issued between September 25, 1991, when the arms embargo was levied against the Federal Republic of Yugoslavia, and November 22, 1995, when the embargo was suspended (United Nations 2024).

The embargo was suspended upon "initialing" of the General Framework Agreement for Peace in Bosnia and Herzegovina (Dayton Peace Accords) in Dayton, Ohio, by the presidents of the Republic of Bosnia and Herzegovina (BiH) (Alija Izetbegovic), the Republic of Croatia (Franjo Tudman), and the Federal Republic of Yugoslavia (FRY) (Slobodan Milosevic). The agreement is contained within the Office of the High Representative document *Bosnia and Herzegovina, Essential Texts* (August 2004).

Sanctions against Yugoslavia were suspended the same day, November 22, 1995. Another four Security Council resolutions were passed by December 14, 1995, when the Dayton Accords were formally signed in Paris by the three presidents.

At the end of December 1995, Security Council resolutions were passed authorizing NATO to replace the UN Protection Force (UNPROFOR), the UN military mission in Bosnia, with the NATO Implementation Force (IFOR), with a six-week overlap for handover purposes, and to establish the UN International Police Task Force (IPTF) in Bosnia. The initial stabilization phase was accomplished.

There were still many stabilization tasks to accomplish involving politicians and diplomats, and international civilians and troops, but the shooting war was over, and one could envision a period of follow-up stabilization overlapping with the reconstruction phase to come. Beyond that were notions of Bosnia, and other former Yugoslav republics, democratizing and joining the expanding European Union.

In the case of a post-conflict America, the end of a stabilization phase would likely be discernible when a democratic, constitutionally valid governance structure was functioning again, and various violent militias were neutralized.

The harbinger of armed intervention is usually an alarmed outcry in the international media and demands in editorial pages to "Do something!" in response to graphic images of refugees and atrocities on TV, coupled with calls for the protection of emergency-relief supplies transported by humanitarian organizations on the scene—the "CNN effect."

Such outcries usually follow ineffective diplomatic conferences and sanctions, which are, in turn, usually followed by conflicted reactionary responses from the

International Community (IC) generally thought of as the United Nations and Western governments. Bosnia was no exception. Neither was Kosovo, initially.

Amid the breakup of the FRY during the fall of 1991, the United Nations High Commissioner for Refugees (UNHCR) in Croatia was deeply involved in a refugee and internally displaced person (IDP) crisis. FRY Serbian forces had invaded the Eastern Slavonia and Western Slavonia territories of Croatia, carrying out a violent ethnic cleansing of non-Serbs from the area, and were intent on incorporating the Serb-majority areas there into Serbia.

During this period, European governments, hoping to avoid a military confrontation, were counting on diplomatic conferences to resolve the crises: the European Community Conference on Yugoslavia (September 1991); the arms embargo (UN Security Council Resolution 713, September 25, 1991 [UN 2024]); and economic sanctions (UNSCR 757, September 30, 1992).

Intervention decision-makers repeatedly issued diplomatic warnings and ultimatums. But, in the end, resolutions without credible use-of-force resolve behind them proved useless, or worse, as Serb armed forces and militias demonstrated time and again by simply ignoring them and pushing ahead with ethnic cleansing and massacres.

It is worth noting that of the ten principles of the Helsinki Final Act of the Conference on Security and Cooperation in Europe (OSCE 1975a,b), signed by thirty-five states on August 1, 1975, five are specific to protecting state sovereignty (OSCE 1998). Ironically, the Helsinki Final Act was supported by some countries, particularly the Soviet Union, to enforce the principle of inviolability of sovereignty and non-interference in the internal affairs of another state.

At the same time, other countries and organizations cited the Helsinki Act as the principal instrument for the protection of human rights and self-determination of national peoples in repressive countries. The OSCE, which succeeded the CSCE in 1995, has become the principal body for promoting and protecting national, human, and minority rights in Europe.

Since the Geneva Conference agreement (November 23, 1991) had the effect of freezing Serbian military gains on the ground in the Serbs' favor in Croatia's Eastern and Western Slavonia and Krajina, Yugoslavia signed the agreement. It concurred with United Nations Security Council Resolution (UNSCR) 721 (November 27, 1991), calling for the establishment of a ceasefire and proceeding with plans to establish a peacekeeping mission in Croatia.

However, when Yugoslav/Serb cooperation was less than forthcoming in real terms on the ground (ceasefire violations), UNSCR 743 (February 21, 1992) was issued establishing the UNPROFOR peacekeeping mission with United Nations Protected Areas (UNPA) in Croatia, but only for two months in anticipation of progress with peace negotiations.

When it was clear that the Serbs were not cooperating, the UN issued UNSCR 749 (April 7, 1992) to renew UNPROFOR for a year and expand its operational mandate to Bosnia, Serbia, Montenegro, and Macedonia, with a liaison office in Slovenia as shown on the United Nations website listing UN resolutions (United Nations 1992).

As war and ethnic cleansing spread, events accelerated rapidly with declarations of independence by Slovenia (June 25, 1991), Croatia (June 25, 1991), Macedonia (September 8, 1991), and Bosnia (March 3, 1992, after an independence referendum), which greatly outpaced other European and UN peacemaking initiatives.

For example, the UN and European Union (EU)-sponsored joint peace talks (International Conference for the Former Yugoslavia [ICFY]), facilitated by UN Special Envoy Cyrus Vance and EU Representative Lord David Owen, proposed the division of Bosnia into ten autonomous cantons. This was rejected by Bosnian-Serbs in a referendum of their own.

EU, US, and UN recognition of the independence of the former Yugoslav republics came quickly after the independence declarations. In May of 1992, the UN recommended membership in the United Nations for Croatia (UNSCR 753), Slovenia (UNSCR 754), and Bosnia and Herzegovina (UNSCR 755) as independent states.

Steven L. Burg (2001) argues that EU and UN negotiation concessions to Serbs, conflicting European and US national interests, and unwillingness by intervenors to use credible force directly led to the strategy developing in 1993–4 to partition Bosnia based on de facto Serbian on-the-ground war gains—an example of coercive diplomacy with no teeth.

The continuing ethnic cleansing by Yugoslav and Bosnian-Serb forces, accompanied by ineffective peace initiatives and hollow declarations of protection by the UN and EU through UNPROFOR, is reflected in a series of fourteen United Nations Security Council resolutions issued between 1992 and 1995. The resolutions included economic sanctions, a no-fly zone, protection of relief convoys, and creation of UN Safe Areas to protect civilians (see United Nations 2024).

Each new resolution was issued because preceding resolutions were ignored. UNSCR 1004 followed the shelling and overrunning of Srebrenica by Bosnian-

Serb forces under the command of General Ratko Mladic in the second week of July 1995. More than 7,000 unarmed civilian men and boys were methodically killed over a period of six days after being handed over to Bosnian-Serb forces by the Dutch UN peacekeeping detachment in Srebrenica, which was responsible for their protection.

Burg (2001) points out that although UNSCR 770 was issued with a UN-Charter Chapter VII "coercive authority" mandate to use "all measures necessary" to get emergency humanitarian aid through to victims of ethnic cleansing, that intent was offset by the "highly restrictive rules of engagement that reflected the original Chapter VI authorization of the UNPROFOR mission, which made it dependent on the cooperation of local forces" (8–9), in other words, local consent.

Although UNSCR 781 (October 9, 1992) established a no-fly zone over Bosnia, which cleared the skies of Serbian war planes, UN concern that UN troops and personnel would be taken hostage by Serb forces in retaliation for air strikes against Serb ground units prevented its effectiveness. The "dual key" system of control in effect at the time permitted a UN Secretary General veto of NATO airstrikes or the escalation of airstrikes.

This continuing scenario of noncredible NATO airstrike action eventually led to the complete ineffectiveness of UNPROFOR as an intervention and protection mission. The dire circumstances of the collapse of UNPROFOR in the latter part of 1994 through the summer of 1995, the Serbian forces massacre of non-Serb civilians in UN safe areas, and shelling of the main market in Sarajevo eventually led to NATO, via the Contact Group, taking full control of the military intervention in Bosnia under US leadership—without a UN dual-key restriction.

It also eventually led to the proactive US diplomatic initiative led by principal US negotiator Richard Holbrooke (1998) to compel all parties to the negotiating table to stop the war.

UNSCR 1010 (August 10, 1995) authorized the Croatian offensive against Serb forces in Croatia and the north and south NATO sectors of Bosnia, lifting the arms embargo. NATO Operation Deliberate Force air strikes (August 30–September 20, 1995) against Serb weapons and munitions' emplacements were carried out to redress the gross imbalance of military capability on the battlefield.

In effect, this shifted the balance of power on the battlefield in favor of Croatian, Bosnian-Croat, and Bosnian-Muslim forces that had, prior to that, been vastly out-matched by Yugoslav and Bosnian-Serb forces.

This new on-the-ground reality included pressure from President Milosevic on Bosnian-Serbs to relent in order to get the economic sanctions against Yugoslavia lifted. It compelled Bosnian-Serbs to eventually accept a ceasefire, and reluctantly accept that Yugoslav President Milosevic would negotiate on their behalf at the peace settlement talks at Wright-Patterson Air Force Base in Dayton, Ohio, in November 1995.

The Contact Group, made up of high-level European diplomats plus the United States, responding to the upgraded interests of the United States, took effective control of negotiations from the UN-EU-sponsored ICFY and moved toward implementing a coercive diplomacy strategy in real terms.

The principal motivation for the new US interest in "doing something" was the realization that an uncontrolled collapse of UNPROFOR amid a continuing Serb ethnic-cleansing onslaught, and loss of the war, would mean that the United States would have to make good on its pledge to evacuate UNPROFOR troops in such an event (Burg 2001).

The new US seriousness about the intervention in Bosnia was a direct result of the associated broader threat to NATO cohesion generally, and therefore to vital US national interests.

A complete intervention collapse in the middle of Europe would have been disastrous for US and NATO organizational integrity and credibility. This fact has clear negative implications with regard to the current Russian invasion of Ukraine and the outcome of the war there.

Although discovery of a post-Westphalian world on the battlefield is not a scientific revelation per se, I think that *resistance to a profound paradigmatic shift concerning a centuries-old conflict protocol is a useful example of adherence to an ingrained older paradigm preventing recognition of a new reality, despite overwhelming evidence to the contrary*—a familiar experience for many in changing times.

Transition to NATO and the Dayton Accords

A ceasefire and negotiated political settlement are normally expected to facilitate a transitional phase between stabilization and reconstruction. In the case of Bosnia, a new ethnicity-based constitution was written into the General Framework for Peace in Bosnia and Herzegovina (Dayton Peace Accords) as an integral state-building feature of the combined ceasefire and peace agreement. Marcus Cox, in his October 1998 article "Strategic Approaches to

International Intervention in Bosnia and Herzegovina," refers to the agreement as "constitutional engineering" (Cox 1998, 3, 6, 12).

The problem of the ethnicity-based structure of the constitution and its mandated ethnic divisions within governmental departments did (and continues to do so to this day) create profound difficulties for normalization of the situation, ethnic relations, and the state. The constitution was not presented for consideration by a legislative body or public referendum in Bosnia.

According to diplomats that I interviewed in Bosnia, the constitution was assumed to be transitional by the original negotiators, but it was never officially designated as such. Therefore, no transitional plan or timeline was set in place to generate a transitional expectation from the Dayton ethno-constitution to a nonethnicity-structured constitution based on individual and minority rights.

The hoped-for transition was placed at the mercy of expedited, fear-based ethno-nationalists' elections that has only served to entrench ultranationalists and obstructionists in power. Structural violence (legal institutional discrimination) was subsequently embedded into the constitution and, hence, the state.

In my view, the following *two factors are the most fundamental, if not fatal, flaws* in the entire Bosnia state-reconfiguring exercise: (1) no declared transitional status and (2) reliance on ethnicity-based elections to resolve constitutional contradictions. They also constitute a lesson to be learned.

However, being cognizant of reality, getting an optimal political settlement/peace agreement in the heat of the moment, as with all things in conflict and intervention, is easier said than done.

In short, criticizing a coercive-trusteeship strategy (imposed conflict management "to do something"), while simultaneously arguing for respect for local consent, reveals the fundamental contradictory dilemma of coercive intervention itself—one of damned if you do and damned if you don't.

Principal Dayton negotiator US diplomat Richard Holbrooke, in his *Washington Post* editorial opinion ("Was Bosnia Worth It?" July 19, 2005), describes the ethnicity-based peace agreement as a necessary compromise to get any agreement at all to stop the war, ethnic cleansing, and sincere efforts at genocide, and to prevent Bosnia from becoming a fundamentally criminal state in the middle of Europe, or another base for al-Qaeda and the associated horrors of an insurgency quagmire that that implies.

I have already pointed out the intervention-conceptual dichotomy between conflict transformation as political settlement and institutional reconstruction versus conflict transformation as relationship change. In this context, the question remains: Does peace enforcement work? Carl Bildt (1998) was a co-negotiator at Dayton and the first EU High Representative for the Office of the High Representative (OHR) for Bosnia and Herzegovina (BiH), which was created to oversee the civilian aspects of the Dayton Agreement in Bosnia.

It was his view that the Dayton Peace Agreement

> balances the reality of division [of ethnic groups] with the structures for cooperation and integration, and is based on the hope that over time the imperative of integration [organically] in the country and the region will be the dominant factor as long as war can be deterred ... I believe that we can only escape the separatist approach when the structures and integrative aspirations of European cooperation begin to have a serious impact on the region as a whole.
>
> (Bildt 1998, 392–3)

In other words, Bildt (1998) was betting on the strength of the eventual assimilation of Bosnia into a civil rights and minority rights-respecting EU (a structural *and* relationship adjustment) to overcome the necessary evil of expedient, ethno-constitutional structures—providing that a lid could be kept on the volatile purpose-built negative peace in the meantime. Over twenty-nine years later, the lid is still holding, but the boiling underneath continues unabated.

A reminder: as I stated early on, *negative peace status will inevitably erupt, eventually, into violent civil disorder or war if not transitioned to a positive peace status at some point.*

I conclude this section with a thought shared by Holbrooke (1998) when discussing the Bosnian intervention in *To End a War*. He comments on Henry Kissinger's general juxtapositions of the foreign policy approaches of "realists"—Nixon, Kissinger, Kennan, and Theodore Roosevelt—with the approaches of "idealists" Woodrow Wilson and Jimmy Carter:

> But based on personal experiences in the late 1970s with authoritarian leaders like Ferdinand Marcos of the Philippines and Park Chung-hee of South Korea—both of whose corrupt strongman regimes were peacefully replaced by democracies—I came to the conclusion that the choice between "realists" and "idealists" was a false one: in the long run, our strategic interests and human rights supported and reinforced each other and could be advanced at the same time. In short, American foreign policy needed to embrace both Theodore Roosevelt and Woodrow Wilson. These thoughts were never far from my mind as we searched for a way to end the war.
>
> (Holbrooke 1998, 366)

When death is at the door, an armed "realist" response offering the illusion of protection ("safe areas") serves victims no better than a no use-of-force policy offered by "idealists." The results are just as unfortunate for victims either way.

To state the obvious, when the moment of truth arrives, decisive action is required in the face of imminent threat, particularly when a known lethal practice (ethnic cleansing/genocide) is repeated again and again with impunity against civilians, as was the case in Bosnia.

Concerning the protection of civilians in Bosnia, the instincts of both realists and idealists failed. Richard Holbrooke, in his call for the simultaneous advancement of mutually reinforcing strategic interests and human rights, is in effect, calling for intervention with cognizant application of what I refer to as human realism, a judicious blend of realism and idealism.

As I conceptualize it, *human realism* describes a fundamental dualism inherent in the human condition—the proven capacity of humanity to deliberately engage in inconsiderate, competitive, self-interested, win/lose acts at others' expense for gain of wealth, territory, prestige, advantage, or survival.

But simultaneously, it also describes the proven capacity of humanity to deliberately engage in empathetic, interactive processes to understand, to change, to overlook or forgive, and to adopt more collaborative methods of interaction for managing and resolving difficult issues and conflict.

In Bosnia, human realism would have called for the simultaneous application of the effective use of negative and positive peace measures, in other words, the use of necessary force to protect life and property (a concept familiar to any law-enforcement agency) and the introduction of constructive conflict—concepts familiar to many judges (restorative justice, victim-offender conferencing, constructive communication), and social scientists, peacebuilders, some political leaders, and concerned citizens.

Hopefully, this insight will be considered in a conflict intervention scenario in the United States or elsewhere when needed.

Reconstruction and Development

Consider this section on reconstruction to be pertinent to all societies and countries at risk—it is what follows (one would hope) polarization, fragmentation, conflict, and collapse. Imagine for a moment, however disturbing that might be, that conflicted circumstances have gotten out of hand where you live.

I repeat that outside intervention would probably not be needed in the United States since there are many informed and trained reconstruction and development organizations and professionals in the country capable of carrying out such tasks (mediation and constructive communication included), although they might be surprised to find themselves called-upon to intervene in the United States as opposed to foreign lands.

The United States is technically a fully technologically developed and politically advanced democracy (although there is slippage politically and civil society-wise of late, we are still learning). My concern is about American patterns of de-democratization and trends toward aggressive nationalism, politically and culturally, that generate destructive forces in societies and nation-states that can, sooner or later, succumb to fragmentation and violent self-destruction.

Yes, it can happen anywhere.

Recent international peace and stabilization interventions (Bosnia, East Timor, Kosovo) and the latter half of the Iraq and Afghanistan interventions have fundamentally become exercises, or at least efforts, at democratization through development, so democratization separate from development is not a distinction easily made now.

In contrast to stabilization, reconstruction has traditionally entailed a more straightforward process of carrying out concrete infrastructure, technical, and institutional rebuilding—as opposed to stabilization's stated aim to suppress violent civil disorder and war—along with an often nefarious struggle to figure out what's going on (determining who among the self-proclaimed authorities are legitimate), who the combatants are, and what to do about it, and to what degree cooperation is possible between intervenors and conflict parties.

Often, intervenors and conflict parties are diametrically opposed in interests and viewpoints, including in their respective camps, as to how, if, and when to bring an end to hostilities.

Previously, reconstruction was assumed to proceed when the shooting was over based on ceasefires and political settlements. However, it appears to be largely accepted policy now, following the latter parts of the Iraq and Afghanistan interventions, that reconstruction overlaps and complements ongoing stabilization efforts before stabilization is adequately secured throughout a conflict zone.

Hence, the concept of Provincial Reconstruction Teams (PRTs) and District Reconstruction Teams (DRTs), which had their advent in Iraq, then became part of the intervention/anti-insurgency effort in Afghanistan (nonlethal aid)—the term attached to my humble efforts in Afghanistan.

In other words, there is initiation of reconstruction tasks while there is still significant instability in an effort to win over public support toward legitimate national and local governance to fill power vacuums, and to neutralize obstructionists, organized crime, predatory militias, and transnational terrorists' groups.

The lessons of Bosnia are still relevant to a post-conflict US scenario. I think it is safe to say that the physical reconstruction of the Bosnian state infrastructure and public institutions has technically been accomplished. Therefore, I focus on implications for re-democratization (if that idea survives in Bosnia, the United States, and elsewhere) and institutional reestablishment in relation to conflict transformation and sustainable positive peace.

This is in contrast to just listing the number of clinics, schools, and hospitals rebuilt, and reliance on coerced suppression of violence in general, that is to say, negative peace. This lesson applies to reconstruction efforts anywhere, including the United States.

The utility of knowing how much material and funding input has gone into reconstruction in Bosnia, or elsewhere, and the number of roads and structures rebuilt is rendered less useful if newly resurrected post-war institutions are ethno-politicized by embedded ethnic discrimination (structural violence). For example, in Bosnia most schools are still ethnically segregated—some by entrances, or schedules, or floors in the same building. The tripartite presidency is a rotating position (every eight months) based on ethnicity.

Being politically sensitive to complete intervention failures in Somalia and Rwanda, and the near catastrophic intervention episode in Bosnia, as well as to ongoing threats to international security elsewhere, the US Department of State established an Office of the Coordinator for Reconstruction and Stabilization (S/CRS) in 2004 and a Bureau of Conflict and Stabilization Operations (CSO) in 2011 (that absorbed S/CRS) to increase the US institutional capacity to "conduct democracy promotion operations in post-conflict states." This is a useful capability, "deep state" function or not.

John R. Schmidt (2008) (the founding deputy coordinator for security and governance in the S/CRS) asks an astute question: "Can Outsiders Bring Democracy to Post-Conflict States?" (107–22). Schmidt lists general conditions that indicate the likelihood of success in the democratization of a post-conflict environment:

- The higher the GNP, the greater the likelihood of success in democratization.
- The lower the acceptance of a political culture of democracy, the less the likelihood of success.
- The greater the religious, ethnic, or factional animosities, the less the likelihood of success (Schmidt 2008).

The same can be said about a re-democratization effort in the United States, or elsewhere, in my opinion.

Schmidt argues that a comprehensive assessment of the roots of a conflict and the popular culture is necessary to fully understand a situation before planning or committing to a democratization or development program in connection with an intervention. Afghanistan comes to mind in this regard.

Schmidt (2008) points out several nuances (110–11): former Communist countries artificially induced low individual incomes and thereby created a "middle-class-in-waiting," which, when stimulated with a market economy and representative government, will more likely succeed in democratization.

Similarly,

> States where the exercise of power is arbitrary or where official corruption is widespread are likely to be highly resistant to democratization, since political elites have a strong stake in maintaining the status quo. Democracy is rare in the Islamic world because Muslim societies lack the clear divide between governance and religion characterizing the secular West.
>
> If the critical mass of political actors are driven primarily by sentiments incompatible with democracy—be it avarice, the desire for power, class hatred, ethnic animosity, or radical Islamic zeal—the result is unlikely to be democracy.
>
> (2008, 119)

...

At the end of the day, what is required for establishing democracy is a willingness to play by democratic rules.

(Schmidt 2008, 112; emphasis mine)

Generally, governmental intervenors tend to advocate for power-sharing arrangements, as indicated by Schmidt (2008) and the Dayton Agreement itself.

At the same time, while acknowledging the grave difficulties of maintaining a conflicted and contradictory status quo (institutionalized discrimination), pairing up international advisors with local governmental officials and civil society organizations is a viable way to embed participatory democracy role models who presumably have a democratic, civil and human rights ethos.

In effect, this describes the UN model that was established and run fairly successfully in Kosovo. The UN embedded international advisors and administrators at all levels in all sectors while retaining state and local authority until such time as specified transparent governance benchmarks were largely met.

In due course, political and institutional instruments of authority were transitioned in Kosovo to national and local officials; a few of whom were removed for corruption or lack of cooperation.

There exists now a fairly coherent matrix of tasks used in post-Bosnia peace and stabilization operations, hence the near axiomatic five-intervention sectors of: governance, security, rule of law, legitimate economy, and social wellbeing.

Robert Muggah (2009) sees the problem of armed groups (militias) and poorly managed "former" combatants in post-conflict environments as high-risk factors, potentially jeopardizing or derailing otherwise satisfactory progress in security and reconstruction gains. There is no question that such groups are of primary concern. If, ultimately, peace settlements degrade, such groups could again be significant obstacles to normalization and democratization in the Balkans or a recently balkanized United States.

For John Paul Lederach (1997) resolution of the former militia/former combatant factor can take twenty or more years. Factors that led him to this conclusion are competitive interactions between conflict prevention/resolution-focused organizations, emergency relief and humanitarian aid organizations, and institution-building organizations—all of which have different priorities, experience, and risks' tolerance (3).

Gerd Junne and William Verkoren (2005) use the phrase "peace versus development in post-conflict situations" to characterize problems encountered by peacebuilding-oriented and development organizations, such as prematurely trying to introduce reconciliation projects when people "have seen their hopes shattered by war and may find it too early to work with a highly traumatized population."

Also, in some cases,

> humanitarian organizations rush in but are neither interested in the causes of the conflict nor in long-term development. Development organizations see these situations as an exception and may find the situation too unstable to resume

their work ... [or] not have much feeling for politics ... [Although the recent] aid effectiveness debate has prompted development scholars and practitioners to look more closely at the role of political and legal structures in stimulating or inhibiting development.

(June and Verkoren 2005, 5)

These circumstances clearly mandate closer scrutiny of governance, security, and rule-of-law structures and practices in connection with reconstruction, peacebuilding, and development projects. Again, I suggest embedding side-by-side, hands-on partnering and coordination by qualified advisors and administrators with local officials, as per the Kosovo model. An added feature would be official collaboration on peacebuilding initiatives between trained international and local facilitators.

Also, I encourage promoting professionalism in governance and economic systems even if they are badly burdened by systemic corruption. The courage shown by individual local nationals—hopefully supported by international officials—pushes against the ills of systemic corruption.

As it is, the profit-motive concept in a corrupt system is already well understood and practiced, but generally for the benefit of a few. Therefore, role-modeling professionalism and transparency in governance is a key factor in demonstrating fairness and supporting local officials inclined in that direction.

The real question to be asked is, should outsiders intervene at all? I have worked with many local nationals in conflict and "post"-conflict environments. With few exceptions, most citizens prefer transparent, representative governance and civic participation, although maybe having little experience of it, to a pre-intervention status of unchecked corruption, brutality, or chaos.

In fact, most local nationals are relieved that something is finally being done about pervasive corruption and discrimination, which are major drivers of conflict and obstacles to sustainable positive peace.

Local ownership of governance responsibility was formally presented as transition policy when adopted in 1995 by the Development and Assistance Committee of the Organization for Economic Cooperation and Development (OECD) (Jeffrey 2007, 7). At the same time, however, the European Union Office of the High Representative in Bosnia was "granted 'final authority in theatre' to interpret the Agreement" (Jeffrey 2007, 12).

However, there is a problem with leaving behind political settlements, reconstructed institutions, and technically democratic enhancements (elections for example), and at the same time leaving behind the same destructive human sentiments that precipitated war and subsequent interventions to begin with.

I note here that there appears to be democratization back-tracking by the current EU High Representative in BiH by imposition of anti-democratic/unlegislated political measures that add, not subtract, polarization and fragmentation stresses in Bosnia (outside imposition of and reinforcement of ethnopolitical divisions in governance)—in other words, a deepening of the negative peace status, which was instituted as an interim measure by the Dayton Accords to stop the war in 1995. Unfortunately, the Dayton Accords (sometimes mistakenly referred to as reconciliation) has yet to be transitioned to a non-ethnopolitical, positive peace constitutional arrangement.

I repeat again that a negative peace status that is not eventually transitioned to positive peace will inevitably erupt again in violent civil disorder or war.

I conclude this section on reconstruction and development with a few thoughts from Pauline H. Baker (2001) who describes a conflict resolution versus technical democratization dilemma as being: "at the heart of the current debate about how best to pursue peace in the twenty-first century." The issue, specifically, is how to "reconcile the two imperatives of peace: conflict resolution, on the one hand and democracy and human rights, on the other" (756)—in other words, enforced negative peace if necessary, or democratic freedoms.

This dilemma has not been resolved as of yet. Baker (2001) asks: "Should peace be sought at any price to end the bloodshed, even if power-sharing arrangements fail to uphold basic human rights and the democratic principle? Or should the objective be a democratic peace that respects human rights, a goal that may prolong the fighting and risk more atrocities in the time that it takes to reach a negotiated solution?" (756).

To my mind, peace at any price essentially describes a negative-peace mandate (of some kind), which has been achieved in Bosnia. A democratic peace respecting human rights, broadly speaking, is a positive-peace mandate of some description that has yet to manifest in Bosnia.

Baker goes on to distinguish between *two types of peacemakers*: (1) *conflict managers* who are involved in conflict mitigation, for example, preventative diplomacy, mediation, dispute resolution, and dispute regulation and (2) *democratizers*, who she describes as "those who advocate human rights, democratic institutions, the rule of law, and the prosecution of those who commit war crimes and atrocities."

Baker (2001) adds:

Conflict managers tend to concentrate on short-term solutions that address the precipitous events that sparked the conflict; above all, they seek a swift and expedient end to the violence. Democratizers tend to concentrate on longer-term solutions that address the root causes of the conflict; they search for enduring democratic stabilization. The former see peace as a precondition for democracy, the latter see democracy as a precondition for peace.

...

Illustrations of conflict resolution that tilted toward the conflict managers' model are Cambodia, Mozambique, Angola, and Sierra Leone ... Basically, settlements in these countries represented power-sharing arrangements with weak democratic foundations.

...

Examples of conflicts settled along the lines of the democratizers' model are South Africa, Namibia, and El Salvador, where real political change included measures to ensure moral accountability and justice in the long term ... in recognition that the crises were basically human rights struggles.

(Baker 2001, 756–60)

In traditional Conflict Analysis and Resolution (CAR) terms, I interpret "*conflict managers*," as described by Baker, as essentially track 1 diplomatic, political, and military/security officials tasked primarily with immediate crises management, security, and basic governance objectives (I would add Bosnia to Baker's list of conflict manager-outcome countries), and "democratizers" as track 2+ reconstruction and development intervenors.

As Baker (2001) qualifies, there is an overlap of tasks and objectives, but fundamentally I think that her categorizations apply. My question here is: To what degree is genuine conflict transformation carried out by either "conflict managers" or "democratizers"?

Put another way, are root causes and conditions of conflict being addressed either by conflict managers or democratizers? Baker (2001) indicates above that democratizers "tend to concentrate on longer-term solutions that address the root causes of the conflict"—thereby leaning toward positive peace-oriented initiatives in my view. A second question then is: Is a distinction to be made between democratization and conflict transformation? Are they the same thing?

Although long term in perspective, democratizers might or might not promote relationship change and getting at the root causes and conditions of a conflict. If the intent is to simply institutionalize elections, with some orientation on civil and human rights, then I would say no, such democratization is not conflict transformation.

Conflict transformation, as generally interpreted by track 2 scholars and practitioners, focuses on relationship and narrative change.

Perhaps the US State Department has promoted the idea of conflict transformation but the contrary seems to be the case currently in Bosnia with active support for an EU initiative to further institutionalize ethnic divisions in Bosnian governance—in effect, to deepen the negative peace status.

Bosnia is still stuck in Dayton Accord ethnopolitical purgatory, a variation on negative peace with no end in sight. Certainly, this is better than being stuck in perpetual war or violent disorder, but the agony needs to come to an end.

In this regard, a shift in perspective on the part of all concerned would be aided by better understanding the *war to sustainable positive peace continuum* and *negative and positive peace parameters*—lessons for Americans and other concerned citizens in stressed societies.

19

Assessing a Negative and Positive Peace Status

There are currently a number of familiar and troubling conflict patterns at work in the United States that resonate with the polarization and fragmentation dynamics that I have seen elsewhere, in the Balkans in particular. Therefore, I continue my focus on the Bosnia situation, by way of example, to get a better understanding of how we can avoid such circumstances with minimal damage.

For four and a half months in 2009, I interviewed and surveyed fifty international intervention officials and staff in Bosnia, along with fifty Bosnians from different ethnicities and societal levels. I would have stayed longer and interviewed many more for a larger statistical sampling but the enterprise was at my own expense.

Having become aware of Johan Galtung's (1969) concepts of negative and positive peace and structural and cultural violence, and having observed dynamics in conflict zones that seemed to be better explained by such concepts, I built my assessment framework around negative- and positive-peace parameters.

Maybe such an understanding would help explain the problem of wars reigniting after a political settlement or peace agreement is signed and reconstruction tasks are finished. Maybe such an understanding would help explain why stabilization and peacebuilding interventions stall in fragile, hostile peace or a negative peace, as Galtung (1969) would describe it.

The usual measures of a conflict's end are a ceasefire, stabilization, a political settlement or peace agreement, and accomplishment of reconstruction if needed. Political and reconstruction inputs and outputs are calculated. Those steps were accomplished in Bosnia. The actual outcome is another matter.

Yet, in 2009 when I carried out my Bosnia doctoral field research, roughly thirteen years after the shooting stopped, deep ethnic animosity and serious state dysfunctionality continued, and still does to this day. Bosnia is said to be almost as fragile and explosive today as it was in the 1990s. Serbian ultranationalists are still pushing for the breakup of Bosnia.

Something was/is clearly missing from the assessment picture, from the political perspective, and from the original Dayton Peace Accords. Therefore, I developed a composite conflict transformation assessment model to help explain the Bosnia situation and maybe similar conflict situations elsewhere.

I wanted to draw the picture so that I could see, so that others can better see, what is happening in their conflict circumstances. The following is an abbreviated explanation of that framework and model. For a full explanation, see my book *Analytic Reflections from Conflict Zones* (Adams 2021).

Measuring Progress in Conflict Environments (MPICE)

My framework identifies sectors and elements for the analysis of peace and stabilization environments. However, I was not the only one wondering about missing pieces at the time and contemplating a different assessment framework. As it turns out, a US government interagency team and I had been independently and simultaneously (unknown to each other) developing a similar conflict-transformation (the term also used by the interagency team at the time) assessment framework.

I began the development of my framework in 2006, Assessing Interventions Stalled in Negative Peace, which I also based on a conflict-transformation perspective.

The US government interagency project (*Interagency Metrics Framework for Assessing Conflict Transformation and Stabilization*, Version 1.0, US Institute of Peace, August 2008) was unknown to me until retired Army Colonel, Professor Dave Davis, director of George Mason University's Peace Operation Policy Program, brought it to my attention and referred me to one of its authors (Michael Dziedzic at the US Institute for Peace).

Our two versions (mine considerably smaller) cited many of the same elements involved in peace and stabilization environments; however, I distinguished structural elements from relationship elements, and attempted to locate them within negative and positive peace parameters on a war to positive peace continuum.

I later adopted the five primary sector "end states" (activity categories) of the MPICE framework, which I placed on the structural side of my model, while retaining seven of my original ten relationship elements on the relationship side.

As it happens, there was a lively debate within the field of conflict resolution in the 1980s and 1990s about structural change versus relationship change to get at resolutions—that is to say, that the genuine resolution of intractable, deep-rooted conflict is a matter of restructuring inherently unjust systems that thwart fair access and distribution versus changing destructive relationships that are inherent in such systems.

This discussion was well captured by the John Burton-Jim Laue debate with Burton (a former diplomat) on the side of the structural change imperative, and Laue (a George Mason University conflict-resolution professor) on the side of the relationship change imperative (Rubenstein 1999). That debate continues to this day in academia and government.

My impression is that most of the adherents of structural change still tend to be track 1 representatives (governmental), and adherents of relationship change still tend to be track 2+ nongovernmental scholar-practitioners (although, that is changing somewhat). My recommendation is simply to respond structurally and/or relationship-wise on a contingency basis when possible and where possible as needed—a human realism perspective.

In my framework, I separated all key elements (indicators) of conflict transformation to structural or relationship sub-branches. I indicate the actual survey response statistical means (averages) using a 1–7 Likert scale based on actual interviewee answers to thirty closed-ended questions. Additionally, I asked four open-ended questions in an attempt to get some triangulation on the statistical results (confirmation of results using different analytical approaches).

The idea is that the survey will indicate *the perceived actual status of the structural and relationship elements in the conflict environment* and, therefore, *the level of effectiveness of the intervention and where intervention imbalances might be*.

Since such a composite framework and methodology did not exist for the purpose, I designed one. I take full responsibility for any inherent flaws.

An example of a structural element is the level of corruption in government. An example of a relationship element is the level of trust between different ethnic groups. The survey asks eighteen questions about structural elements and twelve questions about relationship elements. The answers given indicate the perceived status of structural or relationship elements in the "post"-conflict zone.

I emphasize here that my aim is not to list the actual material inputs (money, materials, troops, etc.) or the technically exact outcomes, but rather to record the perceptions and opinions of intervenors and individual Bosnian citizens as to the status of key structural and relationship elements of conflict transformation in Bosnia.

Given that perceptions often drive conflicts, I focus on perceptions in this study. The sectors selected for examination were governance, security, rule of law, the economy, and social wellbeing.

As I say, I used my 1–7 Likert scale survey, which was administered by me personally in the one hundred face-to-face interviews that I conducted in Bosnia.

Interviewees answered the thirty closed-ended questions by selecting one of seven possible answers for each question, which were scaled as follows:

1. nil;
2. very low;
3. low;
4. moderate;
5. high;
6. very high;
7. completely;

(DK for "don't know" was available for selection).

Examples:

> The statistical average for Question Number 6 (*To what degree is political leadership polarized along ethnic lines?*) was 6.3
>
> (very high).

> The statistical average for Question Number 7 (*To what degree does legitimate institutional capacity outweigh corruption and lawlessness?*) was 2.8
>
> (very low).

All thirty questions and statistical results are given below in the "Survey Results" heading.

I assessed the resulting data within inferred negative- and positive peace parameters with implications for stabilization and peacebuilding. The placement of the resulting data on the War to Positive Peace Continuum (Figure 19.1) is in relation to known war, stabilization, and peacebuilding thresholds.

Answers to the thirty closed-ended questions were calculated to compare respondents' answers. Answers to the four open-ended questions were subjected to content analysis to explore for similar and dissimilar themes.

I used a mixed quantitative and qualitative methodology and an exploratory abduction theory approach (inference to the best estimation) to explore the validity of the findings based on my field experience and the concurrence, or not, of subject matter experts and conflict party members themselves (see Burton [1990a,b] and Charles Sanders Pierce in *Stanford Encyclopedia of Philosophy* [2024] for descriptions of "abduction" theory).

On my subsequent composite War to Sustainable Positive Peace Continuum model (see Figure 19.1 below), I have superimposed elements of Jock Covey, Micheal Dziedzic, and Leonard Hawley's (2005) conflict transformation analytical concepts (*drivers of conflict, institutional performance, viable peace, imposed stability, assisted stability,* and *self-sustaining peace*) over my 1–7 *structural* and *relationship descriptive scales* and *negative* and *positive peace parameters.*

Covey et al. (2005) drew on drivers of conflict modeling from a Grossman-Vermass, Robert, David Redding, and Brenda Wyler PowerPoint presentation given at the Cornwallis Peacekeeping Conference of 2008. Cornwallis, Nova Scotia, Canada: *Through a Glass Darkly: Measuring Policy in Conflict Environments or, Careful What You Wish For: Planning Assessment and Implications for Policy.*

A statistical average (mean) for an element is indicated on the *Structural Elements* (institutions) 1–7 scale or the *Relational Elements* (relationships) 1–7 scale, respectively.

Also shown in Figure 19.1 are segmented arrows dropping straight down from a statistic on the Structural Elements scale or Relational Elements scale into the War to Sustainable Peace Continuum. The arrows indicate where a particular statistic falls along the continuum.

For example, the statistical grand total means (average) for all structural elements is 3.6; inferring that the perceived status of all structural elements combined can be associated with a status of *fragile peace, imposed stability,* and *negative peace* along the war to positive peace continuum.

Note: Although my assessment framework and War to Sustainable Positive Peace Continuum model seem to work in practical terms, they are not proven

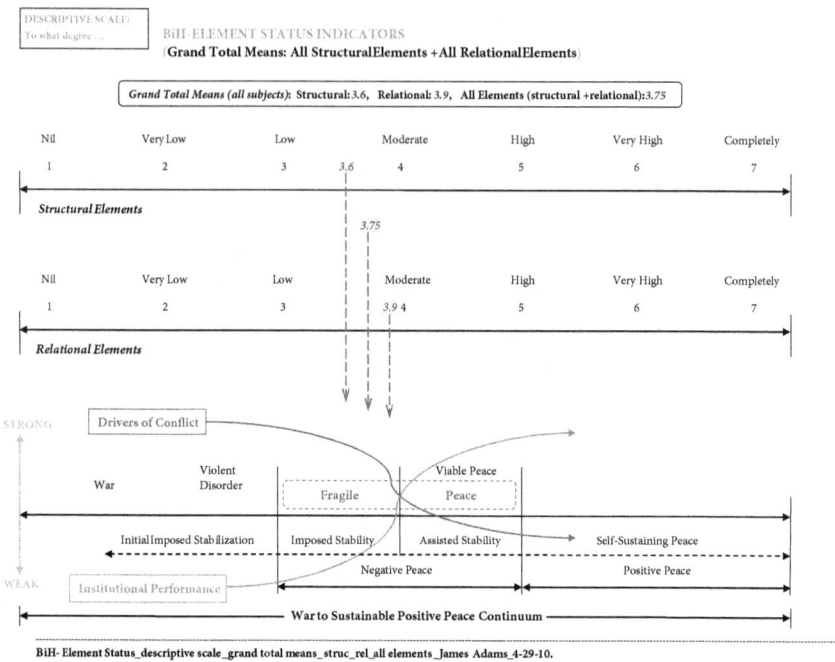

Figure 19.1 War to Sustainable Positive Peace Continuum Model Grand Total Means: All Structural Elements + All Relationship Elements.
Source: Diagram by James R. Adams, 2010.

instruments for substantiating statistical significance. Nevertheless, I did make limited progress in this regard, and I think that the model works well enough for situational awareness and discussion purposes—a proof of concept first step. A dedicated statistician will have to carry on with substantiating statistical significance.

Referencing the War to Sustainable Positive Peace Continuum

The work of Covey, Dziedzic, and Hawley (2005) is an excellent example of field experience-based theoretical and practical analysis. Covey et al. (2005) set out an analytical framework containing stages and strategies of "conflict transformation," much of which is based on actual peace and stabilization operation interventions in the Balkans and intended for practical use in the field.

The analysis could have been described as grounded theory-based abduction if the authors had been so inclined.

The *Drivers of Conflict and Institutional Performance* labels in the War to Positive Peace Continuum section of Figure 19.1 (bottom third of the graphic) indicate the status and strength of destructive and constructive elements respectively in the conflict zone/post-conflict zone.

The curving arrow from the Drivers of Conflict label tracks the increasing or decreasing strength of such elements (corruption, criminalized governance, illegitimate economy, illegitimate militias, warlords, organized crime, etc.).

The curving arrow from the Institutional Performance label tracks the increasing or decreasing strength of the institutions of legitimate governance, a legitimate economy, rule of law, and other public and private institutions.

Covey et al. (2005) use the term *viable peace* to define the point in an intervention in which the "capacity of legitimate institutions" overcomes the "power of obstructionists." They use the term "conflict transformation" to describe "the way in which power is obtained, maintained, and exercised," entailing "diminishing the means and motivations for violent conflict while developing more attractive, peaceful alternatives for the competitive pursuit of political and economic aspirations" (13–17).

I emphasize my opinion that such an analytical perspective would usefully apply whether the intervention is managed by outside intervenors or is being handled internally by local or national intervenors.

In Figure 19.1, *imposed peace* indicates coercive peace enforcement and onsite conflict management and settlement by outside intervenors (as in the case of Bosnia). *Viable peace* is the point at which national/local legitimate institutions can hold their own against the drivers of conflict (obstructionists), but the international presence and assistance are still needed (*assisted stability*). *Sustainable peace* is the institutional capacity point at which peace can be maintained independent of outside intervenors (Covy et al. 2005a).

I reference Covey et al. (2005) in particular to make the point that different intervention approaches, for instance, an academic or purely theoretical approach, in contrast to a largely track 1 approach, are sometimes a matter of semantics, but other times might reflect a fundamental conceptual difference about how to think about and respond to conflict.

To clarify, in the definition of conflict transformation provided by Covey et al. (2005), which I see as capturing the essence of the track 1 governmental/state-driven approach, "viable peace" and "sustainable peace" are to be taken as markers of conflict transformation based on, essentially, successful implementation of security measures, a political settlement, and technical reconstruction—that is to say, sufficient establishment or re-establishment of legitimate institutions and democratic governance.

This approach may well be the only viable option during a stabilization phase. However, any priority consideration given to improving relationships is largely focused on improving relationships between intervention officials and national elites (or warlords) as needed to ensure the attainment of political settlements and technical mission benchmarks, not on improving relationships between conflict parties per se.

I acknowledge that stabilization or achievement of negative peace or viable peace in a conflict zone is an extraordinarily difficult thing to accomplish, and that the use of force is sometimes necessary to prepare conditions for positive peace initiatives.

Conversely, conflict-transformation, in much of the track 2+ world—see Vamik D. Volkan, Joseph V. Montville, and Demetrios A. Julius (1991); David P. Barash and Charles P. Webel (2002); Robert A. Baruch Bush and Joseph P. Folger (1994); John Paul Lederach (1997); Chrisopher Mitchell and Michael Banks (1996); Ronald J. Fisher (1997); Dennis J. D. Sandole (2010), Harold H. Saunders (1999); James H. Laue (1987); and Solon Simmons (2020)—is taken to mean that fundamental changes in personal and societal narratives have been achieved—that is to say, changes in personal perspectives and human relationships.

Barash and Webel (2002) refer to this human-level interpretation (as I think of it) as "personal transformation" and "societal transformation." This is not purely the accomplishment of reconstruction or the reconfiguration of institutions, or the re-educating, intimidating, bribing, jailing, or otherwise successful marginalization of a sufficient number of obstructionists, be they ultranationalists, organized crime elements, or more mundane political and commercial opportunists.

In the end, it appears that real transformation and sustainable positive peace lie beyond purely political or economic power, or the power of coercion, although such may be foundational. I know personally that many track 1 officials in the field know this and strive to address the issue. It is the balancing and timing of approaches that I am focusing on for both negative- and positive peace efforts.

My impression is that the conceptualization of conflict transformation is manifested in two related but distinctly different ways—that is, *transformation primarily through structural change and structural means* or *transformation through primarily relationship change and relationship means.*

For scholar-practitioners in the field of conflict resolution, that is to say principally track 2+ actors, conflict transformation generally implies a fundamental change of relationship between conflict parties, from that of mutual antagonists (position-based opponents) often having the worst assumptions about each other's intentions and character, to that of mutually supportive, or perhaps mutually tolerant, problem solvers who have acquired an appreciation of the interests, security, perspectives, and welfare of the Other—let's say a measure of empathy.

This is said to be accomplished by skilled facilitated dialogues that get at underlying causes, conditions, and narratives of a conflict with mutually developed solutions; see Baruch Bush and Folger (1994), Lederach (1997), Burton (1990a), Laue (1987), Saunders (1999), and Simmons (2020). This is based fundamentally on improved common experiences among conflict party representatives. This goes beyond typical confidence-building measures.

It appears that the relationship change interpretation of "transformation" is intended to indicate a deeper psychological or sociological attitude and behavioral change than traditional diplomacy, political settlements, administrative directives, and security enforcement measures are assumed to accommodate.

A relationship-based interpretation also appears to go beyond the technical accomplishment, strictly speaking, of institutional reconstruction, notwithstanding how vitally important that is.

Another factor surfaces in the consideration of different interpretations of conflict transformation. There seems to be a growing number of intervenors who recognize that peace and stability, despite the best efforts of diplomatic, administrative, and military peacemakers, are unlikely if the root causes and conditions of a conflict remain unaddressed.

Root causes and conditions are typically described as chronic political oppression, abuse of civil, human, and minority rights, extreme poverty, creation of refugees and internally displaced persons (genocide, ethnic cleansing), ineffective and discriminatory governance and institutions, and corrupt, criminalized political economies, to name only a few.

These factors are certainly drivers of conflict, but perhaps more so as symptoms than causes. It seems that if these conditions are indeed symptoms of deeper-level causes, and if concepts of relationship are to be taken seriously, then a step beyond treating symptoms is needed, and a deeper level of conflict deconstruction is warranted—in short, working on relationship and sociological dynamics specifically, as opposed to sole reliance on negotiated political compromises.

This seems to be the conceptual crux: the control of violence with a focus on fundamental relationship and attitudinal change (narrative change), or control of violence through political settlement, law enforcement, and economic and structural/institutional change.

What remains is the matter of how to get it done, and with what degree of expediency and balance, and how to maintain that state of affairs. What is clear at this point is that policy for relational matters is generally missing from track 1 management of peace and stabilization operations.

In practical terms, political and security efforts call for enforcement expediency (minimalist negative peace measures), whereas deeper relationship work, which seems to take more time, only comes when that option is prioritized, if considered at all (maximalist positive peace measures).

The question then is which intervention outcome—negative peace or positive peace (or a combination thereof)—must actually be achieved for a declaration of sustainable peace, positive peace, or a mission-accomplished declaration. This is a matter of one's conception of conflict transformation, and therefore success.

Is success the achievement of technical-structural benchmarks or a fundamental relationship and narrative change? To complicate conceptual considerations further, are sustainable peace and positive peace the same thing? It could be a case of sustainable negative peace.

In philosophical terms, is this line of questioning merely a new chapter in humanity's ancient journey from natural human to enlightened human? And now, perhaps, on to transformed human? My opinion is that some manner of cognitive blending of relationship-based and structural-based approaches will prove to be more productive than a case of either/or.

Prior to arriving in Bosnia and conducting the survey, I fully expected that the total mean score for structural elements would be significantly higher than the total mean score for relationship elements, given that the reconstruction of BiH (in structural and institutional terms) is essentially complete. As it turned out, the grand total mean (average) of all structural elements was 3.6; for relationship elements it was 3.9.

I expected that, given the general lack of symbolic apologies or amends, relations and hostile sentiments would be worse. So, are the statistical means indicated inaccurate and questionable?

I believe the answer is both yes and no. As discussed earlier, the fundamental flaws in the Dayton Peace Accord-based, ethnopolitical constitution (which was intended to be only temporary) rendered the associated governance structures and institutions highly divisive, discriminatory, and dysfunctional. Ethnic discrimination has been institutionalized, constituting a significant degree of structural violence, to use Galtung's (1969) term.

In other words, a system of serious structural violence is deeply embedded in the Bosnia post-war political structure. This would explain the low structural element mean score, even though, on paper, governance and structural elements are essentially in place and completed. In fact, the view that Bosnian governance is largely corrupt and dysfunctional is almost universal among all ethnic groups and international representatives in Bosnia.

Why is there a relatively moderate total mean score (nearly at the Viable Peace Threshold) for relationship overall when there are lower mean scores on individual relationship elements? Again, drawing on the qualitative data, based on open-ended question comments in face-to-face interviews, I suspect that the 3.9 score is both accurate and not accurate.

It is not accurate in that a few interviewees, in response to questions such as "To what degree is reconciliation possible between ethnic groups?" expressed cautious optimism by telling me afterward, "Well, I checked a higher score because I have to hope, don't I?"

At the same time, the 3.9 score is accurate in that subjects told me that nothing has been done to improve relations, and as soon as another crisis comes people will quickly fall back into familiar verbal and physical hostilities. In other words, as some interviewees explained to me, when political/conflict opportunists stir fear-based ethnic passions again.

Most Bosnians told me that there are relatively neutral relations and little manifest personal hostility between ethnic groups now because most people are war weary, and international and national authorities and police are usually careful to keep small incidents from exploding into crises.

In the end, while local authorities are actively suppressing cultural violence, little is being done to meaningfully improve relations (re-relating?). The serious institutional (structural) dysfunctionalities clearly work against improving relationship elements.

Survey Results

Findings from the Structural and Relationship Elements Status Survey resulted from administration of the survey in face-to-face meetings with each interviewee. I interviewed all one hundred interviewees myself. I used a scheduled-structured interview format.

I distinguish three types of results revealed in the findings:

1. the raw data itself (quantitative and qualitative) that provides direct-assessment indicators and empirical data on the perceived status of structural and relationship elements in Bosnia in 2009;
2. inferred indications in connection with conflict, intervention, and peacebuilding thresholds, within negative and positive-peace parameters (as indicated on the War to Sustainable Positive Peace Continuum, Figure 19.1); and
3. indirect indications of the viability of the survey.

There are three types of responses given by interviewees:

1. quantitative answers to thirty closed-ended questions;
2. qualitative comments with regard to their answers; and
3. qualitative answers to four open-ended questions.

Although I have not worked in Bosnia specifically, I added commentary with regard to intervention factors based on my observations there and other conflict zones.

I believe that if this survey were to be given today in the United States or many other stressed nations, the answers would be very similar, especially after an armed conflict.

Survey Questions Posed to Interviewees with Their Answers

Some interviewees qualified some of their answers or otherwise added a comment—for example, question 1, which enquires about the level of support that political leaders have for the peace agreement. A typical comment pertaining to that question is that each ethnic group supports only those parts of the peace agreement that are advantageous to their own group.

An example with regard to particular ethnicities—many non-Serbs claim that Serbs support the Dayton Peace Agreement much more than Bosniaks or Croats because it "legitimizes Serb war gains" and prevents a one-state union, which Bosniaks want, and precludes a three-state union which Croats want, so non-Serb respondents selected the middle ground (a moderate 3.89 on the 1–7 scale) in response to the question.

At the same time, most Serbs claimed to be opposed to the peace agreement since they wanted a state of their own. This type of response occurred in connection with some other questions, and that is why, following the survey-pilot test, I added a Qualification Comments section next to the questions section on the survey form. This accommodated interviewee elaboration on their answers to closed-ended questions.

Below, I include a sampling of actual qualifications by subjects for each of the eighteen structural questions and twelve relationship questions.

In the Structural Questions section, I paraphrase or summarize, or add an observation of my own, as needed. In the Relationship Questions section, I show only actual interviewee responses with no paraphrasing or summarizing by me. The answers speak for themselves.

Closed-ended questions 1–30 were scaled as follows:

1. nil;
2. very low;
3. low;
4. moderate;
5. high;
6. very high;
7. completely.

(DK for "don't know" was available for selection).

The grand total mean (average) for all answers to each question is shown in parentheses next to each question.

Answers to Structural Element Questions

1. To what degree do political leaders fully support the peace agreement (3.9)?
   - Comment provided above.
2. To what degree are government institutions re-established (4.4)?

- Subjects consistently qualified that the institutions of government were all in place but were mostly dysfunctional and corrupt along ethnic lines, as per the Dayton Agreement ethnopolitical/constitutional criteria and nationalist dominated elections. Some subjects qualified that some local municipal governments were less corrupt, more effective, and cooperative with each other.
3. To what degree is the election process fair and transparent (4.9)?
    - Generally, subjects qualified that elections were fair and transparent, but nevertheless marked their answers lower because of the use of fear tactics and intimidation by ethno-politicized nationalist parties (usually headed by hardliners or ultranationalists, or war criminals in some cases) to get re-elected. Moderate parties generally did poorly.
4. To what degree is there civic group participation in governance (3.1)?
    - A number of NGOs have been created since the war (many were supported by UN or Western aid agencies) to advocate for civil and human rights, as well as mental-health and education services, and so forth. However, as some NGO managers have explained to me, there are too few of them and they have very limited access to political offices that are often ethno-politicized and corrupt. A number of NGOs are arms of ethnopolitical parties. There is little sense of personal civil participation or opportunity.
5. To what degree is political leadership polarized along ethnic lines (6.3)?
    - Response to this question drew one of the highest levels of consensus (lowest standard deviation) scores corroborated by the fact that hardline or ultra-hardline ethno-nationalists continue to dominate national politics, including a Bosniak president who was favored by Western diplomats as a promising moderate who later became an ultranationalist.
6. To what degree does the government have a mechanism to facilitate peaceful dialogue between ethnic groups (2.8)?
    - Subject response to this question essentially repeats that for questions 2, 4, and 5. No concrete example of such a mechanism was given.
7. To what degree does legitimate institutional capacity outweigh corruption and lawlessness (2.8)?
    - This is another example of high consensus among interviewees with regard to an issue. Interviewees clearly believe that governance and the political economy have not yet reached a moderate level of controlling corruption and lawlessness.

8. To what degree do police and security forces provide a safe and secure environment for everyone, regardless of their ethnicity (4.5)?
   - Subjects qualified that they felt generally safe in the cities and when staying in areas predominantly of their own ethnicity. Also, there was consensus that police generally are very attuned to keeping interethnic confrontations to a minimum. Nevertheless, a qualification given a number of times is that some are very uncomfortable living or traveling in areas where they see police or authorities on the street that are known war criminals and/or rapists, etc.
9. To what degree can all refugees and IDPs return and live safely in their villages of origin anywhere in BiH (3.6)?
   - The great majority of subjects qualified that they could indeed return to and probably live safely in their villages of origin, but significant qualifications were specified, e.g., (1) someone else might be living in their house and/or have taken over their business property, and it could take years to get it back if ever; (2) discrimination based on ethnicity makes it nearly impossible to get a job, or a decent job; (3) their family, or their business, would be shunned by the community if it was now made up of a majority of a different ethnicity, which applies now to many villages and towns in Bosnia.
10. To what degree is an international presence needed for security (4.6)?
    - Although some Bosniaks were ambivalent on this point, most preferred that the international presence continue in order to safeguard their interests. Most Serbs want the presence to end as soon as possible. Croats were in between on this point.
11. To what degree are laws fair for all ethnic groups (4.2)?
    - The moderate mean score on this question is, as a number of Subjects explained to me, not so much because the laws discriminate against some and not others, but that the systemic ethnopolitical constitutional mandates induce discrimination equally against all minorities, regardless of ethnicity.
12. To what degree are laws applied equally to all ethnic groups (3.8)?
    - See response to question 11.
13. To what degree do government institutions discriminate against members of particular ethnic communities (4.2)?
    - See response to question 11.
14. To what degree is reconstruction of infrastructure accomplished (3.9)?

- Reconstruction in this case, as explained to interviewees, refers to physical infrastructure: roads, railways, bridges, transportation, communication facilities, electric and water supply, schools, hospitals, etc.

15. To what degree can people of any ethnic community have a business anywhere in the country (4.4)?
    - The responses to this question parallel those of question 9. The great majority of interviewees qualified that they felt that they had the right to have a business anywhere in the country and that that principle would not be challenged. The difficulties are that (1) someone else might be occupying their former business property and it could take years to get it back, if ever; (2) new ethnic-majority officials make the licensing/permit process very difficult, and residents and other businesspeople would effectively boycott their re-established business. In other words, they would not be welcome.

16. To what degree are corruption and crime factors in the economy (5.7)?
    - Essentially, the great majority of Bosnians of all ethnicities believe that corruption in the economy is high or very high, referring to the situation as a widespread system of corruption-cooperation and bribery demands at all levels in the economy.

17. To what degree is corruption a factor in the government (5.6)?
    - According to interviewees, corruption in the government is closely tied to getting government jobs and corruption in the economy—that is to say, it is a corrupt politicized economy with close collusion between government officials and organized crime syndicates at macro-levels, and common bribe demands at local levels for services to be handled without delays or other difficulties. The problem increases in instances of ethnic-minority applications and requests.

18. To what degree can people of any ethnic community buy and live in a house anywhere in Bosnia and Herzegovina (4.5)?
    - Generally, the same response applies as given for questions 9 and 15. Interviewees generally did not believe that their right to buy and live in a house anywhere in Bosnia would be questioned, but that the process of doing so would be made difficult and they would be harassed, shunned, and made to feel unwelcome if they were in a minority status in the new location.

Answers to Relationship Element Questions (Actual)

19. To what degree is there trust between neighbors of different ethnic groups (3.8)?
    - Although interaction might be normal on the surface, deep down a sense of betrayal is now embedded.
    - But doesn't work when people with extremist views are involved.
    - My sense is that individuals trust one another. It is group distrust that is more the issue.
    - People of different ethnic groups have helped each other, and common people were always getting along; they are easily tricked and manipulated by political leadership; same in the First World War, the Second World War and 1991–5.
    - The issue here is that of pre-war neighbors or post-war neighbors.
    - The system forces segregation and distrust, especially among the youth via schools and ethnically cleansed areas.
    - There has been no serious discussion between ethnic groups about the war. I feel pressure of Ustase on my neck.
    - This improved slowly after 1995, but has dropped considerably because of political polarization since 2006.
    - Trust toward people you know but not toward an ethnic group.
    - Trust toward the 5th Column people in Sarajevo—No!
    - A lot of distrust amplified by politicians who benefit from it.
20. To what degree is respect shown between different ethnic groups (3.8)?
    - Respect is not possible when Serbs use heavy equipment to dig up mass graves and rebury bodies in more dispersed mass graves.
    - 3.0 generally, but at individual level the situation is better.
    - Depends on locale (local football team in Zvornik is named Genocide); it's OK in Sarajevo, Banja Luka.
    - Depends on the person.
    - Ethnicity always comes first. Though in the absence of direct conflict, respect and cooperation do exist.
    - There are some striking instances of disrespect; older, more sophisticated people show more respect; younger people and villagers, less.
    - When there is no trouble, everybody is friendly; when there is trouble, fast/hard separation follows.

21. To what degree is tolerance shown between ethnic groups (3.9)?
    - Depends on location: city is more tolerant, village is least tolerant, town is in between. Bosniaks in general are more tolerant than Serbs or Croats.
    - Young more problematic than old.
22. To what degree do people of different ethnicities interact in your area (4.5)?
    - Communities try to stick to themselves; for friends, this rule does not apply.
    - In Sarajevo yes, otherwise …
    - Less mixing of population after the war.
    - Most places are ethnically cleansed now; people can enter hotels, restaurants, buildings, etc., dominated by another ethnicity but generally do not.
    - Not many integrated areas left to try interacting in.
    - Segregation is growing all the time; people don't know people anymore from different ethnic groups.
    - The presence of the International Community (IC) allows people to interact.
23. To what degree do students of any ethnicity feel accepted in any classroom in Bosnia and Herzegovina (3.2)?
    - 6.0 in Federation of BiH, and 2.0 in Republika Srpska (RS).
    - Education segregated, ethnocentric; Sarajevo much less multiethnic now than before the war; previous long-time Sarajevans more tolerant than newer war-related urban migrants from villages/small towns.
    - From my local experience, on the surface—higher (5.0), otherwise moderate (4.0); 5.0 for Canton 1; 4.0 for Canton Prijedor.
    - Many schools are officially or de facto segregated.
    - My experience shows bad and getting worse.
    - Newer teachers work to separate kids as opposed to integrate them.
    - Only university students.
    - Special events may be OK, but on a daily basis, no.
    - Special problem: two-schools-one roof, separate schedules, floors, or entrances. Some cantons in FBiH, also RS.
    - Still many separate classes and curricula.

- Teachers do not allow children to interact. Students are manipulated by political elites, parents, and religious leaders to disassociate from children of other ethnic groups.
- The problem is that school curricula and teaching are biased toward one ethnicity. Teachers emphasize their own ethnic perspective in instruction.
- There is some mixing at the secondary school level, but not at the primary school level.

24. To what degree is reconciliation possible between ethnic groups (4.5)?
    - Again, this depends on the locale and the situation. On a national level, there is a long way to go.
    - Collectively, Serbs deny wrongdoing, individually, Serbs wish for reconciliation. Different responses between intellectual levels, and different groups.
    - Depends on where. Urban areas tend to be more reconciliation friendly.
    - First, conflict parties need to reconcile within their own groups, within their own pain, then work on reconciling with other ethnic groups (many felt betrayed by their own groups and leaders).
    - Generational change is necessary and reinterpretation of personal values.
    - If we exclude extremist minorities.
    - In fifteen to twenty years, Serbia will have a major impact on BiH. When Serbia matures past its nationalist episode, it can/will have a major positive influence on RS (things in RS will settle down).
    - Maybe in 100 years.
    - Obstacles are unenlightened population, influence of religion, low cultural standard, emotional factor, character traits (hate, envy, spite), influence of Communism, incapability of humility.
    - One has to hope, but (1) election system should be changed, (2) it took other countries forty years, so why should it be quickly done here? Reconciliation is when ethnicity doesn't matter.
    - Only with change in the political system.
    - People of different ethnicities don't talk about important things such as religion, the war, harm done; we need to be able to speak frankly about differences.

- Reconciliation has not taken place yet; there is still much stoking of open wounds in the media; reconciliation needs a solid foundation; bridges need to be built; IC needs to build linkages.
- Reconciliation: if there is remorse, and a desire, reconciliation will go forward.
- Structural divisions created by the constitution; therefore, structure causes obstructions to improvement in ethnic relations. Timeframe sensitive: people have to see a future for themselves and their families.
- Very high if/when citizens get courageous and have visionary leadership.
- With time, and possibly better with future economic investment, jobs, and recruitment on Western models.
- We have more than one truth.

25. To what degree do people feel that amends have been made for past injuries (2.7)?
    - Difficult to prosecute and discover crimes at the same time; first discover the crimes, then prosecute; allow families of victims to get their dead back; admit that not all Serbs are killers.
    - For Bosniaks, wreath laying by Serbian leaders at Srebrenica would be more meaningful than jailing Milosevic and Karadzic.
    - Justice is needed; criminals walk freely among their own people.
    - Legally mostly yes, emotionally no.
    - Need better economy and less pressure from religious leaders.
    - Nonwar crimes are prosecuted, but there is no cooperation on the prosecution of war crimes.
    - Offers of amends-making are subject to political pressures.
    - People feel there is no justice and no way for victims to ask the guilty for justice; houses not rebuilt for victims without connections (corruption/favoritism).
    - Politicians have not done anything to make up for me having to spend my teenage years in the war in Sarajevo.
    - Really don't know how people feel; what is felt and what is reported may well be very different.
    - Returnees are not satisfied with regard to amends.
    - The idea of Transitional Justice has only recently been introduced to the people of BiH.

- The method is "let's not talk about it," or one group outbidding another on who is the greater victim, but no real amends are made. There is competition about who was the most wronged.
- The whole BiH society has PTSD. Serbs say that there were logically more Serbs killed than Muslims since there are more Muslims proportionately, so proportionately more Serbs were killed.
- There are thousands of war crimes on record for which no action has been taken.
- There is no justice, e.g., Srebrenica.
- This is the Balkans; even educated people have their own version of history.
- Very little, the problem goes back for centuries.
- Very little. Hard to see beyond Mladic's arrest-trial and stepped-up prosecutions of local-level war criminals.
- Was high, but is decreasing rapidly.

26. To what degree is there violence against individuals due to ethnic hostility (3.1)?
    - 3.0 for FBiH, 6.0 for RS.
    - Depends on the region.
    - Generally, not a problem though there is random unorganized incidents. Hooliganism can be a trigger.
    - If discrimination, then high.
    - In schools, I'm hearing.
    - Mental vs. physical violence.
    - Mostly at sports events or around them; there is a lot of potential for violence against individuals.
    - No, except for violence against Roma persons.
    - Not so much because of segregated living; graffiti is indicative of latent violence.
    - This is not widespread, but the fear of it keeps people segregated.

27. To what degree is society polarized along ethnic lines (5.4)?
    - Depends on region.
    - Everything divides: press, political parties, societal issues.
    - The very purpose of the current constitution is to divide and feed the negatives of ethnic division; constitutional/institutional reform would dissolve ethnic animosities.
    - There are more divisions arising than unifying forces.

28. To what degree do I have hope that normalization of relations is possible between former warring parties in Bosnia and Herzegovina (4.9)?
    - At the moment, low, due to the fact that education is totally divided.
    - Not in my lifetime.
    - But only with force and political changes.
    - I am an optimist.
    - I have confidence that a common denominator can be found, but not without a radical change that breaks the current oligarchical political system.
    - If BiH splits, then chances are very low; if BiH proceeds reasonably well to EU accession, then chances are high for normalization.
    - It would be possible if it weren't for the leadership which makes it impossible to normalize relations.
    - None.
    - Ordinary people want normal relations, but politicians don't; politicians push politics of fear.
    - Some days I have hope, and others not.
    - The EU is making things technical (arrangements) as opposed to emotional/nationalistic.
    - Time and prosperity heal things, open issues up; after that, deal with immigration and separation activities/systems, i.e., elections, etc.
29. To what degree have attitudes that led to the war changed since the war (3.6)?
    - Attitudes are worse now than before the war.
    - Attitudes that led to the war were not of those people in the country; it came from outside (initially); the attitudes that led to the war are still around although tempered.
    - Attitudes, despite recent nationalistic fervor, have changed in terms of no appetite for war by anyone.
    - Before the war, I didn't look at people as Croat, Serb, or Muslim, now I do; now most people do; now there is little inter-marriage; before the war there was.
    - Causes of war were power struggles coupled with brain washing and media campaigns; I think you can do that with any people in the world however civilized; only now many people don't want another war.
    - Gotten worse.

- Leaders that prepared the war are gone; war continues by other means; attitudes haven't overcome the fact that no one won the war, so war objectives are still being pursued.
- People's minds are not flexible with regard to attitudes: to feel better about one's actions/history: (1) don't talk about it, (2) if we hadn't done it, they would have done it to us, (3) by not knowing, they protect themselves.
- Strong human insecurities (class, ethnicity) led to the war; there is still a sense of ethnic/human insecurity.
- The opinions that led to the war are still there; Serbs don't see themselves as aggressors; Serbs think, "If we don't stop them/kill them, then they will kill us."
- The primary change is that people are more aware of the dangers of escalation.
- The war was not generated from inside. The question would be better put this way—the question of attitudes is regional capitols.
- There are serious disagreements about what led to the war. There was no real reconciliation after the Second World War.
- They have been maintained as a means to keep power; the war did not come from below; it was a forced mass mobilization from political/military/nationalist elite.
- Very little among opinion framers/politicians.
- We have solidarity on dealing with natural disasters (civil emergencies), but not about war. People don't talk about problems outside of their own ethnic group.

30. To what degree can people of different ethnic groups have empathy toward each other (4.1)?
    - Absolutely, 120 percent.
    - Between 4.0 and 5.0.
    - Between common people there is not a problem generally speaking—except when there is a crisis.
    - Depends on location/area of conflict.
    - Depends on the person, but generally low.
    - Find mutual interest and people can be pragmatic.
    - How can youth have empathy when they have no experience of the other. Before the war, 40–60 percent of marriages in Sarajevo were interethnic; now almost no new marriages are interethnic.

- Moderate but highly variable; war forced everyone to focus on one identity (ethnic) vs. other comprehensive identities; IC has not given a context for locals to come together—no strategy between two points.
- More are over thirty years old than under thirty years old.
- Need outsider facilitation.
- On the basis of personal relationships.
- Only if A. admits and apologizes then B. will respond favorably (a vicious cycle).
- Politicians have none; people are normal.
- Some people do not want to understand others.
- These are not ethnic but religious groups.
- Very high if they as individuals talk to each other, but if generalized, then there is low empathy.

Answers to Survey Open-Ended Questions

The open-ended questions on the survey are:

1. What is the result of intervention by outsiders?
2. Why do some conflict-resolution or peacebuilding ideas not work?
3. How would you improve relations between ethnic groups?
4. What other thoughts would you like to share?

The purpose of posing the four open-ended questions was to draw out elaboration from interviewees on their answers and attempt some triangulation (confirmation) of closed-ended question data.

The complete lengthy responses to open-ended questions 1, 2, and 3 are provided in Appendix A of *Analytic Reflections from Conflict Zones* (Adams 2021). Otherwise, I summarize the answers to open-ended questions 1, 2, and 3 below.

I do not include the answers to open-ended question 4 since they essentially repeat the answers given for questions 1, 2, and 3.

Open-Ended Question 1: My Analysis of Interviewee Responses

What Is the Result of Intervention by Outsiders?

There are definite trends and patterns in the responses, although different words or expressions are used to make essentially the same point.

A review of the responses to the open-ended questions about the intervention reveals that there is a very high level of consensus and appreciation for the intervention having stopped the war. However, qualifications have been made.

For example: "Yes, the war was stopped, but it could have and should have been stopped much sooner." Some respondents point out that much has been done to reconstruct BiH, but there is still as much ethnic tension as before the intervention. Several point out that the Dayton Peace Accord stopped the war, but it is seriously flawed and has resulted in seriously flawed governance and institutions.

I think the answers to open-ended question 1 capture fairly well the complexities of conditions in BiH and the intervention, and provide some indication of the contrast between success in terms of structural reconstruction, albeit flawed, and relationship and tolerance improvement, which has not been successful at all.

Open-Ended Question 2: My Analysis of Interviewee Responses

Why Do Some Conflict Resolution or Peacebuilding Ideas Not Work?

There is a high degree of consensus with regard to the idea of doing something, anything, just to stop the war, which the Dayton Accords did. But the process has left massive problems that continue to seriously undermine any real return to a normalized nation-state or normalized relations between ethnic groups.

Two points stand out here: (1) the Dayton Accords-based reconstruction has established seriously dysfunctional and discriminatory institutions and governance mechanisms; and (2) the peace agreement, and any peacebuilding efforts intended to address underlying causes and conditions, and presumably to improve relations between the ethnic groups, have been very weak and mostly failed.

This implies two things: (1) the degree to which primary structural elements are flawed is high to very high and (2) the status constitutes a state of serious structural violence, which is unlikely to be reduced until flaws inherent in the structures and Dayton Accords-based constitution are remedied.

The agreement that stopped the war became frozen into a constitution, which perpetuates the structural violence and therefore precludes improvement in structural elements. It also seriously inhibits improvement in relationship areas.

Open-Ended Question 3: My Analysis of Interviewee Responses

How Do You Improve Relations between Ethnic Groups?

Open-ended question 3 elicited the most diverse comments and suggestions, making the categorization of trends and patterns less straightforward. A dissertation in its own right could be done on responses to question 3 in regard to peacebuilding and improving relationships, and what can enable or thwart well-intentioned efforts.

It appears that most of the responses here can be separated into structural change or direct relationship change suggestions or comments. Many respondents seemed to understand, directly or intuitively, that there is a connection between structure and relationships. So, the challenge is to decide which approach to take, or what combination thereof.

Although some strong views were given, it still seems largely up to the intervenor to decide, or consult others, on which approach(es) should be attempted.

Based on responses to question 3, it is apparent that no satisfactory formula has been realized or implemented to date in the BiH intervention to improve relations among ethno-national groups. In fact, the opposite effect seems to be the case, largely due to the innate ethnopolitical divisions inherent in the governance design based on the Dayton Accords. However, as everyone pointed out, the Dayton Accords did expedite a negotiated political settlement and stopped the war—with some hoping that the underlying conflict issues could be sorted out later.

It appears that the Dayton Accords brought negative peace to Bosnia, which is still in effect, with little sign of any meaningful movement toward positive peace, which would require a meaningful degree of relationship improvement.

Open-Ended Question 4: My Analysis of Interviewee Responses

What Other Thoughts Would You Like to Share?

Answers to question 4 essentially repeat answers given to the previous three questions, so I have not included them here.

A Few Post-Survey Comments from Interviewees

While still in Bosnia, after all interviews were completed and survey forms filled out, *I asked some of the interviewees to locate the status of various elements directly on the War to Sustainable Positive Peace Continuum model.*

With very little explanation from me, and almost intuitively on the part of the individuals, and consistently among diverse ethnicities, they located the status of a given element in nearly the same spot along the *war to positive peace continuum*. The individuals felt that their chosen point on the continuum, within the indicated thresholds, did reflect reality fairly well.

When I asked a few individuals to locate directly on the War to Positive Peace Continuum model (Figure 19.1) the overall status of all structural or relationship elements (all things considered), or the overall situation in BiH in general, they consistently pointed to somewhere just before or just after the *Viable Peace* threshold line, but qualified that the situation was deteriorating.

Also, they qualified that some elements were pushing into the *Self-sustaining Peace* zone, for example, in some municipalities, but that other elements were regressing, for example, state institutions.

One astute individual told me that when international officials were paying close attention to an element, it moved past the *Viable Peace* threshold, but when international officials were not paying attention, it regressed behind the *Viable Peace* threshold.

Many Bosnians told me that nothing has been done to improve relations, and as soon as another crisis comes along people will quickly fall back into familiar verbal and physical hostilities.

In other words, while local authorities are actively suppressing cultural violence, little is being done to meaningfully improve relations (re-relating?). The serious institutional (structural) dysfunctionalities clearly work against improving relationship elements, and vice versa.

I also asked a handful of individuals, after interviews, what they thought needed to be fixed first, structure or relationships? in order to have normalization. Some immediately said that the structure needed to be fixed first, then everything else would follow. Some immediately said that fixing relations had to occur first or there would be no progress, no cooperation, with fixing the structure. Some said both had to be worked on simultaneously.

Then I asked what is holding up fixing the structure the most: the structure itself or the relationship problem? Some of those who at first said "fix the structure first" then switched over, and said that relations are holding up progress on structure.

Also, meaningfully, *I found that, of those who had suffered serious personal losses during the war, nearly all said relations needed to be fixed first.*

My *War to Sustainable Positive Peace Continuum* model reflects the sentiments expressed by Bosnians and intervenors on-the-ground in 2009. It appears that circumstances and opinions have changed little since then, or have, in some regards, deteriorated.

For those interested in learning more about my Bosnia research, further explanations are available in "Analytic Reflections from Conflict Zones" (2021 hardback, 2022 paperback) with a dedicated fold-out section of color figures and graphics in the book.

A next step for future research with this type of survey would be to have all interviewees locate the status of each element directly onto a 1—7 scale embedded in a War to Sustainable Positive Peace Continuum (Figure 19.1) in the survey.

Comprehensive Multilevel Framework

The models that I include in this section reflect progressive stages of development of my abduction-based analytical tools for analysis and understanding of why interventions stall in negative peace, and why conflicts reignite after peace agreements are signed. With that in mind, I elaborate below on background circumstances leading to the origins of my Comprehensive Multilevel Framework (CMF), which I started developing earlier Africa. But first, some further contextual comments are necessary.

Most intervention diplomats, decision-makers, and officials involved in peace and stabilization operations have been trained in nation-state adversarial, competitive systems and disciplines such as political science, diplomacy, international relations, law, military studies, and management. These areas of expertise are crucial in analyzing many issues of concern. However, given the current strong resistance of intra-state conflict to traditional nation-state protocols, additional perspectives and protocols are needed.

In response to this growing problem, former track 1 diplomats, civilians, and military officials and track 2 scholar-practitioners have been working steadily on trying to better understand the nature of this resistance and what can be done about it. Consequently, within the past roughly fifty years the field of *conflict resolution* (a term generally encompassing conflict analysis, prevention, management, settlement, resolution, and transformation) has been brought into existence to study the problem.

I built my CMF on that foundation to aid in the analysis and identification of viable intervention measures for stabilization and peacebuilding. I believe that, with minimal adaptation, my framework and models can be used for analyzing smaller or larger-scale conflicts and interventions.

The idea is to have on hand additional tools by which someone trained in Conflict Analysis and Resolution (CAR) theory and practice can efficiently analyze a situation and project intervention outcomes from a more informed standpoint.

On a practical note, any measures that can help clarify matters will ease stresses on officials and staff (civilian and military) who are subject to very tight timelines, limited resources, and sometimes literal agitation at the gates in the form of protests or violence.

The nature of work in humanitarian, stabilization, and peacebuilding operations involves continuous interactions *vertically* within and *horizontally* among international and local governmental and nongovernmental organizations.

Tasks are usually carried out within a multicultural context. Consequently, officials often find themselves engaged in some manner of mediation, negotiation, or coordination activity. At some point, some manner of mediation, negotiation, or facilitation is engaged in (formally or informally) by almost every type of intervention official (prepared or not) at every level of interaction.

The models presented here are intended to capture and work out individual conflict processes, adding depth and accuracy. To begin, the basic orientation of my CMF incorporates facets of the following five frameworks/models:

1. Máire A. Dugan's (1996) Nested Paradigm concept, which I expanded on, to indicate the inter-level interactions (see Figure 19.2).
2. My Humanitarian and Peace Operation Activity Levels (1–6) (see Figure 19.3).
3. A slightly modified Kenneth N. Waltz's (1959) Framework (my Equivalent Generic Levels) for better distinguishing the structural levels of activities, conflict parties, and their interactions. This in turn enables easier discussion among analysts and decision-makers about the identities of particular actors and associated conflict dynamics (see Figure 19.3).
4. Robert Carver North's (1990) Global Factors Framework focusing on transnational groups and events with global implications (level 6, see Figure 19.3).
5. My Intervention Assessment and Intervention Approach Selection Framework (see Figure 19.4).

In 1997, as a senior operations officer with the International Organization for Migration (IOM), I made an assessment of my organization's formal and informal mediation and facilitation activities in Africa. In constructing a situational-awareness report for the purpose, I identified five primary levels at which interactions typically occur (levels 1 through 5 indicated below) inclusive of interlocutors.

They can be contrasted with the modified Waltz's (1959) framework (images I, II, and III; individual, society, and international), which I have expanded on and now refer to as Equivalent Generic Levels. I added North's (1990) Global and Ecological framework to make the sixth level. The first five interaction levels indicated below pertain to typical field activities of track 1 and track 2 actors (and beyond: international, national, and local).

I placed my resulting 1997 assessment results into my adapted Dugan's (1996) Nested Paradigm model. It is the genesis of my Humanitarian and Peace Operation Activity Levels model (see Figure 19.3). I added my original 1997 listing to the generic level indicators (inspired by Waltz) as well as North's global systems indicators.

Nested Paradigm Determination

My Conflict Nested Paradigm Determination model (Figure 19.2), shown below, is adapted to Dugan's (1996) Nested Paradigm model and my earlier field-based organizational activity levels 1–5.

The model indicates the connectedness of parties, issues, and dynamics at all six humanitarian and peace operation activity levels inclusive of global transnational dynamics. As described earlier, each member of the various groups has his or her own worldviews, mandates, and needs, and acts consciously or unconsciously accordingly.

The need for basic safety, security, and belonging, as outlined in A. H. Maslow's (1943; 1954) *Hierarchy of Needs and Burton's Basic Human Needs Theory* (1990a,b; 1997), is of paramount importance.

Dugan (1996) describes her nested paradigm concept this way:

> It approaches conflict by identifying on what level its source lies—at the structural level of the system as a whole, within the structure of a sub-system, at the relationship or issue-specific level—and stresses the extent to which these levels are related, nested within one another.
>
> (Dugan 1996, 9)

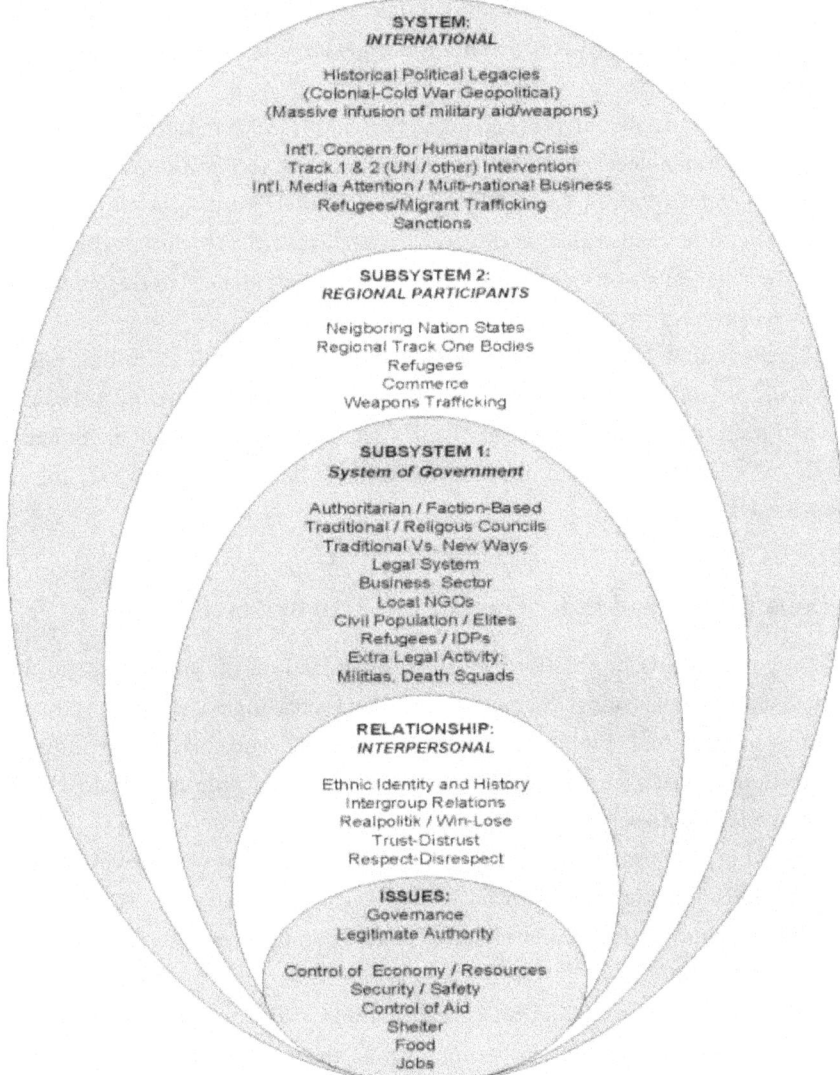

Figure 19.2 Adapted Conflict Nested Paradigm Determination.
Source: Diagram by James R. Adams, 2012.

This model aids in understanding how conflicting parties can be looking at the same conflict from different perspectives or paradigms without knowing it because they are looking from different levels with different embedded issues and meanings. The model is helpful in understanding issues or events coming from "out of nowhere" that are simply interactions between levels.

Needless to say, fundamentally different perspectives about what is happening, especially when non-negotiable values and personal security are at stake, can cause a lot of trouble.

In connection with different perspectives, Burton (1990a,b; 1997) has specified that basic human needs, such as the need for security, recognition, and identity, must be met to ensure sustainable peace. In other words, certain political, cultural, and religious values and security needs are critical to sustainable peace and are essentially non-negotiable. Such things are matters of perception as to what is or is not a problem.

I believe that if intervention decision-makers and planners (military and civilian) in earlier missions had been more cognizant of nested-paradigm dynamics, such as in relation to the United Nations Operation in Somalia (UNOSOM) mission, the outcomes would likely have come out better for all concerned.

Humanitarian and Peace Operations: Activity Levels

Many governments, international and local organizations, and conflict parties are impacted by global factors, for example, rapidly increasing populations, resource and environmental problems, economic turmoil, and massive worldwide migration and refugee movements, along with a worldwide pandemic. North (1990) refers to these phenomena as lateral pressures.

Drawing on Dugan's (1996) Nested Paradigm concept, my five levels of field interactions/activities, and North's Global and Ecological systems concept, I built the composite Humanitarian and Peace Operations Activity Levels model shown in Figure 19.3.

For a contextual sense of an overall conflict situation, including possible linkages between elements and parties, I locate groups and organizations within levels 1–6 and contrast them with Equivalent Generic Levels on the left side of a model.

With the basic operating environment in mind, and the aim of furthering analysis of negative and positive-peace processes, I used two models from a previous project. The original project consisted of my Field Guide for Conflict Briefings. The two models—Humanitarian and Peace Operation Activity Levels (Figure 19.3) and the Intervention Assessment and Approach Selection

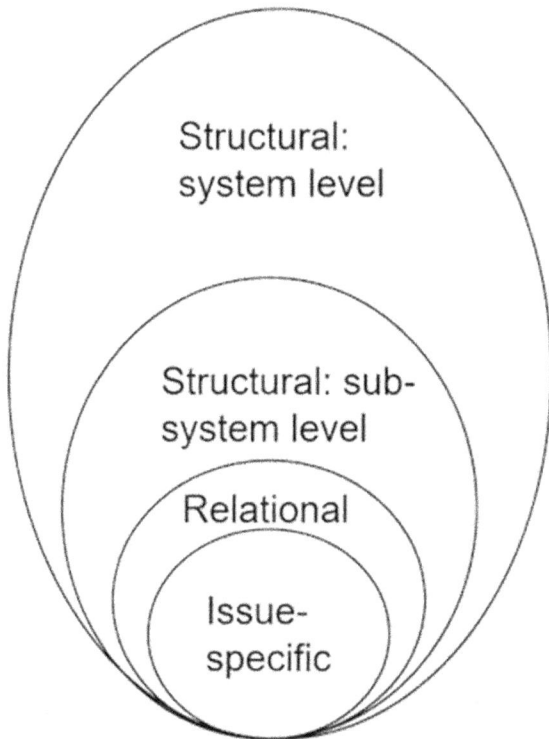

Figure 19.3 Humanitarian and Peace Operations Activity Levels.

Source: Adapted from Máire A. Dugan's original model published in the Leadership Journal (1996) by Heidi Burgess, of "Beyond Intractability." Used with permission.

model (Figure 19.4)—illustrate the positioning and relationship of various key dynamics in a conflict environment.

The models provide an initial orientation to many of the current concepts, frameworks, and responses with regard to conflict, stabilization, and peacebuilding. I acknowledge that some of the terms contained in the models are subjective. Also, I point out that no single graph, chart, or illustration can capture all possible complexities of a concept or situation. What I attempt in my CMF models is a reasonably useful framework for general orientation, analysis, briefings, and discussions pertaining to hypothetical and actual conflicts.

As the reader can see in the models, the names of theorists are superimposed next to key concepts that they initiated. The purpose of indicating concepts on the models is to better illustrate the underlying rationale.

I emphasize here that I believe that a *contingency* approach toward intervention planning is more effective overall (Fisher and Kealshly 1991; Fisher 1997). Different conflicts have different origins, reside at different levels within a society, community, or organization, and respond to different approaches. Also, I emphasize that it may be important to implement simultaneous multilevel, multisector interventions when and where possible.

Intervention Assessment and Approach Selection

The Intervention Assessment and Approach Selection model shown in Figure 19.4 is designed to assist with determining an overall intervention strategy based on desired outcomes and, importantly, awareness of the intrinsic elements and dynamics associated with different approaches.

The model reflects three primary kinds of information by which to consider what type of intervention approach(es) would be appropriate for a given situation. Although I cite numerous terms and authors in my models, I alone am responsible for how the terms are used and characterized in the models.

The Intervention Assessment and Approach Selection model contains three sections, as follows:

Section A: General Nature of an Intervention Approach
Section B: Specific Intervention Approaches
Section C: Dynamics Associated with Intervention Approaches (Figure 19.4)

To use the model, an analyst or practitioner can place a vertical line along a given intervention approach under consideration (Section B), and run the line up through Section C (*Dynamics Associated with Intervention Approaches*), then run the line down through Section A (*General Nature of an Intervention Approach*).

All dynamics that the vertical line intersects in Sections A and C are dynamics commonly associated with the type of intervention selected for consideration in Section A. Ranges of particular dynamics (listed horizontally) are indicated by arrows with end brackets.

As an example of an intervention approach selection, I have highlighted *Sustained Dialogue* (circled in red) for consideration. As can be seen, the red

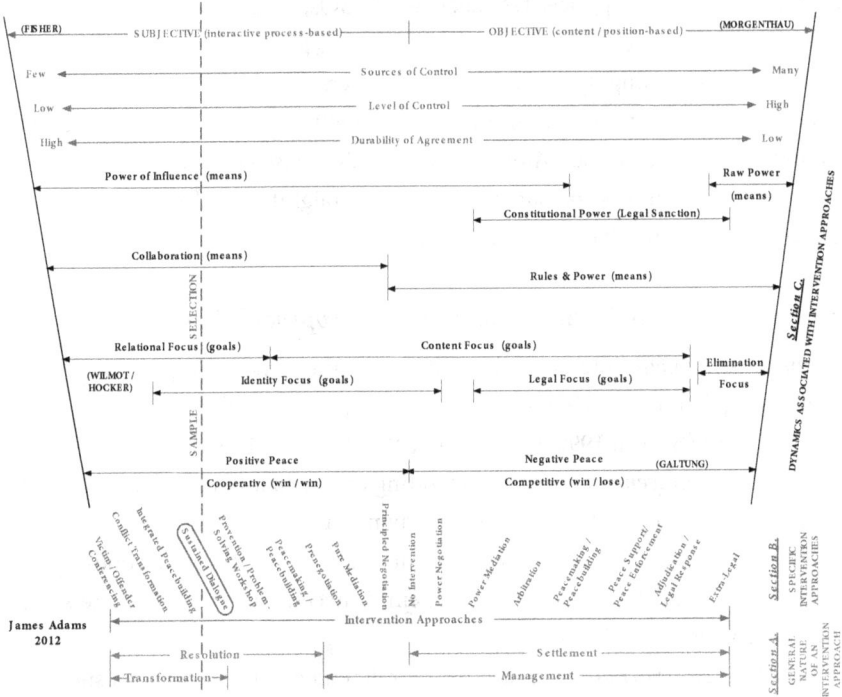

Figure 19.4 Intervention Assessment and Approach Selection.
Source: Diagram by James R. Adams, 2012.

vertical hyphenated line intersects *Resolution and Transformation* in Section A. This indicates that the general nature of the intervention is designed and intended to get at resolution and possibly transformation.

Going upward through Section C, the red line intersects positive peace as a notional intent, *Identity Focus* as a goal, *Relationship Focus* as a goal, *Collaboration* as a means, and *Power of Influence* as a means (versus legal or raw power as an intervention means).

Continuing upward, the red line intersects *Durability of Agreement* close to the high end of the durability range (versus a low durability expectation toward the right of the durability range). The red line intersects the *Level of Control* range on the low end. This indicates that a *Sustained Dialogue* intervention would require a low level of control over the conflict parties as opposed to a *Peace Support* or *Adjudication* intervention in which there is a high level of control over the conflicting parties and situation would be expected.

The red line intersects *Sources of Control* toward the few in number needed to control the situation (a high number of sources required typically involves diplomatic, military, police, UN agencies, NGOs, etc., needed in response to complex emergencies).

Finally, continuing upward, the red line intersects the *Subjective* (interactive process based) range. This indicates that interactive processes are subjective by nature as compared to, say, *Adjudication*, which is based on the implementation of codified law and is, presumably, a more straightforward objective process requiring less subjective considerations.

Section A: General Nature of Intervention Approach, Terms

Conflict Settlement interrupts hostilities for the time being without either identifying their underlying sources or creating a system of constructive-conflict management (Burton 1990a; Rubenstein 1999) (forcefully stop violence).

Conflict Management aims at moderating or "civilizing" the effects of conflict without necessarily addressing the underlying causes and conditions.

Conflict Resolution attempts to get at the root causes and conditions of destructive conflict and to eliminate them, if necessary, by altering the system that embodies or produces them.

Conflict Transformation: a change or refinement in the consciousness and character of individuals or societies. Implies individual moral development, although this kind of change will very likely lead to changes in social institutions as well (Baruch Bush and Folger 1994).

Conflict transformation facilitates a different perspective—a changed sense of what is real and what is possible. Parties shift from identity statements, which include answers, accusations, negative energy, and breast beating, to a joint search for solutions—a critical mass wherein change is possible, a transformation ultimately of the issues and positions. This often requires redistribution of resources, recognition, or at least acceptance, of common needs, and a sharing of power (Laue 1987).

A paradigmatic shift is articulated in the movement away from a concern with compromising positions toward a frame of reference that focuses on the restoration and rebuilding of relationships (Lederach 1997).

Section B: Specific Intervention Approaches, Terms

Extra-legal: outside of legal or constitutional context, without due process.

Adjudication/Legal Response: court-ordered legal processes; litigation.

Peace Support/Peace Enforcement: military and police actions in support of peacemaking and peacebuilding, for example, observation, command and control, force, liaison, logistics, presence, and security (D. Davis 2008a).

Peacemaking/Peacebuilding: (Boutros-Ghali 1992; Davis 2008a).

Arbitration: a legitimate and authoritative third party provides a binding judgment through consideration of the merits of the opposing positions, and imposes a settlement deemed to be fair and just (often by court order) (R. J. Fisher 1997).

Power Mediation: the intermediary provides the functions of pure mediation and adds the use of leverage in the form of promised rewards or threatened punishments to move the parties toward a settlement (R. J. Fisher 1997).

Power Negotiation: conflict parties used various realpolitik negotiating techniques to apply positive and negative pressures to the opposing conflict party or parties to protect or gain leverage for their respective positions at the expense of the opposing party or parties.

No Intervention: self-explanatory.

Principled Negotiation: negotiating parties focus on basic interests (not positions or persons) and shared problem solving to generate mutually satisfying outcomes while utilizing fair, objective standards to efficiently arrive at agreements that meet the legitimate interests of each negotiating side (and associated communities) to the extent possible, and are durable (R. Fisher and Ury 1981).

Pure Mediation: the facilitation of a negotiated settlement on a set of specific substantive issues through the use of reasoning, persuasion, control of information, and suggestion of alternatives (R. J. Fisher 1997).

Pre-negotiation functions to structure negotiation by specifying the boundaries, participants, and potentially agenda in an exploratory, noncommittal manner. Improves the relationship between the conflict parties before dealing with substantive issues; helps decision-makers reduce uncertainty and manage complexity in a low-risk and low-cost manner (R. J. Fisher 1997).

Problem Solving Workshop assist parties in a conflict in making a deep analysis of their conflicted relationships, revealing the hidden data of goals and motivations, enabling an accurate costing of their tactics and policies, and assisting in the discovery of acceptable options; define accurately the interests that are negotiable, and the basic needs and values that are not, and to assist the parties to discover options that are acceptable in terms of their interests and that satisfy their needs (Burton and Dukes 1990).

Prevention: steps taken to remove sources of conflict, and more positively to promote conditions in which collaborative and valued relationships control behaviors; a decision-making process in which the future is analyzed and anticipated, and as a result policy decisions are taken to remove the sources of likely disputes and conflict (Burton 1990b; Burton and Dukes 1990).

Sustained Dialogue: a facilitated five-stage interactive process that brings conflict parties together to change the nature of their relationships—not to negotiate for assets or political settlements. It is intended to probe the dynamics of contentious relationships that underlie the causes and conditions of a conflict and gradually develop a capacity for jointly designing actions to change the relationships for the better. Then, participants go on to decide how to take those insights and steps to the wider community (Saunders 1999).

Integrated Peacebuilding: development of local capacity to design and positively affect social change and structures by linking crisis management and long-term, future-oriented timeframes; generate understanding of crisis issues as connected to systemic roots and develop approaches that explicitly anchor issues within a set of relationships and subsystems; involve grassroots and top leadership in conflict resolution transformation processes, especially mid-range leadership who can cultivate relationships and influence groups vertically within societies and horizontally across societal divides (Lederach 1997).

Psychopolitical Dialogue: an interactive process whereby facilitators guide a five-stage process containing the following elements: establishing safety, communalization and bereavement, rebuilding trust and the capacity to trust, re-establishing personal and social morality, and reintegrating and restoring democratic discourse (Volkan 1999).

Victim-Offender Conferencing: a process whereby the offender and victim meet face to face; the offender has already admitted the offense; the meeting is facilitated and chaired by a trained mediator, preferably a community volunteer. Both parties are encouraged to tell their stories. Both get a chance to ask questions. They also talk about the impact and implication of this experience. When they have done this, they decide together what will be done about it. Once they come to an agreement, they sign a written contract for restitution in the form of financial compensation or means such as community service (Zehr 1990; Umbreit 1994).

Section C: Dynamics Associated with Intervention Approaches

Section C contains a variety of key dynamics common to conflict situations and interventions. The listing of dynamics in Section C is, of course, not exhaustive, but intended to provide a general starting-place orientation for analysis (a tentative first look at some of the primary facets of a particular intervention for consideration) and an initial feel for an intervention's appropriateness and viability of implementation.

General Instructions for Intervention Assessment and Approach Selection

1. Based on all available information, considerations, and desired outcomes, an analyst and practitioner would assess approaches (Section B) and associated general category types (Section A) ranged across the bottom of the model that appear to be the most suited to the desired intervention strategy.
2. They would review the dynamics associated with the potential intervention approach(es) (Section C) for confirmation of desired intervention qualities or indications that the intended intervention contains dynamics or elements not desired, in which case other interventions might need to be considered.
3. They would consult pertinent literature and other resources specific to the tentative approach(es).
4. They would consult appropriate organizations, decision-makers, conflict parties, and other pertinent actors with regard to the viability and appropriateness of the tentative intervention and associated objectives, timeframe, availability of expertise, funds, and other resources needed.
5. They would select an intervention approach or approaches (Section B) appropriate to the situation and desired objectives. They would advise on and coordinate implementation as needed.

20

Implications, Conclusions, and Recommendations

The following comprises my overall conclusions and recommendations concerning the problem of interventions stalled in negative peace as suggested by findings, analysis, observations, and experience:

- Add positive peace/constructive conflict processes as intentional peace operation tasks in the core peace operation components of diplomacy, aid, security, and civil society building.
- Informed positive peace initiatives within a constructive conflict framework can generate better outcomes within civil society-building efforts as well as general diplomacy, aid, and security components of peace and stabilization efforts.
- The status of peace and stabilization interventions can be assessed in structural and relationship terms, and in inferred association with negative and positive peace parameters.
- Structural violence is suggested in the status of structural elements.
- Positive peace processes support negative peace achievements but often are not standalone actions.
- Negative peace measures alone can ensure sustainable negative peace until the inevitable political and social eruption if not transitioned eventually to a positive peace status, or until combined negative and positive peace measures push the overall status of structural and relationship elements past the viable peace and positive peace thresholds into sustainable positive-peace.

The perception-derived statistics from my Bosnia survey might or might not be precisely accurate. Nevertheless, in my opinion, perceptions matter because they drive conflicts.

In my analysis, I posed the question of whether structural and relationship elements can be identified in relation to specific operational tasks such as diplomacy, security, political, economic, institutional, reconstruction, and civil society building.

I believe that question can be answered now, at least indirectly, within the five basic operational sectors of: (1) Good Governance, (2) Security, (3) Rule-of-Law, (4) Legitimate Economy, and (5) Social Wellbeing.

Also, essentially, the same answer applies to the identification of operational tasks in relation to negative and positive peace. The distinction is that relationship elements are more narrowly focused on personal, group, community, or societal relationship improvement, along with values, narrative, and consciousness shifting (track 2+ types of conflict transformation).

This principle could apply to any task in any sector. The distinction is a matter of focus. Structural and negative peace-oriented measures tend to involve imposed institutional and technical solutions (track 1 types of conflict-transformation), whether relationship improvement or consciousness shifting is expected or not.

There is no overriding reason, beyond a political one, that relationship-focused activities cannot be carried out within diplomatic, security, political, economic, and institutional reconstruction contexts, as well as in more traditionally relationship-oriented civil society peacebuilding efforts.

Essentially, what is needed is awareness raising and training on the part of intervenors and conflict parties with regard to the processes involved and expected benefits.

In my opinion, negative and positive peace-oriented measures can and should, when possible, proceed simultaneously and in concert for optimal progress.

Having just stated my overall conclusions, I make a somewhat arbitrary division below between findings for further research, theory, and practice, and for peace and stabilization interventions, since there is overlap.

I make the distinction between findings for scholar-practitioners and for peace and stabilization operation intervenors (decision makers) to indicate that I understand that "practice" is a term commonly used in scholastic and legal contexts, whereby stabilization and peacekeeping managers use terms like implement or execute, and might not readily understand the meaning intended by scholar-practitioners' use of the term "practice" in a mission context.

To elaborate a little, theory for intervenors, whether scholar-practitioners or peace and stabilization operation administrators and commanders, is essentially the same thing, except that scholar-practitioners are more focused on applied conflict resolution theory (broadly speaking), and administrators and commanders are focused more on the operationalization of policy and planning, which might or might not knowingly incorporate theory.

In fact, there is a kind of parallel universe of intervention of which to take note. Track 1 (governments) typically proceeds according to political imperatives, followed in turn by strategy and policy development, followed by implementation (planning and execution if military).

Track 2+ (I am thinking of scholar-practitioners in particular) typically proceeds according to theory imperatives conditioned by peer-reviewed discourse, followed in turn by applied theory practice in the field by trained facilitators. As discussed earlier, both track 1 and track 2+ actors carry out conflict-transformation tasks according to their respective understanding of what conflict transformation means.

Policy for the construction, or reconstruction, of transparent democratic institutions and systems (structural elements) is well understood and receives the predominant share of planning, funding, and resources. *Generally speaking, policy and funding for relationship and narrative change work is missing, and is a significant gap in the overall intervention picture.*

Peace and stabilization interventions are now very generalized enterprises, involving a wide range of sector activities and skill specialties. Such operations are track 1 managed and controlled, although many projects are subcontracted to track 2+ actors (International Nongovernmental Organizations [INGOs] or for-profit contractors) but according to track 1 criteria.

The conceptualization of approaches, whether policy or theory derived, is a definable distinction between track 1 and track 2+ interventions, and perhaps a meeting ground between the two, as there is overlap. And so, in this concluding section, I reference some findings (according to the respective approaches of track 1 and track 2) of interest to scholar practitioners and facilitators, and, separately, of interest to peace and stabilization operation administrators and commanders.

Essentially, the distinctions I make with regard to theory and practice are research oriented, and the distinctions with regard to peace and stabilization interventions are policy and operations oriented.

There is precious little time for administrators and commanders to do focused relationship work, and far too little time and resources are allowed to scholar practitioners to do the kind of peacebuilding research on the ground needed to carry out meaningful relationship studies and mediation or narrative facilitation.

There is some overlap in implications for further research, theory, and practice, and for peace and stabilization operations. Therefore, I ask for indulgence on points of commonality or repetition. In any case, I would think that, generally, intervenors, regardless of orientation, have an interest in, if not a stake, knowing more about the approaches of their various intervention colleagues.

For Further Research, Theory, and Practice

Restating *The Problem:*
Peace and stabilization operations sometimes achieve negative peace status—in essence, a negotiated political settlement and cessation or suppression of overt hostilities. But, despite intense diplomatic and reconstruction efforts, often stall without creating positive peace.

In this context, a stabilization and peacekeeping intervention presence holds open warfare or violent civil disorder in check and engages in a variety of reconstruction/state-building projects, but conflict party sentiments that precipitated the intervention are still in place and remain largely unchanged.

The Problem was examined empirically and qualitatively in this study by looking at the recent international intervention in Bosnia and Herzegovina (BiH). *The overall aim of this research was to assess the problem of a peace and stabilization intervention and environment stalled in negative peace, and to explore parameters of negative peace and sustainable positive peace.*

Fundamentally, this study has been a qualitatively driven exercise in conceptualizations with a quantified kickstart (primary source, scaled-survey) to start an exploration into relatively unknown conceptual territory.

There was not a pre-existing methodology for assessing interventions and environments in structural and relationship or negative and positive-peace terms.

Much of my work in this study has been to create the needed methodology; therefore, I used a grounded-theory, abduction-based approach (inference to the best estimation), which will have to suffice until a deeper statistical analysis is carried out for confirmation of statistical significance and viability.

The Comprehensive Multilevel Framework (CMF) that I constructed is intended to provide a cross-section of analytic tools and perspectives by which someone trained in Conflict Analysis and Resolution (CAR) theory and practice can efficiently analyze a conflict situation and advise on findings and potential intervention measures.

For Peace and Stabilization Operations

Different conceptualizations of conflict transformation imply different responses and possible cross-purposed actions. This can also mean an implementation void or imbalance.

Using the composite War to Sustainable Positive Peace Continuum (Figure 19.1) framework, model, and data collection instrument provide a viable set of tools for accommodating discussions and identifying elements, issues, trends, and priorities, and where adjustments might be made.

It also appears that the structural and relationship data and scales can notionally identify the status and dynamics of various peace and conflict circumstances. Consequently, policy and planning are better informed and focus and resources can be more readily adjusted to move toward positive peace outcomes.

In essence, the framework and composite model draw a picture of key conflict and peacebuilding elements, dynamics, and thresholds that are tangible for all to see and discuss. This is particularly useful for those who are new to fieldwork or not familiar with peace and stabilization environments.

It is also useful in aiding informed discussions between conflict parties who are focused on conflict circumstances, but perhaps without benefit of a broader perspective or awareness of more recent conflict mitigation or transformation processes (a fresh eye on the problem).

The use of the comprehensive multilevel framework and graphic models in face-to-face briefings with intervenors and conflict parties is likely to improve the chances of mutual understanding and collaboration. This capability can better enable all concerned to literally operate from the same page. This can apply to peacebuilding efforts regardless of scale, whether local, societal, or global.

Below, I expand a little further on two crucial facets of conflict that I believe warrant emphasis in terms of implications for peace and stabilization interventions—memory and conflict, and the violentization process.

With Regard to Memory and Conflict Factors

Most of the sentiments that precipitated the recent wars in the Balkans are still largely unaddressed. The root causes and conditions of the conflict, inclusive of problematic historical memory factors, remain untouched in the drive to get political settlements and compliance, however laudable.

Implications might suggest a kind of restorative justice or mutual victim-mutual offender process, or perhaps a series of facilitated dialogues at local and national levels. However, I think that such processes would need to be creatively reframed to encourage participation and any likelihood of success.

Although I think that such processes have the potential for success in Bosnia and elsewhere, I have great reservations about using the term "reconciliation," which in the Balkan context immediately drives deep into problematic memory dynamics and reactions. Generally, I think that the term is used much too loosely by the media and politicians, and by intervention managers and military commanders.

Use of the term reconciliation tends to pose a highly provocative emotional challenge right up front to participants before they even get a chance to warm up to the idea of communicating with each other about sensitive matters.

Also, if reconciliation is immediately and openly proclaimed as the objective, it can strike potential participants as naive and insulting on the part of intervenors. It can unnecessarily generate intense emotions, deeply jarring instincts for defense and confrontation, and can induce predictable further entrenchment.

I suggest offering options conducive to more organically timed mutual acceptance, trust-building experiences such as Harold Saunders' public peace process dialogues. I recommend initially characterizing an otherwise dialogue or reconciliation-intended encounter as an effort toward improving working relationships, community building, or perhaps as a mutual problem-solving effort.

With Regard to Violentization Factors

I believe that Lonnie H. Athens and Jeffery T. Ulmer's (2003) theory of *violentization* has clear implications for dealing with chronic, violent conflicts. I believe that greater familiarity with violentization processes would afford more realistic and effective intervention analyses, strategies, and mechanisms for interrupting or reversing such trends.

Richard Rhodes (in Athens and Ulmer 2003) applies violentization-process analysis to the violentization of "ordinary citizens into mass murderers." Rhodes (1999) concludes that "the experiences and difficulties of the SS-Einsatzgruppen and Order Police on the Eastern Front during the Second World War test and strongly support Athens's violent socialization model of violence development":

> The SS leadership systematically extended the range of EG victims by categories that Athens's model predicts would maximize virulency ... Athens's violent socialization model evidently applies to the training and activities of military and police and of mass killers as well as of violent criminals.
>
> (Athens and Ulmer 2003, 106)

Joshua Sanborn (in Athens and Ulmer 2003) further examines parallels between Athens's violentization process and the military indoctrination of soldiers:

> The comparison of the production of violent soldiers and the production of violent criminals has the potential for important insights into the bloody history of the modern age on battlefields and city streets alike.
>
> It is highly significant that the processes by which young men are transformed into violent criminals so closely parallels the way that they are trained as soldiers. In each case, "violent coaches" undertake a process to "break down" young men by making their "will" to commit violent acts stronger than what Dragomirov called their intellectual desire for self-preservation ... They become new social beings with new outlooks on the world that are patently dangerous for those around them and for themselves.
>
> (Sanborn, qtd. in Athens and Ulmer 2003, 122)

Additionally, if Athens is right—and I think he is—attempts at openly advertised reconciliation are likely to have no positive effect on individuals or communities that are, or are well on their way, to achieving virulency or malignant status, to use Athens's terms.

Also, pertinent and of concern is that the Brahimi Report released by the United Nations in 2000—which offered analyses of peace operations and measures to improve effectiveness—did not include in its recommendations any specific measures to address violentization processes.

The report's recommendations focus on better political consultation, the "robust" use of force, and better coordination and logistics for rapid deployments (United Nations 2000, 183–212)—in other words, a traditional governmental approach to the problem.

I point out an irony here that the Brahimi Report recommendations to reduce or end violence do not address perhaps the most insidious element of conflict—violentization processes (beyond the use of robust force to suppress it).

The Brahimi recommendations clearly lay out steps for achieving negative peace. However, as I said earlier, *use of force—negative peace—even as a necessary initial measure, is of little use in creating anything beyond itself.*

I believe that promulgating Athens and Ulmer's (2003) understanding of violentization would improve the odds for interrupting violentization processes in a peace and stabilization environment—in effect, a violentization-process awareness-raising and mitigation effort. This also would apply at any scale.

21

What Now?

I reiterate an observation that I made earlier: *The pressing problem now is what to do when a political settlement, and stabilization and reconstruction as we know it, are not enough to break a deep-rooted protracted conflict cycle.*

I propose the following measures to improve the odds for addressing the problem of interventions stalled in negative peace:

1. Directly field test the War to Sustainable Positive Peace Continuum (Figure 19.1) model in Bosnia, or elsewhere. This would have intervenors and conflict-party citizens record their perceptions as to the status of various structural and relationship elements directly onto a scaled *war to sustainable positive peace continuum* model in an attempt to fully establish survey statistical significance and an a priori statistical basis for it.
2. Have a thorough statistical analysis of existing and future data done.
3. Follow up on mutual-victim and mutual-offender restorative justice concepts.
4. Follow up on the application of constructive-conflict public peace processes.
5. Follow up on the Dialogue Support Unit concept for onsite application in stabilization and peacebuilding situations and timely transfer to local management (see Figure 16.1).
6. Advance and promulgate Athens and Ulmer's (2003) explanation of violentization processes.
7. Establish a pilot project for testing and refining the Comprehensive Multilevel Framework (CMF) model as analytical and briefing tools.
8. Research and apply the principles and models in this book toward the use of law enforcement reform approaches and community building scenarios in the United States and elsewhere.
9. Advance and promote Insight Approach and Insight Policing training and practices.

These tools and perspectives are designed to improve the odds for reaching a judicious balance of negative- and positive peace initiatives, and realism and idealism imperatives when responding to conflict.

Such human-realism approaches, I believe, provide crucial missing pieces of clarity.

A human-realism approach is readily adaptable to conflicted group, community, and societal level circumstances, given that human-behavior fundamentals are involved at all levels.

The insights and capabilities discussed are needed for improving our understanding of conflict, and changing the toxic tone of discourse around differing perspectives. I believe that such a profoundly human approach is a needed missing piece in today's world.

Final Thoughts

I hope that my note-to-file (note-to-humanity?) is helpful. I have confidence that humanity will continue to self-correct toward decency, civility, and compassionate justice, although it will take ever-present vigilance, awareness raising, wise leadership, and patience.

Humanity, in general, is no longer living in the near absolute darkness of mind and heart of previous ages. That threshold has been crossed. If I were to take a survey of humanity, it appears to me that, as a whole, we have crossed the viable peace threshold. We are in a fragile peace. We still need assisted stability.

As I say, viable peace is where positive peace initiatives are born. This offers the possibility of a sustainable positive peace. I suggested earlier that informed negative- and positive peace initiatives should be used prudently whenever and wherever possible in a conflict zone.

I make the same suggestion with regard to the world and humanity in general. The War to Sustainable Positive Peace Continuum is something we can see and understand. I suggest we use it. We, humanity, can help pull each other from self-destructive ways by focusing on what we want our world to be. I suggest freedoms, civility, dignity, and fairness.

A word of caution here to those eager to divide. A few proud politicians and citizens have recently called for the secession of Texas and Georgia from the United States. They should very carefully consider the hard lessons about divisiveness learned from the Yugoslav wars.

How will the status of a Texan or Georgian be decided, and who decides? Ethnicity, race, and ideological firestorms burn everyone for a very, very long time. It is a sure path to pain and destruction that awaits along the avenging-angel road.

There is no doubt, from what I have seen, that ever-increasing divisions only bring further pain and destruction. Is that what we want for those generations who come after us? For our children?

A caution to anarchists, extremists, or want-to-be authoritarians/fascists eager for a fight, eager to burn something. Whether an avenging angel fire is lit, literally, by someone on the extreme left or the extreme right doesn't seem to matter much. Everything burns.

Oops! War again.

Violence rarely warms the heart or wins minds. As my Mama once told me: "You can't keep hitting someone over the head with a hammer and get them to like it." Perhaps it satisfies an impulse to rage on the highway or start a war, but it is dangerous. Perhaps it can satisfy self-righteous indignation, but, in the end, everyone gets burned.

To be clear, I have no objection to self-defense. The protection of one's own is essential. Finding equilibrium in a polarizing America and world is a different effort. It is a different perspective. I suggest a human-realism perspective. I suggest acknowledging the virtue and vice in each of us and finding the equilibrium in our midst.

I think that it is a matter of dialogue, of communication, of listening. I suggest civil dialogue. In the home. In our communities. In our nation. In our humanity. I do not mean "no shouting allowed." Call it "civil shouting," if necessary. But shouting that allows listening—or, perhaps better put, passion that allows listening. Passion that allows empathy and seeing. Passion that allows change.

There are organizations that promote constructive conflict by advocating constructive communication (nonviolent communication, empathy building)—a curiosity approach vs. retaliatory approach for example, which has proven helpful in law enforcement and community interactions (see Megan Price, Insight Policing.com).

As I say, fundamentally, *self-sustaining peace—of the positive kind—is the ultimate challenge and needed future of conflict discussion.*

Final questions. What do we want our world to be? What future do we want for our children and grandchildren?

Humanity continues to search for balance in freedoms, civility, dignity, and fairness. Many civil society and professional organizations are working toward this end with an emphasis on cooperative, nonviolent communication, and empathy awareness building (constructive conflict). Moreover, there is hope.

I hope that my explanations and observations on peace and conflict dynamics are helpful.

A good place to become better informed about who is doing what, and where, is to check out the website for the Alliance for Peacebuilding (2024) (https://www.allianceforpeacebuilding.org), which is comprised of about 180 organizations worldwide containing many concerned citizens working toward peaceful resolutions of human conflict.

For a final thought, I repeat that *viable peace* is where positive peace initiatives are born. Perhaps there is something you can do to support humanity's effort to live together more constructively. There is always a place for those wanting to lend a hand.

Well, it's time to file this note. I continue my journey. I wish you well in yours, and ours.

PS—As an offering of hope and perhaps ridiculous humor, I include a short story at the end of this book (Appendix: A Day at Boot Camp Peace in Our Time), which I figure is a right-of-passage for a free-range scholar-practitioner such as myself. See you on the trail.

Appendix

A Day at Boot Camp Peace-in-Our-Time
James R. Adams

Nighttime

Narrator: Another sun has long since retreated from Boot Camp Peace-in-Our-Time. It's quiet now. A few night birds are chatting about the returned summer breeze. The moon plays with shadows and rustling leaves while cadets slumber heavily in their bunks, some content, some disturbed. In dreams, the day's emotions transition and take stage deep in the night, only more thoughtfully and without restraint.

In daylight, we ask of each other questions of truth, but during these night performances, our essence, our senses—for a little while—ally with other actors, and deep truths ask questions of us. Elusive dream agents probe for known yet forgotten insights to convey to our mortal vaguely aware selves who—in our awakened state—must reckon with all that we are, and each other: the inevitable displays of kindness and tragedy.

In sleeping darkness, deeper and deeper, mind and emotion and soul commune. Speaking quietly. Speaking boldly. Probing. Ever closer, fragile night truths strain to simultaneously reach mind and clarity, and daylight.

Narrator: Shhh ... A dreaming cadet is resonating insight.

Dreaming Cadet: What are they saying?—Yes, I'm listening. What's that? Ah yes, of course. So basic. Conflict is a web of small tragedies; major conflict is the logical extreme of small tragedies unattended to. Why didn't I see that before? Wait, another question please, wait, wait—what, what did you say? Slower, slower, I don't understand ... Idaho potatoes—what!?

Daylight at Camp Peace-in-Our-Time

DI Wars-a-Fact (Drill instructor enters barracks at 5:00 a.m. banging 50 gal. trash can): I said, KP (Kitchen Police) duty. If you don't get your sorry excuses for a higher-self out of those bunks right now, you'll be skinnin spuds and sloppin garbage pails for the rest of your miserable days here at Camp Peace-in-Our-Time; Or maybe that's just the kind of thing you like (DI Wars-a-Fact's darting-glares land on Cadet Help-Me-Jesus); What are you staring at cadet? You some kinda hippie weirdo? Hit the floor and give me twenty!

Cadet Help-Me-Jesus: (Hits floor doing push-ups and shouting the core basic human needs drill) identity, security, recognition, identity, security, recognition …

DI Wars-a-Fact: The kind of material they send me these days—God help us!

Morning Roll Call

DI Wars-a-Fact: Conflict Cadet So-Much-Fuss, front and center, where are you from boy?

Cadet So-Much-Fuss: Sir, Texas, Sir.

DI Wars-a-Fact: It's all right son, it's not your fault!

DI Wars-a-Fact: Conflict Cadet Gone-Awry. Where the hell are you?

Cadet Gone-Awry: Over here sir!

DI Wars-a-Fact: Where you from boy?

Cadet Gone-Awry: I don't know Sir.

DI Wars-a-Fact: Well, do you know where you're going?

Cadet Gone-Awry: Sir, to resolve conflict sir!

DI Wars-a-Fact: To resolve conflict, Well ain't that somethin. And just what makes you think you ought to go around sticking your big nose into other people's business?

Cadet Gone-Awry: I don't exactly know sir, it, it just seems like something ought to be done, sir.

DI Wars-a-Fact: And why is that Gone-Awry? Come on, out with it! What makes you so special?

Cadet Gone-Awry: Nothing, nothing, sir. It's just that something has to be done about the world, sir.

DI Wars-a-Fact: So, you're gonna save the world. Recruits can't even spell paradigm. A recruit is the lowest form of humane existence there is, so since I can't bust you any lower than you already are, I guess I'll just cry!

DI Wars-a-Fact: Come on, out with it Gone-Awry! Why are you here wise guy?

Cadet Gone-Awry: Uh, uh, everybody beating me up in the sixth grade!—and, and I got no place else to go!

DI Wars-a-Fact: All right, good work Gone-Awry. We'll teach you a thing or two about conflict analyticals here—and work on your wayfaring inclinations too.

Cadet Gone-Awry: Sir, yes sir!

DI Wars-a-Fact: Cadet Maxi-Heart, you look like you're about to go AWOL (Absent Without Leave). What's your problem? You get beat up in the sixth grade too?

Cadet Maxi-Heart: Sir, no sir, but I saw lots of others get beat up in the sixth grade, and it was just awful. The world's just awful. And I don't know where I'm going either, Sir!

DI Wars-a-Fact: Well don't you worry. You have a home with us now, Cadet. The Peace-in-Our-Time Academy takes care of its own.

DI Wars-a-Fact: Cadet Love-and-Trouble, what are you looking at boy?

Cadet Love-and-Trouble: Sir, that cadet passing by over there, she looks very knowledgeable, so bold, so confident.

DI Wars-a-Fact: Cadet, that there is an ABD—All but dissertation—You got less knowledge, skills, and abilities in your entire pathetic imagination than she does in one itty bitty footnote. The next step for an ABD is full-fledged Conflict Resolver—a genuine peace warrior you might say. Cadet, don't you even dare gaze upon that ABD, lest you go blind! You just came within a gnat's whisker of rank disequilibrium son—damn near a goner. Thank me boy!

Cadet Love-and-Trouble: Sir, thank you sir!

DI Wars-a-Fact: You Conflict Cadets keep your heads on straight, stay sober most of the time, and by God we'll make conflict analyticals and resolvers out of your puny-toolbox selves yet! And maybe you'll even learn some polite manners to boot!

Classroom

Instructor Deep-Essence: What we have here is your basic Conflict Resolver Survival Kit. For the next two years your Conflict Resolver Survival Kit will be your wife, your husband, your girlfriend, your boyfriend; you will study with it, write papers of enlightenment with it, discourse on weighty points of Kuhnarian theory with it, eat with it and sleep with it, and don't be caught going to the bathroom without it.

In your Conflict Resolver Kit, you have your basic Moore's "Circle-of-Conflict." You have one complete set of Kuhn's Top Ten Tricky Paradigm Situations. You have got your copy of Deep Essence's 10 Worlds: A Model of Everything That Could Possibly Be Going On—You're welcome! And in cases of imminent danger in a field situation, you have got your Blechspeak's Who done it? So What, Who's Gonna Be Next? Where's the Exit? handy dandy emergency Get Me Out of This One pocketsize guidebook with tear-out instructions (chocolate included).

Instructor Deep-Essence: Cadet Hothead, you're lookin kinda peculiar. Are you conflicted son?

Cadet Hothead: Sir, yes sir. That's why I like it here sir! I'm a pent-up fireball of conflicted emotions, sir!

Instructor Deep-Essence: Well, by golly, make it work for you, cadet. This here outfit had just you in mind when we included in your Conflict Resolver Survival Kit, Dollard's (1939) most interesting discourse on frustration and aggression, which I think should come in right handy for you.

Instructor Deep-Essence: All right Maxi-Heart, demonstrate for us that conflict resolution technique I told you about that can get at the root causes and conditions of intractable conflict when nothing else will. … Well, what are you waiting for cadet!

Cadet Maxi-Heart: (Perplexed and rather desperate looking) Sir, yes sir! (Maxi-Heart turns and starts strangling the cadet next to her).

Instructor Deep Essence: Maxi-Heart! What are you doing!?

Cadet Maxi-Heart: Well, you said try strangulation sir!

Instructor Deep Essence: I said triangulation, cadet!—the use of three different analytical approaches to corroborate a hypothesis—although maybe you're on to something there Maxi-Heart.

Narrator: Research is an ongoing focus at Peace-in-Our-Time Academy.

Break Time around the Barracks

Narrator: Cadets talk among themselves while nursing sore copier start-button finger injuries and contemplating universal values.

A Cadet: Man, these instructors are busting our chops. If I hear "Has anybody read the book?" one more time, I'm over-the-wall.

Narrator: Mysterious Instructor Power-to-the-People is hanging around the barracks during break.

Instructor Power-to-the-People (Peeking around the corner of a barrack): Psst, hey, cadet, you heard of Senator Fulbright on "The Arrogance of Power?" I've got an original copy right here; still has an excellent-condition dust cover. Martin Luther King? Ghandi? I've got 'em all. You can pay me later. Remember the people! (power to the people salute); (The cadet fumbles a people-power salute).

Mysterious *Instructor Power-to-the-People*: Don't worry. I'll show you how to do that.

Narrator: Meanwhile, around the corner, ABD Candidate Nearly-There exchanges urgent whispers with Cadet Love-and-Trouble.

ABD Nearly-There: No! I can't see you again. You are a puny-toolbox cadet with a pathetic imagination, and I am a very knowledgeable, bold, and confident ABD. It is forbidden!

Cadet Love-and-Trouble: But isn't conflict resolution about love? Besides, I haven't gone out with anybody normal in a long time—and you're an ABD!

ABD Nearly-There: Slow down, you're confusing me. Get, get away. I have to go wax lyrically with poignant insight on the Spirituality, Love, and Reality paradox.

Cadet Gone-Awry: I can help you with that!

ABD Nearly-There: I, I must away!

Wormhole (Odd tiny depository of dissertations, theses, and other academic mysteries)

Narrator: Later that day, DI Wars-a-Fact finds ABD Nearly-There in the Wormhole. She's looking pretty down.

DI Wars-a-Fact: ABD Nearly-There, you look like you lost the last copy of your dissertation data-base. What's going on? Talk to me.

ABD Nearly-There: I've got the ABD Blues sir. I don't know any more about where I'm going than a puny-toolbox recruit. What's conflict resolution really all about? I don't think I'm cut out for this, sir.

DI Wars-a-Fact: Well, I can understand how you feel; been there myself. Ain't nothing mysterious. Follow me.

Narrator: Instructor Wars-a-Fact takes ABD Nearly-There to the confidential Peace-in-Our-Time Communications Center deep in a second Alt Reality worm hole.

DI Wars-a-Fact: Have a listen to this radio traffic Nearly-There (They listen).

Narrator: Somewhere in a wormhole, far far away, Conflict Resolver In-The-Middle-of-It, trying to get help, radios-in.

Conflict Resolver In-The-Middle-of-It: Peace-in-Our-Time Comm. Center, this is Conflict Resolver In-the-Middle-of-It at Operation People for Positive Peace Processes, we've got a situation here: Surrounded on all sides. Unmet basic human needs. Ethnic conflict. Political conflict. Conflicting organizational mandates. Cultural conflict. Interpersonal conflict. And it's getting all mixed together. It's getting hard to see!

Peace-in-Our-Time Comm. Center: All right In-the-Middle of it, copy that. It's Ok, take your time, give me some analysis.

Conflict Resolver In-the-Middle-of-It: Conflict as start-up is only a memory. It's all conflict-as-process now; chosen traumas coming from the right, cognitive blindness coming from the left, avoidance behind me, competition in front of me, and disappearing perspective all over the place! It's hell sir!

Peace-in-Our-Time Comm. Center: Tell me what you see right now In-the-Middle-of-It.

Conflict Resolver In-the-Middle-of-It: Lots of shouting and venting.

Peace-in-Our-Time Comm. Center: Hmmm, manifest conflict. Well don't worry about venting In-the-Middle; Watch out for flying chairs.

In-the-Middle-of-It: Chairs, sir, lots of flying chairs! Everybody's getting chaired!

Peace-in-Our-Time Comm. Center: Hmmm, aggressive manifest conflict.

Peace-in-Our-Time Comm. Center: Maintain In-the-Middle. What did conflict theorist Kuhn say about something like this?

In-the-Middle-of-It: I don't know sir. Kuhn didn't mention flying chairs.

Peace-in-Our-Time Comm. Center: Go deeper Conflict Resolver—Burton, Mitchell, Gurr, Volkan, Sandole's complexities, Saunders' sustained dialogue. Dig deep! Elicit!

In-the-Middle-of-It: I've got it sir, Blechspeak's Handy Dandy Get Me Out of This One Pocket Size Emergency Instructions.

Peace-in-Our-Time Comm. Center: Use it man. Use it!

In-The-Middle-of-It: (Fumbling nervously for the right page, In-the-Middle-of-it reads): ... Majority/Minority Population Power-Ratio Dynamics—In a case in which no group has a majority, the former majority may still be a plurality, may still try to claim that its way is THE way. Sometimes, when the ratios are close, everybody realizes that there is no one way. Negotiation ensues. Try empathy and nonviolent communication, a curiosity approach as opposed to a retaliatory approach. Conflict subsides ...

In-the-Middle-of-It: (After a pause) It's, it's working, they've stopped fighting, they're listening to each other; and no more flying chairs. I think we can move on to positive peace processes now, sir.

Peace-in-Our-Time Comm. Center: Copy that. You have a good day now Conflict Resolver.

Visiting Hours at Camp Peace-in-Our-Time

Grandma: ... Speak-up sweetie, Grandpa doesn't hear so well you know.

Grandpa: You're studying conflict revolution you say—Well, that's the spirit Teddy! Show a little backbone I say.

Conflict Cadets Theodore and Susan Scholar-Activists: No, no Grandpa, not revolution; resolution. We're conflict resolvers.

Grandpa: That's right Teddy my boy, revolvers; Why, if I were ten years younger—where's my revolver Grandma!?

Conflict Cadets: Grandpa, we don't work with revolvers, we use active listening.

Grandpa: Active hissing? What kinda dang fool revolution is that!

Grandma: They're talking about resolution dear, R-E-S-O-L- ...

Grandpa: I can spell Grandma! I just want to know how the hell anybody's going to resolve anything by hissing! Damnedest thing I ever heard—Is that what they teach you kids at that fancy college?

Just before Lights Out

Narrator: The mood is reflective in the barracks. Pages turn quietly. Small bottles of contraband open more quietly. Cadet Love-and-Trouble is preparing for the next day. He continues his research on contingency intervention and other theories. Adhering to proper scientific methodology, Love-and-Trouble poses his next research problem statement—Dear ABD Nearly-There, how can I go slow when you make my motor race …

Lights Out

Narrator: Again, it's quiet. Again, the moon looks down and observes shadows and leaves darting about. The day's emotions slowly stir, slipping on shadow clothes to evade their daylight masters and take stage deep in the night to speak freely. The summer breeze brushes the faces of slumbering cadets preparing them for the nightly performance, the lessons, the forgotten realizations in which emotions and memories take odd partners for the occasion.

Deeper and deeper, mind and emotion, and soul commune. Speaking quietly. Speaking boldly. Probing. Revealing. The birds grow still, listening

References

Adams, James R. 2021. *Analytic Reflections from Conflict Zones: A Cautionary Tale for a Polarizing America and World*. Newcastle Upon Tyne: Cambridge Scholars.
Alliance for Peacebuilding. 2024. https://www.allianceforpeacebuilding.org/.
Anzulovic, Branimir. 1998. *Heavenly Serbia: From Myth to Genocide*. New York: New York University Press.
Athens, Lonnie H. 1992. *The Creation of Dangerous Violent Criminals*. Chicago: University of Illinois Press.
Athens, Lonnie H. 1997. *Violent Criminal Acts and Actors Revisited*. Chicago: University of Illinois Press.
Athens, Lonnie H. 2017. *The Creation of Dangerous Violent Criminals*. 2nd ed. New York: Routledge.
Athens, Lonnie [H.], and Jeffery T. Ulmer, eds. 2003. *Violent Acts and Violentization: Assessing, Applying, and Developing Lonnie Athens' Theories*. Sociology of Crime, Law and Deviance 4, series editor Mathieu Deflem. Leeds: Emerald Publishing.
Avruch, Kevin. 1998. *Culture and Conflict Resolution*. Washington, DC: United States Institute of Peace.
Baker, Pauline H. 2001. "Conflict Resolution versus Democratic Governance: Divergent Paths to Peace." In *Turbulent Peace: The Challenges of Managing International Conflict*, edited by Chester A. Crocker, Fen Osler Hampson, and Pamela Aall, 753–64. Washington, DC: United States Institute of Peace.
Barash, David P., and Charles P. Webel. 2002. *Peace and Conflict Studies*. Thousand Oaks, CA: Sage Publications.
Baruch Bush, Robert A., and Joseph P. Folger. 1994. *The Promise of Mediation: Responding to Conflict through Empowerment and Recognition*. San Francisco, CA: Jossey-Bass Publishers.
Bildt, Carl. 1998. *Peace Journey: The Struggle for Peace in Bosnia*. London: Orion.
Boutros-Ghali, Boutros. 1992. *An Agenda for Peace*. New York: United Nations. https://digitallibrary.un.org/record/145749?ln=en&v=pdf (accessed September 3, 2024).
Boutros-Ghali, Boutros. 1995. *An Agenda for Peace*. 2nd ed. New York: United Nations. https://unesdoc.unesco.org/ark:/48223/pf0000103357 (accessed September 3, 2024).
Burg, Steven L. 2001. *Intervention in Internal Conflict: The Case of Bosnia*. Case Study. Center for International and Security Studies, University of Maryland Publications. https://cissm.umd.edu/sites/default/files/2019-08/burg.pdf (accessed September 3, 2024).
Burton, John, ed. 1990a. *Conflict: Human Needs Theory*. London: Macmillan.

Burton, John, ed. 1990b. *Conflict: Resolution and Prevention.* New York: St. Martin's Press.

Burton, John, ed. 1997. *Violence Explained: The Sources of Conflict, Violence and Crime and Their Prevention.* New York: Manchester University Press.

Burton, John, and Frank Dukes. 1990. *Conflict: Practices in Management, Settlement and Resolution.* London: Palgrave Macmillan.

CIA. 2024. *The World Factbook.* Online at https://www.cia.gov/the-world-factbook/countries/bosnia-and-herzegovina/#people-and-society.

Clinton, Bill [Pres.]. 1997. "Managing Complex Contingency Operations." Presidential Decision Directive (PDD 56, May 1997). https://clinton.presidentiallibraries.us/items/show/101150.

Cohen, Philip J. 1996. *Serbia's Secret War: Propaganda and the Deceit of History.* College Station: Texas A&M University Press.

Covey, Jock, Michael Dziedzic, and Leonard Hawley, eds. 2005. *The Quest for Viable Peace: International Intervention and Strategies for Conflict Transformation.* Washington, DC: United States Institute of Peace.

Cox, Marcus. 1998. "Strategic Approaches to Intervention in Bosnia and Herzegovina." https://www.files.ethz.ch/isn/102388/1998_10_Strategic_Approaches_to_International_Intervention.pdf (accessed September 9, 2024).

Curle, Adam. 1971. *Making Peace.* London: Tavistock.

Davis, David. 1999. *CMPO: Civil Order and Social Justice in Peace Operations. Referencing an Unpublished Classroom Lectures.* Peace Operations Policy Program. Arlington, VA: George Mason University. Adapted by James R. Adams.

Davis, David. 2008a. *The Conceptual Model of Peace Operations CMPO.* Information Document from the Department of Public Administration, Peace Operations Policy Program (POPP) 3. Fairfax, VA: George Mason University.

Davis, David. 2008b. *Planning Assessment and Implications for Policy.* Referencing an unpublished classroom handout. Peace Operations Policy Program. Arlington, VA: George Mason University.

Deutsch, Morton, Peter T. Coleman, and Eric C. Marcus. 2006. *The Handbook of Conflict Resolution: Theory and Practice.* 2nd ed. San Francisco, CA: Jossey-Bass.

Diamond, Louise, and John McDonald. 1996. *Multi-Track Diplomacy: A Systems Approach to Peace.* West Hartford, CT: Kumarian Press.

Dollard, John D. 1939. *Frustration and Aggression.* Hew Haven, CT: Yale University Press.

Donnelly, Jack. 2003. *Universal Human Rights: In Theory and Practice.* Ithaca, NY: Cornell University Press.

Douglass, Ana, and Thomas A. Vogler, eds. 2003. *Witness & Memory: The Discourse of Trauma.* London: Taylor & Francis.

Dugan, Máire A. 1996. "A Nested Theory of Conflict." *Leadership Journal: Women in Leadership* 1, no. 1 (July): 9–20. https://emu.edu/cjp/docs/Dugan_Maire_Nested-Model-Original.pdf (accessed September 3, 2024).

Dziedzic, Michael, ed. 2016. *Criminalized Power Structures: The Overlooked Enemies of Peace*. Lanham, MD: Rowman and Littlefield.

Evans, Gareth. 2008. *The Responsibility to Protect: Ending Mass Atrocity Crimes Once and for All*. Washington, DC: Brooking Institution Press.

Fetherston, A. Betts 2000. "Peacekeeping, Conflict Resolution and Peacebuilding: A Reconsideration of Theoretical Framework." *International Peacekeeping* 7, no. 1: 190–218. https://doi.org/10.1080/13533310008413825.

Fisher, Roger, and William Ury. 1981. *Getting to Yes: Negotiating Agreement without Giving In*. New York: Penguin.

Fisher, Ronald J. 1997. *Interactive Conflict Resolution*. Syracuse, NY: Syracuse University Press.

Fisher, Ronald J., and Loraleigh Keashly. 1991. "The Potential Complementarity of Mediation and Consultation within a Contingency Model of Third-Party Intervention." *Journal of Peace Research* 28, no. 1 (February): 29–42. https://doi.org/10.1177/0022343391028001005.

Galtung, Johan. 1969. "Peace, Violence and Peace Research." *Journal of Peace Research* 6, no. 3: 167–91. https://www.jstor.org/stable/422690.

Gambier-Parry, E., Maj. [Parry, E. Gambier]. 1885/2006. *Suakin 1885: Being a Sketch of the Campaign of This Year, Paul and Trench*. London: K. Paul, Trench. https://archive.org/details/suakin1885beings00parrrich/page/n9/mode/1up; East Sussex: Naval & Military Press.

Geertz, Clifford. 2000. *Local Knowledge: Further Essays in Interpretive Anthropology*. 3rd ed. New York: Basic Books.

Halbwachs, Maurice, ed. 1992. *On Collective Memory*. Edited, translated, and Introduction by Lewis A. Coser. Chicago, IL: University of Chicago Press.

Hanson, Marianne. 2001. "Warnings from Bosnia: The Dayton Agreement and the Implementation of Human Rights." In *The Kosovo Tragedy: The Human Rights Dimension*, edited by Ken Booth, 87–104. London: Taylor and Francis.

Hayden, Patrick. 2001. *The Philosophy of Human Rights*. St. Paul, MN: Paragon House.

Hewitt, J. Joseph, Jonathan Wilkenfeld, and Ted Robert Gurr. 2010. *Peace and Conflict 2010*. Center for International Development and Conflict Management, University of Maryland. Boulder, CO: Paradigm.

Hicks, Donna. 2011. *Dignity: The Essential Role It Plays in Resolving Conflict*. New Haven, CT: Yale University Press.

Holbrooke, Richard. 1998. *To End a War: The Conflict in Yugoslavia*. New York: Random House.

Holbrooke, Richard. 2005. "Was Bosnia Worth It?" *Washington Post* (Opinion), July 19. https://www.washingtonpost.com/archive/opinions/2005/07/19/was-bosnia-worth-it/70ac0a67-d2a7-4683-ae4b-d750514bbdf2/ (accessed September 3, 2024).

Huntington, Samuel P. 2011. *The Clash of Civilizations and the Remaking of World Order*. New York: Simon and Schuster.

Jeffrey, Alex. 2007. "The Politics of 'Democratization': Lessons from Bosnia and Iraq." *Review of International Political Economy* 14, no. 3 (May): 444–66. https://doi.org/10.1080/09692290701395718.

Junne, Gerd, and Willemijn Verkoren, eds. 2005. *Postconflict Development: Meeting New Challenges*. Boulder, CO: Rienner.

Kelman, Herbert C. 1990. "Appling a Human Needs Perspective to the Practice of Conflict Resolution: The Israeli–Palestinian Case." In *Conflict: Human Needs Theory*, edited by John Burton, 283–97. New York: Saint Martin's Press.

Kennan, George F. 1985. "Morality and Foreign Policy." *Foreign Affairs* 64, no. 2 (Winter): 205–18. https://doi.org/10.2307/20042569.

Kriesburg, Louis, and Bruce W. Dayton. 2016. *Constructive Conflicts: From Escalation to Resolution*. 5th ed. New York: Rowman and Littlefield.

Kuhn, Thomas S. 1996. *The Structure of Scientific Revolutions*. 3rd ed. Chicago, IL: University of Chicago Press.

Langholtz, Harvey J., ed. 1998. *The Psychology of Peacekeeping*. Westport, CT: Prager.

Laue, James H. 1987. "Resolution: Transforming Conflict and Violence." Institute for Conflict analysis and Resolution, Occasional Paper no. 7. Fairfax, VA: George Mason University. https://mars.gmu.edu/server/api/core/bitstreams/804d76b4-7115-4843-9213-2775e2b03f52/content.

Lederach, John Paul. 1997. *Building Peace: Sustainable Reconciliation in Divided Societies*. Washington, DC: United States Institute of Peace.

Lindner, Evelin Gerda. 2002. "Healing the Cycles of Humiliation: How to Attend to the Emotional Aspects of 'Unsolvable' Conflicts and the Use of 'Humiliation Entrepreneurship.'" *Peace and Conflict: Journal of Peace Psychology* 8, no. 2 (June): 125–38. https://doi.org/10.1207/S15327949PAC0802_02.

Malcom, Noel. 2002. *Bosnia: A Short History*. Revised ed. London: Pan Books.

Malcom, X. April 3, 1964. *Ballot or The Bullet Speech*. Cleveland, OH. https://www.gilderlehrman.org/sites/default/files/inline-pdfs/ballot_or_bullet.pdf (accessed October 28, 2024).

Margalit, Avishai 2004. *The Ethics of Memory*. Cambridge, MA: Harvard University Press.

Maslow, A. [Abraham] H. 1943. "A Theory of Human Motivation." *Psychology Review* 50, no. 4 (July): 370–6. https://doi.org/10.1037/h0054346.

Maslow, A. 1954. *Motivation and Personality*. New York: Harper.

Mitchell, Christopher, and Michael Banks. 1996. *Handbook of Conflict Resolution: The Analytical Problem–Solving Approach*. New York: Pinter.

Muggah, Robert, ed. 2009. *Security and Post-Conflict Reconstruction: Dealing with Fighters in the Aftermath of War*. Routledge Global Security Studies. New York: Routledge.

Newbury, Catharine. 2002. "Ethnicity and the Politics of History in Rwanda." In *Genocide, Collective Violence, and Popular Memory: The Politics of Remembrance in the Twentieth Century*, edited by David E. Lorey, and William H. Beezley, 67–83. Wilmington, DE: Scholarly Resources.

North, Robert Carver. 1990. *War, Peace, Survival: Global Politics and Conceptual Synthesis*. Boulder, CO: Westview Press.

North Atlantic Treaty Organization (NATO). 1999. "Military Technical Agreement." Kosovo. June 9. Naples. JFC NATO. https://jfcnaples.nato.int/kfor/page184922630#:~:text=The%20%22Military%20Technical%20Agreement%22%20is%20signed%20by%20KFOR,for%20the%20withdrawal%20of%20Yugoslav%20forces%20from%20Kosovo (accessed November 3, 2024).

Oakley, Robert B. 1998. "Peacekeeping: Its Evolution and Meaning." *US Foreign Policy Agenda* 3, no. 2 (February): 21–7. https://ciaotest.cc.columbia.edu/olj/fpa/fpa_apr98.pdf.

Office of the High Representative (OHR-European Union). 2004. "General Framework Agreement for Peace in Bosnia and Herzegovina." Sarajevo. August. Now available at https://www.ohr.int/Dayton-peace-agreement (accessed October 23, 2024).

Organization for Security and Cooperation in Europe (OSCE). 1975a. "Final Helsinki Act of 1975." https://www.osce.org/files/f/documents/5/c/39501.pdf (accessed September 3, 2024).

Organization for Security and Cooperation in Europe (OSCE). 1975b. "Helsinki Final Act, 1975." http://www.osce.org/mc/39501 (accessed September 3, 2024).

Organization for Security and Cooperation in Europe (OSCE). 1998. "Kosovo Verification Mission Agreement of October 16, 1998." https://digitallibrary.un.org/record/262304/files/S_1998_991-EN.pdf (accessed September 3, 2024).

Organization for Security and Cooperation in Europe (OSCE). 2003. *Individual Human Rights Complaints: A Handbook for OSCE Field Personnel*. Warsaw. Published by OSCE Office for Democratic Institutions and Human Rights ODIHR. https://www.osce.org/files/f/documents/8/9/20437.pdf (accessed September 3, 2024).

Peirce, Charles S. 2024. "Standford Encyclopedia of Philosophy (for description of abduction Theory)." The Metaphysics Research Lab. Department of Philosophy. Stanford, CA. Stanford University. https://plato.stanford.edu/entries/peirce/#:~:text=Charles%20Sanders%20Peirce%20%281839%E2%80%931914%29%20was%20the%20founder%20of,labelled%20%E2%80%9Cpragmatism%E2%80%9D%29%2C%20a%20theorist%20of%20logic%2C%20language%2C%20communicatio (accessed November 7, 2024).

Prunier, Gérard. 2009. *From Genocide to Continental War: The "Congolese Conflict" and the Crisis of Contemporary Africa*. London: Hurst.

Ramsbotham, Oliver, and Tom Woodhouse, eds. 2000. *Peacekeeping and Conflict Resolution*. Portland, OR: Frank Cass.

Rhodes, Richard. 1999. *Why They Kill: The Discoveries of a Maverick Criminologist*. New York: Vintage.

Ricoeur, Paul. 2004. *Memory, History, Forgetting*. Translated by Kathleen Blamey and David Pellauer. Chicago, IL: University of Chicago Press.

Rubenstein, Richard E., ed. 1999. "Introduction: Conflict Resolution and Social Justice." *Peace and Conflict Studies* 6, no. 1–2: Article 1. https://nsuworks.nova.edu/cgi/viewcontent.cgi?article=1195&context=pcs/ (accessed September 4, 2024).

Sanborn, Joshua. 2003. *Violent Acts and Violentization: Assessing, Applying, and Developing Lonnie Athens' Theories*, edited by Athens, Lonnie [H.] and Jeffery T. Ulmer. Sociology of Crime, Law and Deviance 4, series editor Mathieu Deflem, 107–24. Leeds: Emerald Publishing.

Sandholtz, Wayne. 2002. "Humanitarian Intervention: Global Enforcement of Human Rights?" In *Globalization and Human Rights*, edited by Alison Brysk, 201–25. Berkeley: University of California Press.

Sandole, Dennis J. D. 1999. *Capturing the Complexity of Conflict: Dealing with Violent Ethnic Conflicts of the Post-Cold War Era*. London: Pinter.

Sandole, Dennis J. D. 2010. *Peacebuilding: War and Conflict in the Modern World*. Cambridge: Polity Press.

Saunders, Harold H. 1999. *A Public Peace Process: Sustained Dialogue to Transform Racial and Ethnic Conflicts*. New York: St. Martin's Press.

Schivelbusch, Wolfgang. 2004. *The Culture of Defeat: On National Trauma, Mourning, and Recovery*. Translated by Jefferson Chase. New York: Picador.

Schmidt, John R. 2008. "Can Outsiders Bring Democracy to Post-Conflict States." *Orbis Quarterly* 52, no. 1 (Winter): 107–22. https://doi.org/10.1016/j.orbis.2007.10.008.

Simmons, Solon. 2020. *Root Narrative Theory and Conflict Resolution: Power, Justice, and Values*. New York: Routledge Studies in Peace and Conflict Resolution.

Smith, Michael. 1999. *Humanitarian Intervention: An Overview of the Ethical Issues*. In Hayden 2001, ed., 478–501. St. Paul, MN: Paragon House.

Steger, Manfred B., and Nancy S. Lind, eds. 1999. *Violence and Its Alternatives: An Interdisciplinary Reader*. New York: St. Martin's Press.

Umbreit, Mark S. 1994. *Victim Meets Offender: The Impact of Restorative Justice and Mediation*. New York: Mosey; Criminal Justice Press.

United Nations (UN). 1948a. "Universal Declaration of Human Rights." https://www.un.org/en/about-us/universal-declaration-of-human-rights (accessed September 4, 2024).

United Nations (UN). 1948b. "Convention on the Prevention and Punishment of the Crime of Genocide." https://www.un.org/en/genocideprevention/documents/atrocity-crimes/Doc.1_Convention%20on%20the%20Prevention%20and%20

Punishment%20of%20the%20Crime%20of%20Genocide.pdf (accessed September 6, 2024).

United Nations (UN). 1992. "United Nations Security Council Resolution 749." *Authorization for Full Deployment of UNPROFOR in UNPA's (Croatis)*. 3066th Meeting. April 7. https://www.nato.int/ifor/un/u920407a.htm (accessed September 4, 2024).

United Nations (UN). 1999. "UN High Commissioner for Refugees Policy Research Unit." *Working Paper No. 8. The Humanitarian Operation in Bosnia, 1992-95: Dilemmas of Negotiating Humanitarian Access*. Mark Cutts. May. Geneva. https://www.unhcr.org/sites/default/files/legacy-pdf/3ae6a0c58.pdf#:~:text=By%20December%201995%2C%20out%20of%20a%20pre-war%20population,a%20further%201.3%20million%20had%20become%20internally%20displaced (accessed October 30, 2024).

United Nations (UN). 2000. "Report of the Panel on United Nations Peace Operations (Brahimi Report)—A/55/305." https://www.unv.org/sites/default/files/Report%20of%20the%20Panel%20on%20United%20Nations%20Peace%20Operations%20%28BRAHIMI%20Report%29%20-%20A-55-305.pdf (accessed September 4, 2024).

United Nations (UN). 2005. "United Nations World Summit Resolution A/RES/60/1 Regarding 'The Responsibility to Protect.'" September 16. Office of Genocide Prevention and the Responsibility to Protect: https://www.un.org/en/development/desa/population/migration/generalassembly/docs/globalcompact/A_RES_60_1.pdf (accessed September 4, 2024). https://www.unhcr.org/refugee-statistics/download (accessed October 31, 2024).

United Nations (UN). 2018. "UN High Commissioner for Refugees (UNHCR) Refugee Data Finder." (Country of Origin, Displayed by region: Bosnia): https://www.unhcr.org/refugee-statistics/download?data_finder%5BdataGroup%5D=displacement&data_finder%5Bdataset%5D=population&data_finder%5BdisplayType%5D=totals&data_finder%5BpopulationType%5D%5B%5D=REF&data_finder%5BpopulationType%5D%5B%5D=ASY&data_finder%5BpopulationType%5D%5B%5D=IDP&data_finder%5BpopulationType%5D%5B%5D=OIP&data_finder%5BpopulationType%5D%5B%5D=STA&data_finder%5BpopulationType%5D%5B%5D=HST&data_finder%5BpopulationType%5D%5B%5D=OOC&data_finder%5Byear__filterType%5D=range&data_finder%5Byear__rangeFrom%5D=2018&data_finder%5Byear__rangeTo%5D=2024&data-finder=on&data_finder%5Bcoo__displayType%5D=region&data_finder%5Bcoo__region%5D=7&data_finder%5Bcoa__displayType%5D=doNotDisplay&data_finder%5Byear__%5D=&data_finder%5Bcoo__%5D=&data_finder%5Bcoa__%5D=&data_finder%5Badvanced__%5D=&data_finder%5Bsubmit%5D= (accessed October 30, 2024).

United Nations (UN). 2024. United Nations Security Council. "Ninety-One Security Council Resolutions Were Issued Regarding Bosnia and Herzegovina from September 25, 1991, to November 22, 1995." New York. UNSC online listing of Resolutions regarding Bosnia and Herzegovina. New York: https://main.un.org/securitycouncil/en/content/search?p=Security+Council+resolutions+on+Bosnia+and+Herzegovina+1992-1995https://www.jcs.mil/Portals/36/Documents/Doctrine/pams_hands/jwfcpam_draft.pdf.

United Nations (UN). United States Department of State. 1999. *Understanding the Rambouillet Accords*. Archive. March 1. https://1997-2001.state.gov/regions/eur/fs_990301_rambouillet.html (accessed November 4, 2024).

United States Institute of Peace. 2008. *Interagency Metrics Framework for Assessing Conflict Transformation and Stabilization*. Washington, DC: Version 1.0. https://www.files.ethz.ch/isn/101977/mpice.pdf (accessed September 4, 2024).

Vasquez, John. 1993. *The War Puzzle*. New York: Cambridge University.

Vertzberger, Yaacov Y. I. 1986. "Foreign Policy Decisionmakers as Practical-Intuitive Historians: Applied History and Its Shortcoming." *International Studies Quarterly* 30, no. 2 (June): 223–47: https://doi.org/10.2307/2600677.

Volkan, Vamik. 1999. *Bloodlines: From Ethnic Pride to Ethnic Terrorism*. New York: Farrar, Straus and Giroux.

Volkan, Vamik D., Joseph V. Montville, and Demetrios A. Julius. 1991. *The Psychodynamics of Interpersonal Relationships Volume II: Unofficial Diplomacy at Work*. Lanham, MD: Lexington Books.

Waltz, Kenneth N. 1959. *Man, the State, and War: A Theoretical Analysis*. New York: Columbia University Press.

Waltzer, Michael. 1977. *Just and Unjust Wars*. New York: Basic Books.

Wilmot, William W., and Joyce L. Hocker. 1998. *Interpersonal Conflict*. 5th ed. New York: McGraw-Hill.

Zehr, Howard. 1990. *Changing Lenses: A New Focus for Crime and Justice*. Scottsdale, PA: Herald Press.

Index

Note: Page numbers in italics refer to figures and tables.

Adams, James R., *Analytic Reflections from Conflict Zones* 1–3, 211
adjudication/legal response 222
Afghanistan 117–27, 179–81
Ahmed, Muhammad 43
Alliance for Peacebuilding 238
Anti-bureaucratic Revolution 94
Anzulovic, Branimir 165
arbitration 223
Arusha Peace Accords settlement 82
assisted stability 193, 236
Athens, Lonnie H. 53–7, 86–9, 165, 232–4
automatic prejudice default levels 51–3, *52*
avenging-angel road 3, 7–9, 18, 58, 237
Avruch, Kevin 121–2

Baker, Pauline H. 184–5
Balkans 54, 89, 92, 96, 100, 159–61, 165–7, 182, 187, 192, 232
Barash, David P. 194
al-Bashir, Omar 47
Battle of Kosovo Polje 96, 167
Baud, Andy 101
Belgium 82
Bildt, Carl 177
bin Laden, Osama 117–18
Boot Camp Peace-in-Our-Time 239–46
Bosnia and Herzegovina (BiH) 1, 9, 12, 157–68, 171, 177, 184, 196, 207–8, 211–13, 230
Bosniaks 95, 158–60, 199, 201, 204, 206
Bosnian-Serbs 94, 158, 173–5
Bosnian war 98, 114, 168–86
Boutros-Ghali, Boutros, *An Agenda for Peace* 139–40, 151
Brahimi Report 233–4
brutalization 55–6, 87
Burg, Steven L. 173–4
Burton, John 135, 189, 218

Carter, Jimmy 177
chosen trauma 85–7, 90, 96, 167
Citizen Assistance Center 37
civic group participation 200
Civil-Military Operations Center (CMOC) 58
civil order and social justice 142–3, *143*
Clinton, Bill 114
CNN effect 78, 171
Cohen, Philip J. 164–6
Cold War 60, 78, 92, 123, 132, 139, 146–7
community health worker (CHW) training facility 49
composite process 152
Comprehensive Multilevel Framework (CMF) 214–25, 231, 235
Conceptual Model of Peace Operations (CMPO) model 140, *141, 143*, 143–4
Conflict Analysis and Resolution (CAR) 106, 134, 185, 215, 231
Conflict Analysis Resolution (CAR) 1, 91, 106, 134, 185, 215, 231
Conflict and Stabilization Operations (CSO) 180
conflict management range 75, 134, 145–9, *149*, 151, 184–5, 193, 222
conflict managers 184–5
conflict resolution 11, 86, 103, 106–7, 121, 134, 151, 155, 184–5, 189, 195, 211, 214, 222, 224, 229, 242
conflict settlement 134, 222
conflict transformation 24–5, 32, 131–2, 134–5, 139, 147, 151, 176, 180, 185–6, 188–96, 222, 228–9, 231
constructive conflict 11–12, 16, 19, 24, 26, 54, 57, 104, 135, 222, 227, 237–8
constructive interaction 147, 149
Contact Group 98–9, 174–5

corruption 42, 46–7, 112, 181–3, 189, 202
Covey, Jock 191–4
Cox, Marcus 175–6
crime 91–2, 100, 117–18, 125–6, 129, 134, 180, 202
critical zone 147
Croatia 93–6, 98, 158–63, 167, 171–4
Curle, Adam 145

Davis, Dave 122, 139–40, 142–5, 188
Dayton Accords for Bosnia (1995) 79, 134, 171, 175–8, 184, 211–13
Dayton Agreement 177, 181, 199–200
Dayton, Bruce W. 24
Dayton Peace Accord 171, 175, 188, 197, 211
defiance 56
democracy 2–3, 7–10, 16, 79, 99, 132, 137, 163, 177, 179–82, 184–5
democratization 179–82, 184–6
democratizers 184–6
destructive interaction 147
Diamond, Louise 142, 153–4
Digna, Osman 43
discrimination 81–2, 95, 99–100, 104–5, 115, 134, 180, 183, 197, 201
District Reconstruction Teams (DRTs) 126, 179–80
Djilas, Milovan 164
Dollard, John D. 242
Donnelly, Jack 78
Douglass, Ana 164–5
drivers of conflict 100, 134–5, 144, 183, 191, 193, 196
Dugan, Máire A. 215–16, 218
Dumont, Matthew 55
Dziedzic, Micheal 191–2

Egypt 42–3
Eitz, Maria 39
election process 200
episodic memory 167
ethnic groups 51, 82, 88–9, 115, 133, 158–60, 162, 164, 177, 189, 197–8, 200–1, 203–5, 209–12
ethnic identity 82–3, 117, 147, 162
ethnicity 15, 42, 94, 108, 158, 162, 166, 175–6, 180, 201, 204

ethnocentrism 121
European Union (EU) 93, 101, 171, 173, 177
extra-legal 222
extremism 2–3, 7–8, 117, 119, 157

Federal Republic of Yugoslavia (FRY) 91, 95, 97, 157–8, 161–3, 171–2
Fetherston, A. B. 151
First World War 41, 87, 96, 160, 203

Galtung, Johan 22, 54, 86, 135, 145, 187, 197
Gambier-Parry, E. 43
Geertz, Clifford 121
Geneva Conference agreement 172
Gordon, Charles 43
Greater Croatia 95, 161–3
Greater Serbia 93–5, 161–3

Habyarimana, Agathe 82
Hadendowa 40–1
Halbwachs, Maurice 165
Hanson, Marianne 79
Hawley, Leonard 191–2
Helsinki Final Act 97, 172
Hitler, Adolf 15, 88
Hocker, Joyce L. 120
Holbrooke, Richard 98, 174, 176–8
Hudavendigar, Sultan Murad 96
humanitarian and peace operation 218–20, *219*
humanitarian issues 23, 58, 60, 63, 65, 72, 76–7, 97, 131, 139, 174, 182
humanity 2, 8–9, 12, 17–19, 21, 24–5, 43–4, 91, 115, 123, 178, 236–8
human realism 18, 21, 24–5, 120, 133, 135, 137, 152–3, 178, 236–7
human-realism approach 236
human rights 76–9, 172, 177–8, 184–6
humiliation 52, 85, 87–90, 167
humiliation entrepreneurship 88
Huntington, Samuel P. 44, 76

idealism 24–5, 27, 133, 135, 178, 236
imposed peace 193
integrated framework 154
integrated peacebuilding 224

internally displaced persons (IDPs) 58,
60–2, 65, 71–4, 100–1, 159, 172, 201
return and resettlement unit 58, 61,
71, 73–5
international community (IC) 76, 78, 87,
114, 124, 172, 204, 206, 210
International Organization for Migration
(IOM) 73–4, 81, 84–5, 91, 216
international organizations (IO) 44, 91, 110
international presence 201
Intervention Assessment and Approach
Selection 65, 123, 194, 218–25, *221*
intervention conflict 122–3
intervention dilemmas 76–9
intervention structure 99–102, *102*

Junne, Gerd 182

Kagame, Paul 83
Kennan, George F. 78
Kismayo 71–3
Kosovo 76, 79, 91–115, 182
Kosovo-Albanians 95–100, 102–4,
108–11, 113
Kosovo Liberation Army (KLA) 96
Kosovo National Assembly 96, 114
Kosovo-Serb 95–6, 98–9, 102, 104, 108–9,
111–12
Kriesburg, Louis 24
Kuhn, Thomas S. 120

Langholtz, Harvey J., *The Psychology of Peacekeeping* 89
latent conflict 146–7
Lazar, Knez 167
Lederach, John Paul 151, 154, 182
legitimate institutional capacity 200
Likert Scale 63–5, 189–90
Lindner, Evelin Gerda 87–9
Local Communities Officer (LCO)
104–5, 112

Malcom, Noel 161–2
Malcom X 86–7
Margalit, Avishai 164
Maslow, A. H., *Hierarchy of Needs and Burton's Basic Human Needs Theory* 216

McDonald, John 142, 153–4
Measuring Progress in Conflict
Environments (MPICE) 24, 188–92
Mediation Support Unit 105–6
Medical Volunteers International (MVI)
39, 44–5
Milosevic, Slobodan 15, 93–6, 99, 163,
171, 175, 206
Mladic, Ratko 94, 174, 207
Mogadishu 58–63, 65, 67–75
Moljevic, Stevan 161
Morgan, Mohammed Said Hersi 71–2
Muggah, Robert 182
multilevel public peace process 149, 154
Municipal Communities Office (MCO)
105, 112–13
Mussolini, Benito 15

NATO Kosovo Force (KFOR) 100–3, 105,
110–11
negative peace 9–10, 12, 18, 21–3, 25,
54, 103–4, 133–4, 136–7, 139–40,
144–8, *146*, 151, 169, 177, 180, 184,
186–225, 227–8, 230, 234–5
Nested Paradigm Determination model
216–18, *217*
Newbury, Catherine 166
nongovernmental organizations (NGO)
45–6, 81, 84, 86, 124, 142, 200
North Atlantic Treaty Organization
(NATO) 93, 98–9, 101, 118–19,
171, 174–5
North, Robert Carver, Global Factors
Framework 215–16, 218

Oakley, Robert B., Core Components of
Peace Operations 140, *141*
Office of the Coordinator for
Reconstruction and Stabilization
(S/ CRS) 180
Organization for Economic
Cooperation and Development
(OECD) 183
Organization for Security and
Cooperation in Europe (OSCE) 78,
93, 97–9, 101, 172
Verification Mission 98
Ottoman Empire 42, 96, 158–9, 167

peace agreement 175–7, 187, 198–9, 211
peacebuilding 1, 8, 11–12, 16, 19, 22, 24,
    49, 54–5, 91, 105–6, 122–3, 133,
    135–7, 139–40, 142, 144–5, 151–3,
    182–3, 187, 190, 211–12, 215,
    224–5, 229, 231
peace enforcement 177, 193, 223
peacekeeping 1, 58, 89, 94, 99, 139–40,
    170, 172–4, 228, 230
peacemakers 184
peacemaking 122–3, 142–3, 156, 173
peace support 122, 140, 142, 223
personal horrification 55–6
polarization 3, 7–8, 15, 17, 19, 187
political leadership 200
positive peace 12, 16, 18, 21–3, 54,
    133–7, 144–9, 146, 151–3, 178, 180,
    183–225, 227–8, 230–1, 235–6
positive peace-oriented process 152–6,
    185, 228
power mediation 223
power negotiation 223
pre-negotiation 223
primary conflict 122–3
principled negotiation 223
problem solving dialogue 112, 114, 148–9,
    152, 153, 154–5, 224, 232
problem solving workshop 223
professionalism 183
profit-motive concept 183
Provincial Reconstruction Teams (PRTs)
    179–80
Provisional Institutions of Self-
    Governance (PISG) 101
psychological disorganization 86
psychopolitical dialogue 224
pure mediation 223
Putin, Vladimir 9–10

al-Qaeda 117–19, 176
quest for viable-peace framework 144

rage 8–9, 18, 23–5, 44, 237
Rambouillet Agreement (a peace
    agreement) 99
Ramsbotham, Oliver 151–2
reconciliation 75, 86, 104, 107, 134, 152,
    182, 184, 197, 205–6, 232–3

reconstruction 8, 13, 17, 23, 49, 65, 99–
    102, 104, 119, 125–6, 129, 132–3,
    135, 142, 148, 152, 170–1, 175–6,
    178–87, 194–6, 202, 211, 228–30
respect 18, 44, 97, 103, 203
Rhodes, Richard 55, 233
Ricoeur, Paul 164–6
roadblock/checkpoint 60–3, 65, 74
Russia 9–10, 93
Rwanda 81–90, 98, 166
    Tutsi and Hutu ethnicities 82–4, 88
Rwandan Civil War 83
Rwanda Patriotic Front (RPF) 82–3

Sanborn, Joshua 233
Sandholtz, Wayne 78
Saunders, Harold H., A Public Peace
    Process 103, 106, 148–9, 152–6, 232
Schivelbusch, Wolfgang 167
Schmidt, John R. 180–1
Scramble for Africa 41
Second World War 7, 9, 15, 41, 54, 93, 96,
    160–1, 164, 166–7, 233
self-sustaining peace 213
semantic memory 164, 167
Serbia 79, 93–6, 98–9, 102, 111, 114,
    159–63, 172–3, 205
Smith, Michael 76–8, 115
social justice 142–3, 143
Solana, Javier 99
Somalia 17, 39, 49–79, 84, 97–8, 140,
    180, 218
Somalia National Army (SNA) 65,
    67–71
Somali Joint Peace Committee 75
Soviet Union 93, 125, 149, 172
stabilization 1, 16, 22–4, 45, 52, 54–5,
    57–8, 76–7, 99–100, 113, 118–19,
    121–3, 125, 129, 132–7, 139, 142,
    144–5, 151–2, 170–88, 190, 192,
    194, 196, 214–15, 227–31
    structural and relationship elements 64,
        77, 132–3, 135, 188–91, 196–211,
        213, 227–9, 235
structural violence 95, 134–5, 145, 176,
    180, 197, 211
Sudan 39–47
survey results 190, 198–211

sustainable positive peace 23, 134, 151–2, 180, 183, 191, 193, 195–6, 218, 236
Sustainable Positive Peace Framework model 64
sustained dialogue 106, 148–9, 152–6, *153*, 220–1, 224

Taliban 117–18, 125–6
Tito, Josip Broz 93, 158, 161
tolerance 204
Tomasic, Dinko 164
Trump, Donald J. 15, 94, 152
trust 16, 45, 85, 120, 189, 203
Tudman, Franjo 95

Ukraine 7, 9–10, 93, 175
Ulmer, Jeffery T. 53, 55–6, 232, 234
Uncle Saleh's Restaurant 40–5
UN International Criminal Tribunal for Rwanda 84
United Kingdom 42, 46
United Nations (UN) 37, 49, 58–61, 65–79, 81, 84, 91, 93–4, 97–8, 101–5, 112, 114, 119, 139, 142, 147, 151, 159, 170–5, 182, 200
United Nations Assistance Mission for Rwanda (UNAMIR) 82–3
United Nations Children's Fund (formerly United Nations International Children's Fund) (UNICEF) 40
United Nations High Commissioner for Refugees (UNHCR) 81, 101, 159, 172
United Nations Interim Administration Kosovo (UNMIK) 79, 91, 99–105, 109, 111–13
  Office of Community Affairs 104, 112–14
United Nations Operation in Somalia (UNOSOM) 49, 58–60, 62–3, 65, 69–75, 77, 218
United Nations Protection Force (UNPROFOR) 98, 171, 173–5
United Nations Security Council Resolution (UNSCR) 97–9, 172–4

United States 2–4, 7, 10, 12–14, 16–17, 46, 49, 78, 83, 125, 131–7, 149, 157, 160–1, 169, 175, 178–82, 187
UN Security Council 97–9
  resolutions 170–3
US Agency for International Development (USAID) 49, 125–6

Vasquez, John A. 124
Verkoren, William 182
Vertzberger, Yaacov Y. I. 165
viable peace 144, 193–4, 213, 227, 236, 238
victim-offender conferencing model 106–8, 224
Vietnam 35
violence 2–3, 22–3, 44–5, 52–8, 84–6, 89, 92, 95–8, 104, 111, 120, 133–5, 137, 143–6, 160, 162, 164, 176, 180, 185, 187, 196–7, 207, 211, 213, 215, 233, 237
violent coaching 56
violent dominance engagement 56
violentization 52–7, 87–90, 165, 232–4
violent subjugation 55–6
virulency 56, 89, 233
Vogler, Thomas A. 164–5
Volkan, Vamik 50, 96, 167
  Bloodlines 85–6
  tree model of dialogue 106

Waltzer, Michael 77
Waltz, Kenneth N. 215–16
War Is the Road Rage of Humanity 8, 18
War to Sustainable Positive Peace Continuum 64, 133, 135–7, 186, 190–8, *192*, 213–14, 231, 235–6
Webel, Charles P. 194
Wilmot, William W. 120
Wilson, Woodrow 177
Woodhouse, Tom 151–2
World Food Program (WFP) 101

Yugoslavia 54, 91, 93–5, 98, 104, 117, 160–4, 166, 171–3, 175

Zehr, Howard 106–8

About the Author

James R. Adams, PhD, is a Vietnam veteran and professional field officer, who has extensive on-the-ground experience in peace and stabilization operation roles with the United Nations and other international organizations in Africa, Kosovo, and Afghanistan. In pursuit of a better understanding of conflict and peacebuilding, he acquired an MS and a PhD in Conflict Analysis and Resolution from George Mason University, Fairfax, Virginia, specializing in Peace and Stabilization Operations. He has presented resulting observations, and innovative frameworks and models, field-tested in Bosnia, to civilian and military audiences in Kosovo and at the US National Defense University. His publications include an *Alliance for Peacebuilding* article "Bosnia—Stabilization Stalled in Negative Peace" (2014), and the book *Analytic Reflections from Conflict Zones: A Cautionary Tale for a Polarizing America and World* (2021). For further news, insights, and updates, visit Dr. Adams' website: https://analyticreflections.org/.

www.ingramcontent.com/pod-product-compliance
Lightning Source LLC
Chambersburg PA
CBHW071701160426
43195CB00012B/1545